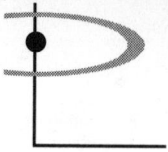

CONTENTS

PREFACE TO THE FOURTH EDITION 2
INTRODUCTION 11

CHAPTER 1 21
The Case Stated

CHAPTER 2 57
Theories and Beginnings

CHAPTER 3 89
Women among the Casual Poor

CHAPTER 4 115
Our Founding Mothers and Convicts

CHAPTER 5 155
The Irish

CHAPTER 6 179
Models for Female Identity Formation in a Frontier Land

CHAPTER 7 221
Into the 1980s!

CHAPTER 8 259
Eager Ghosts

CONCLUSION 293
A KIND OF GLOSSARY 299
INDEX 305

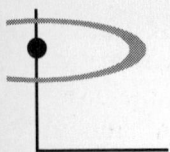

PREFACE TO THE
FOURTH EDITION

Subtitled *Woman and Identity in Australia*, in 1976 *The Real Matilda* was designed as part of the debate on national identity. Until 1994, when Patricia Grimshaw and others published the feminist history *Creating a Nation*, *The Real Matilda* was unique in placing women at the heart of that debate. Though I set the book's argument in an explicit general theory on national identity, at the time the latter was taken to mean male identity; to some it still is. And so in the seventies, and for a long while after, a book could be about national identity, or it could be about women in Australian history. It could not be about both. Thus mainstream debate tended to overlook a work on identity like mine which featured women in the title. And while in the seventies Australian feminists were interested in (if still wary about) identity in general, *national* identity did not feature explicitly in feminist writing until 1990 or so. Now, with its fourth edition, this book's themes might find a wider audience among those interested in both national and gender identity.

The Real Matilda, then, concerns women in the national identity. But what we called national identity in 1976 is better described in these more ethnically diverse times as the Anglo-Celtic core culture. (My 1999 book, *The Imaginary Australian*, explores at length the relation between this core culture and national identity.) Yet if, since 1976, the core culture has shed a former air of universality, it still compels our attention; so therefore does its gender history, the subject of *The Real Matilda*. I believe one reason bears on social cohesion. From 1788, beyond institutions, constitutions and politics, the core culture functioned as the ultimate, the grounding insurance of

Miriam Dixson

THE REAL
MATILDA

WOMAN AND IDENTITY
IN AUSTRALIA
1788 TO THE PRESENT

PRESS

This time, for Helen

A UNSW Press book

Published by
University of New South Wales Press Ltd
University of New South Wales
Sydney 2052 Australia
www.unswpress.com.au

© Miriam Dixson 1976, 1984, 1994, 1999
First published by Penguin Books Australia,
1976; Reprinted 1976, 1978, 1982; Revised
edition 1984; Third edition 1994; Fourth edition
published by UNSW Press 1999

National Library of Australia
Cataloguing-in-Publication entry:

Dixson, Miriam.
The real Matilda: woman and identity
in Australia 1788 to the present.

4th ed.
Includes index.
ISBN 0 86840 737 2. ✓
1. Women — Australia —
Social conditions. 2. Women's rights —
Australia — History. I. Title.

305.420994

Printer Griffin Press, Adelaide

Miriam Dixson was born and educated in
Melbourne, completing a PhD at the
Australian National University. She began her
identity project in 1967, later pursuing it in
England, France, Finland and Sweden. A
member of the former Australian Commission
for the Future, Dixson has been a Senior
Fulbright Scholar and an Honorary Fellow at
Harvard University. She is now an Honorary
Fellow at the University of New England in
Armidale, New South Wales.

Dixson's new book on Australian
identity, *The Imaginary Australian* (1999)
addresses a new century's defining issues.
Along with gender, they include globalisation,
class, racism, gender, intellectuals, and
Australian 'history wars'. This takes Dixson's
thinking on identity further into the psyche of
the individual and nation alike.

social cohesion. Today, it must continue to function as such insurance so as to safeguard national viability during the critical times of consolidation ahead. Providing the core culture does this, the disintegration shadowing much of the world will remain at bay. And an enriching diversity will go on flourishing in safety.

Asking whether Australia's unique past imparted its own spin to female identity today as well as yesterday, *The Real Matilda* targets a range of historical influences. They include the role of colonial urban and rural élites; the role of the free poor; of Aborigines; of the Irish; and, overarchingly, of convictism as founding institution. In a frontier situation, all these were prominent among the influences which produced an unusually masculinist culture.

The book pays special attention to the Irish. Their numbers and confidence far outran those of their fellows in countries like the USA and, as a founding people, they were extraordinarily powerful in helping to determine Australian cultural dynamics. Given the unique degree of individualism characterising the English as the world's first modernisers, what I call the 'residual clan collectivism' among the colonial Irish points to a division in colonial society which was cultural in the deepest sense, which embraced even the psychical. The colonial Irish exerted a major impact on Australian identity in relation to authority, to the work ethic and to gender role. On the latter, *The Real Matilda* argues for the enduring influence on us of a late-eighteenth- to-nineteenth-century and highly polarised peasant idea of Irish gender role.

One main message of *The Real Matilda* is that today, as we explore identity, we need to do so in terms of a remarkable overall achievement based on strange beginnings by no means wholly transcended. Another message is that where our formative historical experience was dark and difficult, the implications were even harsher for women than for men. And they were certainly not confined to convict women or to free poor women. Colouring the identity of all women, they affected the self-confidence of many if not most of them, especially as it related to public and, in particular, political roles.

Australian colonial life was in many respects severe, even ugly, but it was also remarkably varied. It was deeply scarred by convictism and by the racial encounter, for example, yet far from lacking in broad-ranging decency, in courage, sturdy hope and great kindness. As an inevitable by-product of the pioneering experience, a good deal of the early social harshness and personal bleakness was shared by similar pioneering societies. But much was also linked with convictism as a foundational and formative institution.

Consider what that institution meant for respectability, a leitmotif in colonial Australia as throughout the West. Today, the idea of respectability attracts scorn in much of our intellectual culture. But for ordinary men and women in colonial Australia, to be respectable — to be sober rather than drunken, to be hardworking rather than feckless, to be responsible, to be polite — could mean a great deal. It could mean the difference between survival and starvation; or between modest progress up the social ladder and subsistence on its lowest rungs.

Struggling but respectable working-class and middle-class people held strongly negative views about convictism; most emphatically about convict women. Since the 1970s our historians have spent a great deal of effort to establish whether those views were *accurate*. (Were convict women prostitutes? Or were they Little-House-on-the-Prairie good wives and mothers? Perhaps they were productive workers?) This effort drew much of its energy from an assumption that views on convict women would (and certainly should) not have arisen and been handed down unless they were accurate. The effort assumed, in short, that accuracy basically determines cultural influence. But as Hitler's views on the Jews might alone have suggested, inaccuracy will often serve just as well. The key points for us are, first, that irrespective of accuracy, negative attitudes about themselves were internalised only too often by convict women. Second, such attitudes were internalised by the great majority of women — convicts among them — who aimed at, or who had achieved, respectability. Such negative attitudes widely coloured the sense of self of women at large.

One way in which perceptions of convict women affected respectable women was to make them anxious to distance themselves from the unrespectable. The unrespectable was starkly symbolised in convict women and, even where direct racial encounters did not occur, in Aboriginal women. In reaction, for a long time respectability found itself transmuted into what I called the 'ultras' — defensive *ultra*respectability and *ultra*domesticity. Until rather recently — major change began to bite only after the 1970s — the ultras figured importantly among influences which discouraged white women from participating in public life as fully as their sisters in comparable societies. Even though Australian women exercised the vote so early, this applied especially to politics.

As to the life of the mind, female ultrarespectability and ultradomesticity tended to make women back off subjects that weren't — there is no other word for it — 'nice'. In the life of the mind as enchanting, as serious (let alone as transformative — the ultimate magic), very little is 'nice'. As they mother, women transmit across the generations massive orienting concerns, some powerfully enabling, others not. Australian colonial women handed down certain things that, in reaction or conformity, today still play a defining role in this richly diverse culture through our Anglo-Celtic core. Thus for one thing, from the colonial 'ultras' an encompassing timidity about mind enveloped wide areas of Australian thought. As a result, until recent feminist and other initiatives, many of our most creative women chose exile — Miles Franklin, Christina Stead, Peggy Glanville-Hicks, Shirley Hazzard, Jill Ker Conway, Germaine Greer come to mind. This is to name only those whose exile was one of geography, not those who stayed to inhabit an exile of inner space.

Despite public funding and a certain celebration, even now Australian intellectuals endure a degree of illegitimacy I believe to be unique in Western culture. (Note the extraordinary shyness about even describing ourselves as intellectuals!) But women intellectuals are doubly marginalised. They are marginalised as women in a still unusually masculinist culture. They are marginalised as intellectuals in a strongly practical ethos shaped by our closeness to under-examined frontier origins.

How have women fared since 1976, the year of this book's first edition? How likely would today's historian be to write, as I wrote then, that Australian women 'come pretty close to top rating as the "Doormats of the Western World"'?

As we move into the third millennium, Australian women face the best of times and the worst of times. Women in the professional middle class (or 'new class') may in some respects experience the best of times. In the professions, the bureaucracy, the media, the arts, in management and the academy, women know that while there is a long way to go, the advances notched up since the seventies — in vital ways by feminism — are striking. These new-class women, whose capital is in knowledge rather than property, are themselves doing better in status and material terms. But they are also helping to change entrenched social attitudes. For example, where feminism has won legislation against discrimination in education and employment, the spin-off is certainly not confined to post-1970s new-class women. As culturally 'contagious' strata, today the latter function as social pattern-setters in the way the old middle class or bourgeoisie — whose capital was in property — functioned from the seventeenth to the late nineteenth or even the mid-twentieth century.

But for women these are also the worst of times. The gender gulf within classes has certainly decreased since 1976, so the historian today would be hard put indeed to describe Australian women as

'Doormats of the Western World'. On the other hand, the material, educational and cultural gap between the classes has widened, a fact with implications as dire for women as they are for men. Moreover, when we contemplate women, new-class and mainstream alike, in their roles as parents and citizens, we uncover an even more troubling picture. All we Australians, irrespective of class, ethnicity, religion and age, take into our being media- and commodity-driven stereotypes of worth and beauty. But this applies especially and with most distorting results, I think, to women. Thus, in an era when the potential for autonomy and dignity among ordinary people is without historical parallel, the media deliver to a tiny minority a degree of power beyond the dreams of ancient Babylonian potentates.

Furthermore, the media are increasingly shot through with physical and psychic violence. Women, both directly and in their connection with children, are particularly affected by the spread of a kill-culture. In the seventies, radical feminism discerned a new sexual barbarism driven in part by an already-vast pornography industry. This industry is built ultimately upon an inability to experience the Other in terms of the self, and upon an unconscious pleasure in cruelty. Now endowed with lavish chic and an outreach even children cannot avoid, pornography has expanded enormously since then.

The Real Matilda explores the ways history had shaped Australian gender relations. But, in keeping with its 1970s origin, the book also addresses the underlying psychic and cultural roots of the gender script common to any male-dominated society. I drew on two prominent psychoanalysts. One, Erik Erikson, is of special interest to the Australian historian because he identifies frontier countries as lands under the sway of the brother rather than the father: this gives us not so much 'patriarchy' (the rule of the father) as 'fratriarchy'. (I use the more general term 'male domination' to cover both.) Erikson is of interest to all historians because he focusses on the interface between personality and society over time, particularly between childhood and society.

The second psychoanalyst is Melanie Klein, high priestess of the divided self. Her life's work turns on the themes of coherence and fragmentation, themes which, I believe, touched colonial Australians at both personal and social levels as they struggled to take root in a strange land. And they are themes which continue to haunt us today, when a bewildering rate of change threatens to fragment almost all frameworks of being. As Freud's most original and unsettling disciple, Klein has a special interest for feminists: she focusses on the mother and the infant rather than on Freud's three-year-old [boy] and the father.

THE SOURCES MALE DOMINATION

Despite the trivialisation and demeaning of women integral to a vio-lence-ridden mass culture, women today appear far more confident in their sexual role. Indeed some feminists tell us that women can now 'have it all'. It was this, Germaine Greer declared, which fired her to write *The Whole Woman*, a 1999 reprise of *The Female Eunuch* (1970).

Confronting us with the fact that feminism today has largely dumped the big questions it initially posed, Greer insists that women have lost ground since the seventies. Taking the West as a whole, she deplores 'the hammering that women are taking'. Though uncon-cerned with theory on the psychic or cultural roots of male domina-tion, Greer amplifies a defining early theme which feminism now tends to evade: 'men *really* don't like women'. This returns us to other feminists of the seventies whose interests were explicitly theo-retical, like Nancy Chodorow and Dorothy Dinnerstein. They sought the roots of male domination in actual psychic and social relations, where the recent theory of a largely academised, often post-struc-turalist feminism looks for such roots in texts. Most feminist endeav-our since the seventies has gone into softening the practical daily expression of male domination, and in this, the feminist achievement is immensely valuable. But it has left that domination basically intact at psychic source, and so it remains a mystery to us.

At the level of theory, the poetic, burning urgency of the early Greer was matched by Dorothy Dinnerstein's 1976 classic *The Mermaid and the Minotaur*. This was inspired by Freud and Klein, and the later editions of *The Real Matilda* (1984, 1994) used it to probe the roots of male domination. Where Greer flatly insists that 'men *really* don't like women', Dinnerstein targets ambivalence: the deep love and the profound 'hate [and] fear ... that men express toward women'. Such hate and fear, she claims, 'so pervade ... the human atmosphere that we breathe them as casually as the city child breathes smog'.

Dinnerstein's quarry is the ultimate source of this transhistorical ambivalence between men and women. Encapsulated lightly in the old saw — 'you can't live with 'em and you can't live without 'em' — it is a passionate and fateful ambivalence.

Drawing out Klein, Dinnerstein locates the roots of emotional ambivalence between women and men in the immense power which (wildly misreading the real social situation) the infant unconsciously senses in relation to the very early mother. The infant's illusion of an overwhelming maternal power set in a totally perfect love, blocks its life-and-death tasks of separation and individuation. To prosecute those tasks, the infant employs, and thereby forever privileges in mental life, the elemental, fiercely potent mechanisms of splitting and projecting.

The infant splits its own initial, vastly inflated image of the mother into all-Good and all-Bad. The better to hold fast to an inner feeling of life-giving all-Good, the infant then throws (projects) the all-Bad part of itself outside, onto the early mother. The infant associates its all-Good side with the imaginary figure of a father with whom, in terms of history, its physical contact has been relatively slight. In terms of child development, the father appears to the baby as 'vivid' only relatively late, when it is somewhat less under the sway of magic and somewhat more under the sway of reason. The father, and thus male domination, appear to the infant as a life-preserving refuge; as an indispensable step enabling its separation from an imaginary engulfing mother.

Gender is therefore implicated to the hilt in the way the infant, male or female, prosecutes the life-and-death tasks of separation and individuation. They are tasks equally crucial to men and women and so provide the basis for gender collusion. Thus where 1970s feminism tended to picture women as victims — men actively persecuting, women passively suffering — Dinnerstein jarred: indeed the American feminist poet Adrienne Rich saw her as one of women's worst enemies. For to Dinnerstein, while gender was a matter of deadly contest between the sexes, it was also a matter of unending collusion.

Dinnerstein's solution? Women's dominant role in very early childrearing should cease, and the father should play a far stronger, if not equal, part. The infant would then no longer be encouraged to split initial parental imagos into an all-Bad mother, whom it knew so very well, and an all-Bad father, whom it often scarcely saw. Forced to bring together or 'integrate' rather than split its images of the mother and the father, the infant would find itself compelled to imagine two imperfect but more separate and more whole human beings. As such, they were not so radically different from itself after all. Dinnerstein thought this change — one in the first instance concerning gender role — might eventually reshape our whole mental universe. For it meant that the infant would have less crucially formative experience of dealing with *mental life itself* in terms of splitting. It would thus be forced to call rather more on the demanding, developmentally-later mental mechanism of integrating. As a result the infant and ultimately the *adult* would fall back rather less on the seductively simple, early mechanisms of splitting and projecting.

If even partly true, what a blessing! It is, after all, by splitting into all-Good and all-Bad, then projecting the Bad outside, that we create all manner of monsters from the sexual to the ethnic or to the religious.

WOMEN AND BORN-MODERN AUSTRALIA

Accused of being one more movement of Western modernity which hid oppression behind universalising claims, feminism in the 1980s bowed before that charge. Thereby it dimmed the flame that gave it life. For concerns with gender identity, and ultimately with feminism, took shape within the West as integral aspects of the modernising project. The West defined itself in terms of ideals about the dignity of the individual, freedom of belief and speech, rights of association and publication. Such ideals formed a substratum of modern identity *along all its main axes* and, though implicitly masculine, were such that women managed to *deploy them in the service of women*. If that substratum of modern identity embraces the gender identity central to feminist concerns, it also includes the spin given to gender identity by the unique history of a born-modern Australia.

Feminism can still recover aspects of the universality it surrendered too readily, and perhaps thereby can revive its own early life-giving flame. But on the very roots of gender relations, Dinnerstein never made such a surrender. She staked out what remains an abiding feminist claim to universality. For where do women *not* have a dominant role in early childrearing? Which human being does *not* wrestle with the task of separation and thus *not* confront the early mother as her or his imagined, monstrous enemy?

Gender role today — after all too little changed by the feminist project — could well have its sources in the haunting early scripts written by infant and mother: scripts better mapped by classical tragedy than by current mainstream disciplines. Some hailed Dinnerstein's approach as brilliant breakthrough; some as treachery to women. Far more dismissed it as tedious diversion. Feminists, they said, must devote their energies to the practical.

Yet over twenty years have passed and the roots of male domination stand revealed as awesomely tough and supple. How many of us now even ask what makes it so enduring? Some, like Germaine Greer, say that today sexism itself has intensified; some claim it has not decreased by much. But other scourges built, like gender, around a polarising, body-based split into all-Good self and all-Bad Other seem even more rampant than they were in the seventies: resurgent genocide (politely now called 'ethnic cleansing') is an example. Indeed, the experience of the last twenty years suggests that in order to change sexism and racism alike, we need to go beyond the level of the practical. Moreover, precious, dearly-bought practical advances for women are at risk, in part precisely because deeper issues have been sidelined.

•••

The experiences of early generations, *The Real Matilda* argues, had a formative influence on women and identity in Australia, as on the culture as a whole; an influence which, in positive and negative ways alike, energetically inhabits the present. We might see its persistence in the form of 'eager ghosts'. As chapter 8 puts it, 'We are pushed to [our fortune] by the hundreds of days we have buried, eager ghosts. And if you have not the habit of taking counsel with them, you are but an instrument in their hands' (George Meredith, *Harry Richmond*, XXXII). Of course, some of these ghosts are splendid creatures. But if today we want to change the effects of others — certainly some race ghosts and some sex ghosts — we need to take more careful counsel with them. As a community we need to further explore and discuss the subtly coded ways in which these and other ghosts might still exert their power.

•••

Miriam Dixson, *The Imaginary Australian: Anglo-Celts and Identity 1788 to the Present*, UNSW Press, Sydney, 1999.

Miriam Dixson, 'The "Born-Modern" Self: Revisiting *The Real Matilda:* An Exploration of Women and Identity in Australia', *Australian Historical Studies*, vol. 27, no. 106, April 1996, pp. 14–29.

Germaine Greer, *The Whole Woman*, Doubleday, London, 1999.

Patricia Grimshaw, Marilyn Lake, Ann McGrath, Marian Quartly, *Creating a Nation*, McPhee Gribble, Melbourne, 1994.

Introduction

In this exploratory book I propose that Australian women, women in the land of mateship, 'the Ocker', keg-culture, come pretty close to top rating as the 'Doormats of the Western World'. Since I am part of my culture, since it is in me and I am of it, I include myself in all I say about Australian women.

This book is called *The Real Matilda*. Australia's unofficial national anthem is often said to be 'Waltzing Matilda', linked partly with poet Banjo Paterson in the 1890s though possibly originating earlier as a folk song in Western Queensland. The innocent foreigner may be forgiven for thinking the 'anthem' includes a woman called 'Matilda' and some scholars suggest an early English origin which did include a woman. But our anthem does not. The words 'Waltzing Matilda' mean 'carrying a swag', and a swag is a bundle of the possessions or property of a swagman. One might be going too far in describing the swagman as an isolate-reject. On the other hand, Australians would probably not quarrel with the statement that the swagman rejected *women*. Not that the statement isn't questionable: it just isn't worth questioning; let's get on with the action. Matilda, then, is a thing, an item of property of a male who rejects women. This anthem relies more than do formal anthems on its action or story, so we have to note that the actors include a sheep ('jumbuck'), which, unlike the surrogate woman Matilda, is at least alive; horses, troopers mounted on horses (the military aren't far away in an ex-convict colony); and finally a landowner called a squatter. Emotional involvement centres around these players, and Australians, have widely taken the drama to their heart, finding it all part of the natural order of things. Not surprisingly, then, there are also no women in the pantheon of Australian gods. No goddesses: the Norsemen, Greek and Romans didn't know the score. Among the gods of Australia there is, once more, an animal, this time a horse called Phar Lap. The rest tend to be males under all-male and danger-fraught conditions: e.g. mateship-men at Gallipoli and Ned Kelly's all-male gang; or males who are loners and rolling-stones, nineteenth-century Ockers, eternal sexual adolescents, one feels, exuding wariness or fear about women, and often themselves virtually womanless. Henry Lawson and Ned Kelly will do as examples. In short, Australian gods were and are largely misogynist.*

During the formative times of all States, except South Australia, women were widely treated with contempt, in its many variations, and often with brutality. We have never outgrown the former attitude, and our women are still deeply, if unconsciously, impoverished by this dominant cultural characteristic.

Australians are now increasingly discovering their past. But the explorers are mainly males and what they are uncovering tends to concern the lives and achievements of males. Their work is thus a kind of unacknowledged affirmation of their present identity through a celebration of their past selves. They believe, however, that they are uncovering 'the past', and fail to notice that they deny that same affirmation to women through school, university, the novel and the mass media. Thus, in this proud democracy, women figure as pygmies in the culture of the present and are almost obliterated from the annals of the past.

Clinical psychologist Ronald Conway believes we Australians have exaggerated 'the Anglo-Saxon habit of differentiating the sexes to the point of parody'. There's no doubt that Australian men and women are *supposed* to differ from each other in a quite weird way. The 'ideal' Australian male 'should' be insensitive and blockish, while his 'ideal' female counterpart should be so colourless that she seems mentally backward. Happily many of us ignore ideals like these. But still, by adopting such rigid ideal sex-role differences, Australian men and women deny one another too many of the human qualities which the

* For my personal definition of 'misogyny', see the Glossary

sexes share. And so we short-change each other pathetically, stunting possibilities for fellowship and the kind of sexual joy that can only go with a rich sense of shared humanity. That sharing process is taking place more slowly here than in any of our cousin countries: England, the United States, Canada, Sweden . . .

A past, a history, unusually steeped in misogyny, has bequeathed Australians some especially narrow styles of man-woman relations, with nuances specific to Australia. Our task is to look at these specific nuances and the historical influences that shaped them. Why? In order to understand, and then to change, the present. Thus these chapters look at misogynous influences arising from Australia's history so as to shrug off the faster those influences we feel impoverish us as we live out our present. The magic might work like this. Looking at history, we finally decide, yes, all things considerd, our ancestors couldn't have been much different. There but for the grace of God go I . . . in 1788, or 1830, or 1875. But they've landed us with much the same attitudes. The needle has lodged for too long in one groove of an old record. We must exorcise the ghosts of yesterday.

Apart from influences peculiar to the Australian past, twentieth century international consumer society, with its new religion of technology, weaponry, machismo* ('Marlboro Country') maleness, and consumerism, threatens to convert women (as John Kenneth Galbraith puts it) into a 'crypto-servant class'.

I call this an exploratory book, not as a device to disarm critics, but as an honest statement of intent and limitations. Virtually all serious analysis of Australian character – or identity – is *by* males *about* males. So what else could I be doing but throwing up a temporary scaffolding? As things stand at the moment, males unknowingly use history as a way of ensuring that their existence in the present is worthwhile, by exploring its roots in an allegedly national past. At the same time, they effectively deny this to women. So women's virtual obliteration

* For my personal definition of 'machismo', see the Glossary

13

from a communal past has left them without overarching perspectives, generous and airy dwellings within which they can seek their faces in the present with surer direction.

This book explores the issues of woman and identity in Australia from 1788 to the present. I have followed Erik Erikson's use of identity, which he sees as

a process 'located' in the core of the individual and yet also in the core of this communal culture . . . [it] depends on the support which the young individual receives from the collective sense of identity characterizing the social groups significant to him: his class, his nation, his culture . . .[1]

Erikson would not regard this as a definition of identity, for he explicitly refuses to define the concept, letting its sense emerge in the course of his writings, as it does. This very lack of semantic polish serves as an index of the exploratory state of psychohistorical inquiry. Nevertheless one can see that Erikson's use of 'identity' gathers in the unconscious, our sense of the body, social class, the nation, and cultural tradition. All these live as throbbing psychic realities in the individual as he or she moves through the days. Erikson's approach to identity thus allows one to follow a given problem into many disciplines, though, as his readers will know, there is one central to them all: history.

I've had to accept the fact that his conceptual itinerary, as he calls it, takes its point of departure from the life-cycle of males. But his concept of identity seems as good a starting point as one can find, given that women are only beginning to define themselves as culturally authentic existents.

While one must agree with Herbert Marcuse that 'no degree of androgynous* fusion could ever abolish the natural differences between males and females as individuals',[2] my final understanding of man and woman is that in the last instance – not, for example, in bed – they aren't separate beings but two complementary aspects of an entity called 'the human being'. So Tennyson's words on the cover of the *Rules of the Woman-*

---

* For a definition of 'androgynous', see the Glossary

hood Suffrage League of New South Wales, 1895, make a lot of sense to me: 'The Woman's Cause is Man's; they rise or sink together, dwarfed or godlike, bond or free.'

In the long history of patriarchal* societies, certain human qualities have been attributed to the female rather than the male ... 'receptivity, sensitivity, non-violence, tenderness, and so on'. But, Marcuse continues, why 'do these life-protecting characteristics appear as specifically feminine characteristics ?' At this moment, characteristics which males in patriarchal society have tended to deny in themselves are surfacing for increasing numbers of men. Theodore Roszak believes the woman most in need of liberation is the woman 'locked up in the dungeons' of man's psyche.[3] Well, it looks as if she's on her way out, and nothing is going to stop her.

Our species has experience of a wide range of styles of being male, and the 'machismo' or 'macho' style is only one. 'Macho' qualities – a relentless drive to dominance, competitiveness, restlessness, status-obsession, insensitivity and lack of inwardness – characterize those men in Western and Westernizing societies whom David Riesman calls the 'pace-setting and boundary creating men'.[4] If by their domination of major institutions they con other men into believing theirs is the only way of being men, they also con women into believing theirs is the authentic way of being *people*, and that consequently women should be, not female human beings, but *feminine* human beings. That involves 'servicing' the needs of real people – macho males – in the economy, the polity and the home.

Erich Fromm shows that eight 'life-affirmative societies' (the Zuñi Pueblo Indians, the Mountain Arapesh, the Bathonga, the Aranda, the Semangs, the Todas, the Polar Eskimos, and the Mbutus) are not achievement-oriented, nature-destroying or violence-addicted: 'There is little envy, covetousness, greed and exploitativeness. There is also little competition and individualism and a great deal of co-operation.' Our way of being human, then, is not inevitably dictated by nature but

* See the Glossary

shaped by the special type of social arrangements in which, as children, we begin to take form, from the moment we open our eyes. However in Fromm's life-affirming societies, 'women are in general considered equal to men, or at least not exploited or humiliated . . .'[5] This is also a way of saying that, in contrast to the pattern-setting males in our own society, males in the life-affirming societies do not deny and denigrate their *own* qualities of receptivity, sensitivity, non-violence, tenderness, by labelling them 'feminine'. Such males, then, are not machismo males, and the woman in their psyche is not locked in any dungeon.

Men often say that Australian women can be paralytically boring to be with – though I must admit I often find our men that way too. But the frequent flatness of Australian women – if we confine ourselves to women for the moment – is only a variant of what is called 'feminine conservatism'. As Philip Slater puts it, feminine conservatism 'is part of a role into which women are inducted by men . . . Men, like all dominant groups, have generally been successful in getting women (like other "minority" groups) to accept whatever definition of their essential character has been convenient for men.'[6] Feminine conservatism clutches on to power through the family, where the mother plays her part in setting up the same psychic pattern for the rising generation. But now, for better and for worse, the disjuncture between generations has become so sharp that the mother's usual unconscious transmitting devices do not work, and significant layers of younger women, (though not *just* younger women), are failing to be drawn into the substitute-gratification* patterns of earlier generations. They are intuitively moving towards ways of living as 'subjects' in their own right. And the same historical development is also throwing up a complementary, though at present it seems much smaller, layer of men who feel a gut-revulsion over the demand that they relate to women in terms of domination and subordination.

This is happening on an international scale, but we in Australia are lagging seriously, and in any case, we need to get

* For my definition of 'substitute-gratification', see the Glossary

it together in the light of our own specific traditions, which means in the light of our own historical legacy. Men *like* women less in Australia than in any other community I know. However if it is true that, in some final sense, men and women are not separate universes, but two complementary aspects of an entity called 'the human being', the whole starves when the parts are stunted. And in any case, women's progress in Australia will probably finally undergo that odd bogging-down process that Scandinavians seem to be reporting[7] unless men wake up to what *they* are missing out on, and *want* women to go further. That does seem to be happening. For example, Professor Warren Farrell, an American, writes: 'The liberated woman can allow a man more autonomy in his personal life' . . . 'Sexual attractiveness deserts a woman who gives up her sense of freedom and her ability to explore . . .' and 'Men who learn to listen to women . . . acquire a new set of values.'[8]

Since 1788 there has always been a time-lag between major social developments in the rest of the Western world and in Australia, and admittedly in this question of man-woman relations, Australian men, by and large, still look pretty backward. An American male historian I know teaches about civil rights and women's history in an Australian university history department. A student asked one of the American's male Australian colleagues, a fellow historian, what the American's course dealt with, and the Australian historian replied – and amicably told the American later – that he taught about 'coons and cunts'. Still, the particular substitute-gratifications Australian males clutch at in place of authentic human relations with women are shoddier than the ones men have in many other patriarchal countries, and somehow even these grow increasingly sour as the years go by.

As in all patriarchal societies, men in Australia have laid down the basic ground rules for the power structure, itself apparently pivoted around the sexual power-relationship. Having set it up (though many complain – quite rightly and literally – that it's killing them) men still get the bigger power pay-offs from the game itself. So they have more vested interest in keeping the game going than have women. Ronald Sampson writes: 'To the extent that we develop our capacity for power we weaken our capacity for love; and conversely, to the extent that we grow in our ability to love we disqualify ourselves for success in the competition for power.'[9]

Understandably, more men than women feel safer in clinging to power, in the economy, polity and in personal relations, because since our capacity to love has been so much diminished, it is none too sure that love can be rewarding enough to make up for loss of power. This is all worked out unconsciously, and it surfaces, if at all, in terms of a belief that domination-subordination relations are the crux of sexual relations. The paradigm case of defining sexuality as domination and subordination, I think, is exemplified by the Androids inhabiting *Playboy* magazine and its feminine counterparts, *Cosmopolitan*, etc.

This is what Freudians mean when they say people will cling to 'substitute-gratifications' even though they half-realize they are being destroyed by them, because they have no deep-down certainty that there *are* other gratifications. The game men have set up – a game in which women adapt, grasp at compensations, and a game whose patterns they transmit as mothers – is starving both men and women. Australia's history has made that starvation more severe than in analogous patriarchal societies. So men and women alike have the best possible reason for changing the whole game: unadulterated and enlightened self-interest. Put Eros to work!

Notes

1. Erik Erikson, *Gandhi's Truth: On the Origins of Militant Nonviolence*, Faber and Faber, London, 1970, p. 265; *Insight and Responsibility: Lectures on the Ethical Implications of Psychoanalytic Insight*, Faber and Faber, London, 1966, p. 93.

2. H. Marcuse, 'Feminist Socialism: The Hard Core of the Dream', *Nation Review*, 26 July to 1 August 1974.

3. Theodore Roszak, 'The Hard and the Soft: The Force of Feminism in Modern Times', in Betty and Theodore Roszak, eds., *Masculine/Feminine:*

Readings in Sexual Mythology and the Liberation of Women, Harper Colophon Books, New York, 1969, p. 101.

4. David Riesman, 'Two Generations', *Daedalus*, vol. 93, no. 2, Spring 1964, p. 712.

5. Erich Fromm, *The Anatomy of Human Destructiveness*, Jonathan Cape, London, 1974, p. 168.

6. Philip Slater, *The Pursuit of Loneliness*, Beacon Press, Boston, 1970, p. 75. Also available in Penguin Books.

7. For example, Harriet Holter, *Sex Roles and Social Structure*, Universitetsforlaget, Oslo, 1970.

8. Warren Farrell, *The Liberated Man: Beyond Masculinity, Freeing Men and their Relationships*, Random House, New York, 1974.

9. Ronald Sampson, *The Psychology of Power*, Pantheon Books, New York, 1966, p. 2.

Chapter 1

The Case Stated

'Australia is more "a man's country" than other industrial democracies . . .'

(NORMAN MACKENZIE, *Women in Australia*)

With one of the world's strongest trade union movements, Australia is among the most advanced industrial democracies in the world, while the patriarchal system at the core of that tradition is the most enlightened we have. Yet the overall standing of women in Australia comes close to the *lowest* among Western industrial democracies, having a faintly non-Western flavour (maybe because of the role of the Irish). Australian woman's sense of personhood is among the thinnest, the least robust, within this range. Our short history has bequeathed us a marginally more impoverished stock of 'models'* for female identity-formation than has the history of analogous countries.

From the preverbal stages of childhood, the 'once-upon-a-time' months and years, Australian girls begin to acquire a kind of gut knowledge that they are 'outsiders'. It comes across in the looks, the gestures and family customs that constitute the child's first introduction to the values that matter in the big world beyond. So we grow up knowing from wayback that to be a woman – an Australian woman, though we imagine that's the only way there is to be a woman – is to be tip-toe, dull, dolly-bird, blank-faced, 'don't crowd me love, I've got my mates'. As in all communities dominated by what Fromm designates as 'patricentric-acquisitive't values, an Australian

---

* For what I mean by 'models' or 'role models' see the Glossary
† For my definition of the nature of 'patricentric-acquisitive' societies, see the Glossary

woman soon develops an awareness that her country values most highly, and rewards accordingly, those qualities which it decrees she must not have if she is to be a 'real' woman: that is, achievement-drive, initiative, autonomy, true dignity, confidence and courage. These she must not display if she is to be a woman sexually relevant in terms of the values congenial to that small but powerful group, 'the pace-setting and boundary creating men'.

In *Women and Society*, Encel and Tebbutt refer to 'the masculine flavour of social life in . . . [Australia], with its suspicion, hostility and fear of women who step out of an essentially domestic role'.[1] That hostility helps explain the low profile of women in the work structure; lower indeed than for women in the United States. It's not easy even for an American woman, of course, to treat paid work as an integral part of living, though her society estimates human worth very much in terms of payment. Philip Slater catches her predicament quite as much as ours:

. . . when a man asks a woman if she wants a career, it is intimidating. He is saying, are you willing to suppress half of your being as I am, neglect your family as I do, exploit personal relationships as I do, renounce all personal spontaneity as I do? Naturally, she shudders a bit and shuffles back to the broom closet. She even feels a little sorry for him, and bewails the unkind fate that has forced him against his will to become such a despicable person.[2]

Yet while hostility towards Australian women helps explain her lowly position in the work structure, that hostility itself owes something to values associated with the work structure as it took shape historically, during 'formative' decades. Dominant values in any community spring partly from the dominant values in the work structure and, during formative early decades in New South Wales, dominant values became fused with single-male staffed 'robber industries' – sealing, fishing, wool, mining – where in a sense mother earth is raped. Intensive agriculture, family-farmed, has always rated much more highly in the United States where, from formative times, women have enjoyed considerably higher standing than in Australia. In long historical perspective, Lewis Mumford sees man's relation with nature and with the earth as crucial to his feeling about woman and thus to her social standing. With the transition from hunting to cultivating plants and thus, as he puts it, to 'domestication', woman acquired a new dignity and was 'no longer merely a drudging camp-follower of the hunter . . .'[3] In Finland, as an Australian woman, I was deeply moved by a pantheistic affection for lake, forest and field, which came as a startling contrast with 'the Australian ugliness', and my feeling that Australia is like the body of an unloved woman. But I was just as moved to see so many level-eyed tall-walking women, especially among those I call peasant grandmothers. If we could peel back the layers congealed into Australia's misogyny, I think we'd find a stubborn early layer linked with our early robber industries: 'work and love' – Freud's famous twins – are inseparable.

In Australia, the pace-setting and boundary creating men tend to be WASPs, that is, white, Anglo-Saxon, often Protestant and to all intents heterosexual. They've had a fair, though now waning, success in imposing their cramped style of masculinity on other males. Pace-setter males lay down the parameters of what Herbert Marcuse calls 'the performance principle'. Under its influence, 'society is stratified according to the competitive economic performance of its members',[4] and in such a society, if you are a woman, you are a member of an 'underdog group'.[5] 'Modern society', Henrik Ibsen once remarked, 'is not a human society; it is only a society of males',[6] and that is of course true in Australian society. Now sexuality is always experienced within a social context. For patricentric-acquisitive society in general, sexuality is experienced in the setting of a 'sexually-based power hierarchy . . . wherein decision-making and leadership are the prerogative of the male',[7] and for the most part sexuality is thus experienced along a domination-subordination spectrum. Ronald Sampson indeed writes that 'inequality' lies 'at the heart of the sexual relationship'.[8] But sexuality also reflects the *specifics* of given identities, ethnic, class and national, so what might this mean for *Australian* men and women?

'One thing that saddens me about Australian society is that

not only is it male-dominated, but "male" values in the form of power, status, force, and greed, are most influential in our society': Dr H. C. Coombs, Chancellor of the Australian National University, in July 1974.[9] Dr Coombs could be speaking about any patriarchal society, but our history has contributed its own nuances. Russel Ward, for example, writing about the 1840s, lists what he believes are aspects of a uniquely Australian outlook. They deserve close attention: their implications are misogynist to the core. In these lines Ward offers:

. . . the basic elements of that outlook which later came to be thought of as 'typically Australian': a comradely independence based on group solidarity and relative economic plenty, a rough and ready capacity for 'stringy-bark and green-hide' improvization, a light-hearted intolerance of respectable or conventional manners, a reckless improvidence, and a conviction that the working bushman was the 'true Australian' whose privilege it was to despise 'new chums' and city folk. We have seen that this ethos sprang mainly from convict, working-class, Irish and native-born Australian sources . . .[10]

If we assume for the moment that this is a rough sketch of one major configuration of values in our national identity, we can see that it centres around a special *style* of masculinity. It is a style that reeks of womanlessness: 'group solidarity' should read 'male group solidarity'; 'working bush*man*' is accurate, but the final lines need adjusting: '. . . this ethos sprang mainly from *male* convict, working-class, Irish and native-born Australian sources . . .' And the true Australian had a further 'privilege' omitted by Ward: the 'privilege' of despising not only ' "new chums" and city folk' but also human beings who were female. Australian patriarchal society thus threw up a peculiarly limited style of masculinity which owes a lot to that strand of national identity sketched by Ward.

Yesterday's ghosts live on now and help to explain what Ronald Conway describes as 'latent homosexuality on an astounding scale'.[11] Australian women who are close friends with men from other cultures often say Australian men withhold shared humanity from them to a much greater extent, and I suspect this might finally have to be explained in Conway's terms. On the implications of homosexuality *at the unconscious level*, the American feminist psychologist, Dr Phyllis Chesler writes: '. . . male homosexuality, in *patriarchal society* [emphasis in original] is a basic and extreme expression of phallus worship . . . [and] misogyny . . .'[12] It goes without saying that unconscious and bodily rejection may, but need not, exclude friendship on other levels: we know this perfectly well from our daily experience. But it still holds a frightening potential for a community's overall regard for woman, and thus for her dignity.

Many historical influences combined to give Australian women a standing relatively lower than women in comparable Western communities. The following chapters explore some of those influences, throwing up in so doing a scaffolding designed to be dismantled, not to endure. Until recently, the low standing of Australian women seems to have been a 'secret' known to most people except Australians. Foreign friends first alerted me to the secret, a year overseas convinced me in a new way, but as is only logical, a foreign male made the earliest definitive public statement of the 'secret' about Australian women. Invited in 1958 by the Social Science Research Council of Australia to investigate the position of women in Australia, Norman MacKenzie subsequently wrote a book called *Women in Australia*. He said:

. . . it is felt by many Australians and by overseas visitors that women have a less significant role in the professions and public life, that they encounter more formal and informal discrimination, and that, in short, Australia is still more 'a man's country' than other industrial democracies.[13]

He went on:

Almost every book about Australian social life has contained some reference to its strong masculine overtones and its emphasis on the domestic virtues for women; similar comments recur in articles about Australia published overseas; and it is a commonplace subject for anyone who reads the Australian press. Scarcely a week passes without a newspaper report that an overseas visitor has criticized the position of women in Australia. The visitors may vary in authority. Some are distinguished public figures, such as Sir Sydney Caine, the director of the London School of Economics; some are writers; some are entertainers. The critics in 1960 included both Alfred Hitchcock, the film director, and Cherrie Butlin, the actress daughter of the English millionaire showman, who said in the Sydney *Sun* that she was 'furious at the way married women are treated in Australia' – and much more in the same vein. Some are prominent members of women's organizations overseas, and others are academics, such as the American social scientist, Professor Margaret Myers Beckhart, who summed up her impressions in these words: 'Many women in Australia seem contented, but much of this is resignation rather than satisfaction . . . I have already found a strong undercurrent of bitterness in the tones in which Australian women discuss their men.'[14]

In 1974, Professor S. Encel and Ms Margaret Tebbutt updated and considerably rewrote MacKenzie's pioneer work. Their book, *Women and Society*, is a mine of excellent information and one of the most valuable studies on women we have to hand. Like him, and as we saw earlier, they point to '. . . the masculine flavour of social life in this country, with its suspicion, hostility and fear of women who step out of an essentially domestic role'.[15] But in introducing the work, Encel differs from MacKenzie over the *comparative* international status of Australian women. While, Encel says, women in Australia have a tradition of regarding themselves as worse off than their sisters in other 'advanced' countries, he himself prefers to 'underline the similarities rather than the differences'. In the concluding chapter Encel writes that these differences are 'marginal by comparison with the essential similarity':

It is undeniable that differences do exist, but they relate chiefly to the fine grain of social relations, whose exploration lies in the realm of subjective experience and artistic imagination rather than science.

Without doubt, from certain perspectives, differences can be seen as 'marginal by comparison with the essential similarity'. But first I propose to look at the question of 'the fine grain of social relations'.

Even if differences felt by Australian women did only concern this fine grain, 'the fine grain of social relations' are essentially what human beings are about. I don't comprehend any view of social science that contraposes 'subjective experience' to 'science' – though an impressive string of 'objective' relative disadvantages and differences are scattered throughout the book: we'll look at them shortly. Women may find crippling, subjective 'differences' which demean them, as do central aspects of Australian folkways and myths (e.g. mateship, Ockerism, and other equally deep, if not as manifestly grotesque, currents). These may be more significant than objective projections stipulating that long-run tendencies will bring us to the situation of women in analogous communities. As to 'long runs', of course one always has to watch they are not *Keynesian* 'long runs': in the long run, John Maynard Keynes once remarked, we are all dead.

If sexuality reflects not only the general but also the specific features of a particular patriarchal society, it is not surprising Australians are increasingly articulating the view that, within the Western democratic context, there is something marginally more impoverished about Australian sociosexual patterns. In 1966 a young and well-travelled journalist, Craig McGregor wrote:

many Australians . . . regard women merely as sexual providers, things to sleep with but not to talk to, and the extraordinary prevalence of phrases such as 'they're all the same in the dark' and 'makes no difference with a bag over her head' illustrates an attitude to women which is narrow, cynical and immature.[16]

The immaturity is ugly and astonishing, and is probably well illustrated by Craig McGregor's remark that 'one of the commonest words used by Australian men to describe sexual intercourse is "a naughty".'*

* As one would expect, Australian women have complementary views. Investigating 'body notions' among Melbourne wives in 1971, demographer Helen Ware reported 'a considerable feeling . . . that touching one's own sexual organs is not altogether nice'.[17]

This immaturity reflects attitudes stemming from an early stage of the individual's development, where sex is often seen as 'naughty' and 'dirty'. But it also stems from an early stage of Australian history, and is in keeping with Hartz's 'fragment' theory, which we'll look at in the next chapter. Lacking the tug-of-war from deeply opposing social forces that coaxed and pushed England forward as the nineteenth century unfolded, Australia, 'a fragment' of England ('the whole'), remained in many of its folkways, 'frozen' in the archaic postures characterizing its formative experiences. And so in describing sexual intercourse as a 'naughty', Australian men are manifesting a retarded quality that is both personally backward and socially or historically backward, expressing attitudes stemming from as far back perhaps, as the mid-nineteenth century. Thus McGregor explains that many men

think of women who have consented to sleep with them as 'common' or 'dirt' because, though they desire sex, they regard it guiltily as immoral and rather dirty. It is a fantastic situation, in which a society accepts a *stern neo-Victorian morality* as correct, transgresses it at every opportunity and then feels guilty about it afterwards. [My emphasis][18]

Frederick C. Folkard said that 'woman, in a way, has always been a bit of an embarrassment to the Australian. He does not quite know what to do with her. He accepts love casually, is regarded as an inept wooer and shies away from passionate protestations.'[19] In 1967, English authoress Elspeth Huxley attacked the relegation of women 'almost to the status of chattels' in a weirdly-segregated 'booze society'.[20] Discussing 'The Girls of Australia', a journalist in *Playboy* wrote during 1969:

One of the dominant themes in Australian social history has been a strong, intrasexual loyalty among men, an inheritance from the cell-block isolation of the penal days and the outback isolation of the pastoral era, which has led more than one sociologist to suggest it drowns male sex lives in a sublimatory sea of heavy drinking, aggressive masculinity and loyalty not to mistresses but to mates . . .

Australian girls are treated by their own men with a casualness that borders on sheer neglect.[21]

On 1 June 1973, *The Times* (London) summed up the main themes dealt with by 'The big three Australian playwrights in 1972', claiming they

all celebrate another national obsession, the unique awfulness of the Australian male. Nowhere in the world, if you are to believe Australian playwrights, are there more male chauvinist pigs a square foot than in Australia. They are even more ubiquitous than Merino sheep. Buzo in *Rooted*, Hibberd in *White with Wire Wheels*, Williamson in *Don's Party*, put them on the stage in all their appalling vulgarity: swilling beer, loving and betraying their mates, murdering the language, using and abusing women.

According to Kevon Kemp, theatre critic in the *National Times*, Jack Hibberd's play describes

three young Australian city men, at various heights up the executive ladder . . . their beer-drinking, their drunken driving, their non-committal sex lives are all cruelly painted in a tough and recognizable vernacular; they are very much the hollow men of our coastal cities . . . Their only serious talk is about cars; sex is a fullness to be relieved by a girl with suitably large nongs (their favoured term) and a quiet nature. A woman's true life, however, is an unknown nightmare to them, much better lost in a mass of performance details of the new Valiant one of them has just bought.[22]

This play reveals the 'insensitivity of our sexual mores'.[23] Xavier Herbert, widely accepted as a leading and 'typically Australian' novelist, revealed the extent of his intuitive understanding of women in an interview given in July 1974. When he came to write *Soldiers' Women*, he told journalist Elizabeth Riddell, '. . . I . . . found that I didn't know anything about women . . . From then on I researched women, their clothes and the way they talked, piling up cuttings from the Sunday papers and so on . . .'[24]

As recently as November 1974 Al Grassby, special consultant to the Federal Government on community relations, felt we were still 'tagged [as] a man's country',[25] while another writer saw our recent flowering of 'new nationalism' as marked by some 'utterly Ocker' qualities.[26] The Ocker's way of being a male is so lacking in sensitivity, compassion, gentleness, inwardness and insight, as to render him not just an impoverished, but almost a caricatured, human being.

And increasingly, Australian women begin to spell out their awareness of mainline Australian male definitions of them. Here is *Pol*, making the point (while over-estimating 'the foreigner'):

The nice thing about the foreigner is that he actually likes women. He doesn't think there's something very weakening about them and that it's much more masculine to be with the boys around the bar. The foreigner also stays and talks to you, gets you drinks and lights your cigarettes at parties too, which is a nice change if you've been used to being marooned with the girls. While the Australian builds his empire of Fosters and lays siege to it with the boys until it's time to drag you off home to bed.[27]

Jenny Ham, thirty-four, former fashion model, public relations company owner and one-time Melbourne City Council candidate, said this:

'For [Australian men] point one in importance is going to the football; point two, putting money on the races; point three, drinking with the boys; point four, conglomerating at a party and talking business or telling risqué jokes while women talk babies.' Rather than feature as a priority at the bottom of the list, Miss Ham prefers the company of European or English men.[28]

Helen Violaris, thirty-one, married, businesswoman and jazz singer, said much the same: 'Australian men are inclined to put their beer first, sport second and women third . . .'[29] The American, Dennis Brogan reports that Australian women 'lament' that, when given the choice 'between women and horses, the Australian man, like that most phony of gallants, the modern Irishman, chooses horses'.[30] We noted that the American, Professor Margaret Myers Beckhart, found 'a strong undercurrent of bitterness in the tones in which Australian women discuss their men'. Similarly commenting on our women, Frank Doczy, a Hungarian sociologist married to an Englishwoman and living in Australia, wrote: '. . . the depth of their bitterness has shocked me at times . . .'[31]

Vincent Buckley, Australian author, poet and critic, writes: 'We are in general astonishingly insensitive to one another as persons, and this insensitivity is most marked in the attitude of the sexes for each other.'[32] Another author and critic, Ronald Conway, Senior Psychologist at Saint Vincent's Hospital in Collingwood, Melbourne, is more explicit as to this 'insensitivity':

Listening to the average Australian adult male, it becomes clear that his concept of sex remains a pretty bovine affair. The sturdy leg that kicks a football often seems less assured when it must straddle the nuptial bed . . . Contrary to what he thinks of himself, many a manly Australian 'sport' is apt to be a desultory lover and rather naïve sexual partner. Too much sunning, surfing, footballing and beer-drinking are in fact all alternative expressions of libido which can help to keep many Australian males stuck fast at a pubescent level of sexual response.

But finally, perhaps the cruellest blow of all: Australian males, Conway concludes, appear

to have an elementary pelvic concept of sex which tends to bustle them towards vaginal entry with the minimum of delicate preliminaries which distinguish human coitus from mere animal release. Less well educated Australian working men often stare blankly when questions about preliminary love play are put to them in interview.[33]

Jenny Ham says something similar: 'Generally, the Australian man doesn't consider the woman's role to be very important sexually . . . He doesn't make love to her, he just gratifies himself. I think we have a whole lot of virtual masturbators on our hands because that's all they're doing really'; though 'men who travel overseas, who have studied in universities or lived abroad' are not like this, she adds.[34]

One of Australia's leading historians, Manning Clark, whose sense of the way beginnings and the past have shaped our present folkways will be invoked in this book, points to a significantly underplayed aspect of one of the current larrikin-heroes, Barry ('Bazza') McKenzie: '[He has] . . . not the slightest bit of interest in romantic love. His only interest is in how to get it in.'[35] True sexual potency implies a capacity for a fairly sustained and full-hearted human relationship. Our Bazza-heroes, 'stuck fast at a pubescent level of sexual response', interested only in 'getting it in', 'virtual masturbators', must be sadly lacking in such a capacity.

The critic Phillip Adams finds Bazza's creator, Barry Humphries, 'extraordinarily interesting', a 'soulmate' to Patrick White with whom he 'dominates Australia culturally'.[36] There is, to me at least, one similarity of 'soul' which, if these men *are* in any sense culturally dominant, adds up to a devastating comment on the feeling for women in our culture: the similarity of the sense of awkwardness or fear about the flesh of woman one gains from reading them, much as one does from Lawson, Penton, Xavier Herbert, Vance Palmer or Joseph Furphy.

About Furphy, the English literary critic Barry Argyle writes: 'There is nevertheless a good deal of anti-feminine bias which is gratuitously offensive . . . The only men in *Such is Life* who find women desirable are Sunday-School teachers and Willoughby, the English man, all objects of Furphy's contempt.'[37] Furphy carefully explored the soul of Colonial Man, but as for Colonial Woman, Jill Roe thinks Furphy was a bit vague except 'that she would be more likely to have a moustache',[38] while Argyle notes that Nosey Alf 'like the rest of Furphy's Australiennes, has a moustache and she wears trousers'.

Jeanne MacKenzie, writing in *Australian Paradox*, proposes that one 'rarely' finds 'any expression of rich human emotion, of young love, or any profound relationship between two people of the opposite sex. There are few Australian love poems . . . "nearly all Australian fiction reveals some aspect of sexual loneliness".'[39] In 1973 Max Harris could still endorse a similar view. He wrote:

Geoffrey Dutton has examined the almost complete absence of amatory themes in Australian writing. As far as Australian writers are concerned, right up to modern times, male-female relationships have no potential literary substance. There are no Australian love-poems. There are few detailed studies of women in the Australian novel.[40]

If many Australian writers of high standing deal at best awkwardly with the body, sexuality and women, and often demonstrate aversion and hostility, what does this imply about their sense of woman's humanity? And thus of their own?

In *Women and Society*, the book by Encel and Tebbutt based on MacKenzie's work, to which we referred earlier, we noted Encel felt the 'undeniable' 'differences' between Australian women and other women chiefly concerned 'subjective experience' and thus were not relevant to the 'realm of ... science'. Yet if one reads carefully through *Women and Society*, the work itself offers some interesting items of 'difference' we might well classify as belonging to the 'realm of ... science' and not to mere 'subjective experience'. For example the writers point out that 'both absolutely and relatively access to and participation at the professional level is difficult [for women] in Australia.'[41] They note that 'Australia has one of the highest female suicide rates in the world'[42] and that 'a study of drinking behaviour in Sydney ... suggests that women drink rather more in Australia than they do in a number of other countries.'[43] They note the 'slow development of the [nineteenth century] feminist movement' which they see – correctly I think – as 'partly due to a lack of educated and articulate women'.[44] Later in the book Encel and Tebbutt write: 'the role of women in public employment is a major influence on the employment of women in general',[45] and then describe the public service's archaic and insulting slowness in allowing women access to positions of any substance.

For example, in 1951, a United Nations inquiry found that only five out of forty-four countries replying to a questionnaire about civil service employment retained the marriage bar: 'Australia was one of the five.' In 1962 Ronald Taft could write, 'There is probably no other industrialized nation in which married women are subject to so many bars, both formal and informal, against their employment or their elevation to executive or professional positions.'[46] Though the 1973 equal pay principle was to be phased in over three years, it was introduced immediately in the Australian Public Service. But even here, women are severely over-represented in the lower-paid rungs and similarly under-represented in the higher-paid rungs. The number of women in class ten of the third division and above, for example, is statistically insignificant.

Regarding social work in Australia, Encel and Tebbutt note we have lacked women like Jane Addams and Florence Nightingale – 'commanding figures', as they aptly style them. The lack of 'educated and articulate women' and of 'commanding figures' both finally stem, as I will argue shortly, from the fact that Australian élite strata have been stamped by what some Marxists see as a thinness quite normal for a colony (Rosa Luxemburg and Trotsky bring this out well). The class structure of a colony tends not to produce robust native bourgeois strata, which tends to hold back the growth of confident, innovative, professional, intellectual and liberal groups. But in many countries (for example England, the United States, Sweden), women – and men – from such groups have made crucial contributions to the women's movement.

Despite their fairly small incomes, women are vital to Australia's economy. In any 'modern economy', Galbraith remarks, 'the servant role of woman is critical for the expansion of consumption . . .' and he concludes that women's 'conversion into a crypto-servant class was an economic accomplishment of the first importance'.[47] This is as true of democratic Australia as it is of any other 'modern economy'. But is it not morally *uglier* because we are so democratic a democracy? Women save private and State employers millions of dollars by virtue of the fact that they produce (give birth to) the producer, then make it possible for him to turn up at work every Monday, clean, clothed, and more or less emotionally functioning. This is not paid for, because it is not 'counted'. It is 'woman's work', so it is not 'real' work.[48] But, on an increasing scale, women now also participate directly in the *paid* workforce, though for the most part in its lowest-status and lowest-paid rungs.

In so democratic a democracy as ours, where unions have played such a big part in moulding national values, the historian must find both challenging and paradoxical some aspects of the way women are treated in the workforce and unions. It was not until 10 December 1974 that the Australian Government – a Labor Party Government – ratified the 1951 Equal Remuneration Convention of the International Labour Organization (Convention 100).[49] As late as 1969, it could be said that women here experienced discrimination in employment, education and training on a scale which 'would receive widespread publicity and outraged condemnation if it were directed in the same overt fashion at colour or religion'.[50]

In 1970 Professor Jean Martin, then head of the Sociology Department at La Trobe University, objected to 'nineteenth century attitudes' towards 'working women in Australia';[51] while in 1973, Alice Cook, Emeritus Professor of Labor and Industrial Relations at Cornell University felt 'that Australia was lagging well behind much of the Western world in its attitudes to women workers . . .'[52] It is just as strange to read in a 1974 Commonwealth Department of Labour publication: 'There is a claim that the estimated level of female unemployment is higher than the official figure and represents a degree of unemployment which would not be tolerated in Australia for the general labour force.'[53]

Women are thus being slowly brought to ask whether there is some curious anthropological male-bonding quality 'imprinted' into trade unionism through the circumstances of its origins in the nineteenth century. Having been slowly driven from many areas of the productive process after the seventeenth century, women's status stood very low by the nineteenth, when the industrial phase of capitalism took firm shape in England. Indeed Geoffrey Gorer believes 'women of all classes were more exploited in the nineteenth century than in any previous period of European history.'[54] Thus one regular contributor to the *National Times*, Lyndsay Connors, wrote in 1974:

Women are becoming increasingly aware that they have been continually done down in their search for equality in employment – *as much by their own trade unions* [my emphasis] as by employers and politicians. For instance, on an A.B.C. 'Monday Conference' last year, Bob Hawke showed his indifference to urgent extension of the minimum wage to women when he preferred to talk about the need for some rearrangement of social services first. And who knows how long that might take?[55]

R. J. Hawke is the leading trade union figure in Australia, a man of outstanding stature who has achieved a great deal for unionists. On 2 May 1974 the Commonwealth Conciliation and Arbitration Commission extended the adult minimum wage to women, and on 5 January 1975 Prime Minister Whitlam announced that 'the full implementation of this decision is to be achieved by 30th June, 1975 . . . [a step] given full support by the Government in the 1974 National Wage Case.'[56] There does seem to be some ground for the feeling in the women's movement that, in terms of grasping the historical significance of women's slow rise to fuller human status, Prime Minister Whitlam is far more a man of the seventies than union leader Hawke.

The equal pay decision of 1973 was a most important step forward – though as Minister for Labour Clyde Cameron told a forum on Women and the Workforce on 14 December 1973, far more formidable obstacles lie ahead: 'questions of equal opportunity and equal representation in the workforce at all levels'.[57] But there are still serious problems about the equal pay decision itself. A 1974 study made by the Women's Bureau of the Department of Labour and the O.E.C.D. expressed concern 'for the flow on of equal pay for work of equal value to the estimated 80 per cent of women still not receiving it'.[58] However Margaret Power suggests the answer to such a curious delay lies in the 'segmented nature of the occupation structure':

Despite recent moves towards 'equal pay', increase in aggregate female incomes has been small. The way in which equal pay is being implemented in Australia ensures that this is so. Because of the segmented nature of the occupation structure most women are unable to show that they do work 'equal' to the work of men and thus fail to qualify for increased wages.[59]

At the moment of writing, the underlying intent of the equal pay decision is being threatened as union officials (male) join employers (male) in defining new classifications for most women employees which will place them in a permanently inferior situation. This of course intensifies the 'segmented nature of the occupation structure'.

We are internationally proud of our commitment to egalitarianism and justice, which includes justice in the workforce. We have a right to be proud. But in a democracy where trade unions have lodged high in the priority of national values so firm a devotion to wage and work justice, the situation of that large and growing part of the workforce who are female moves beyond mere anomaly to a mockery of those very values. And so, as a committed member of the Labor Party, as an historian of the labour movement as well as of the role of women, I had to ask myself the question: was women's situation in the workforce a mockery of some of our finest values *in spite of* the trade unions or *because of* them? It was not a happy question to find myself asking. But at first sight the answer seemed even less happy.

From the seventeenth century, women have been steadily pushed out of areas of the work structure.[60] While still working over a wide range of trades in the eighteenth and early nineteenth centuries, later in the nineteenth century women incurred the special wrath of men as industrialization gathered momentum and employers preferred women for their docility and readiness to accept lower wages.[61] With enormous difficulty, the men learned to defend wages for themselves and their families, by forming unions. But as Professor Coral Lansbury, an Australian now teaching in the United States, writes: 'Organized labour meant the organization of men by men, with the clearly voiced intention of driving out women.'[62] In the United States, despite superb women like Mother Jones ('mobbed, beaten, and jailed, she never failed to return to the embattled mining camps and to the miners who called her

"Mother" ')",[63] despite women like Elizabeth Gurley Flynn and Emma Goldman, 'union labour had no interest in . . . women . . . As in England, many unions barred women from membership. Most union leaders thought women's place was in the home . . .'[64] 'Do [unions] not tend to unsex [women] and make them masculine?', an A.F.L. official asked Agnes Nestor, president of the women glove-makers' union.[65] Gunnar Myrdal sums up: 'All over the world men have used the trade unions to keep women out of competition.'[66] Organized labour in Australia has not been an exception. Thus Alice Henry, who did a great deal to encourage women to enter the Australian labour movement, was in 1944 reported as 'reproaching the unions in Australia for backwardness . . . [regarding women] especially in view of the long time the Labour Movement . . . had flourished in this country.'[67]

To return to our question: is the *inferior* position of women in the Australian workforce to be explained, at least partly, in terms of the *superior* position of the trade union movement here relative to, perhaps, most other democracies? At first sight the answer looks discouraging. But things are changing. At this moment in time, for the most part the Australian union movement may seem to be clinging to its historical contempt for women, clinging to its role as an embattled male citadel. Yet younger working class men are showing themselves increasingly receptive – both at the level of personal relations with women and within the union movement – to broad community currents which contain a sense of women as companions, friends, comrades, people . . . Surprising numbers of older trade unionists seem to be moving towards a similar sense. So to any of my readers who, like me, are labour movement women, my message would be – it's over to us. Right On!

Endorsing Evelyne Sullerot's belief that 'the changing status of women can be assessed most particularly by examining their position at the highest occupational levels, i.e. the professions, which represent the heights of prestige, authority, learning and income', Encel and Tebbutt add that entering these areas has been 'difficult if not impossible' for women 'in all countries . . .

[but] there is no doubt that both absolutely and relatively access to and participation at the professional level is difficult in Australia.'[68] Difficulties at higher educational and professional levels are in no small part influenced by lower educational levels. In a 1972 survey aimed at assessing the sex roles and self-images of 1,200 Victorian teenagers, Dr Don Edgar, Reader in Sociology at La Trobe University, said '. . . our education system produces women who are incompetent, dependent and self-denigrating . . . Australian society is sexist . . . it makes girls develop a negative self-image and believe that women have a lower status than men . . . Girls . . . have been locked into a narrow and vicious cycle of incompetence . . .'[69]

Dany Torsh offers some sober facts suggesting that if we are in fact a democratic community dedicated to principles of justice and a 'fair go', it is a fair go to men rather than women. Of the women in the workforce, 80.7 per cent have no training as compared with 67.6 per cent of males: in numbers women are the lowest educated group in the workforce, and this goes far towards explaining the fact that they are also the lowest-status and lowest-paid group. All apprenticeship training at technical colleges is open to women, but in 1970, even if we count 'ladies hairdressing', only 2.4 per cent of the students taking stage one trade courses were female. Girls' schooling on any appreciable scale in Australia dates back about sixty years, and is chiefly an extension of the system designed for boys. Ms Torsh describes it as predominantly a male, white and Anglo-Saxon interpretation of the universe. It certainly always seemed that way to me.

Turning to the area of tertiary education, we might begin by noting what Dr H. C. ('Nugget') Coombs has to say about the university of which he is Chancellor:

I believe that a university such as the A.N.U., that doesn't have even one woman professor, is just about the most male-dominated of all in Australia, even if the discriminatory attitude is unconscious.[70]

In 1975 sociologist Bettina Cass presented a paper on 'Women in the Academic Professions . . .' at the forty-sixth congress

of the Australian and New Zealand Association for the Advancement of Science. She found that for 1972, 1 per cent of all
Australian professors were female, 20 per cent of all associate-
professors and readers, 33 per cent of senior lecturers and
lecturers, while women occupied 64 per cent of all junior
positions. Relating this to the crucial question of role models,
Ms Cass asks: '. . . to what extent do the 16 per cent of the
academic workforce, who are women, supply positive role
models for 35 per cent of the student population [who are
girls] ?'[71]

Jessie Bernard found highly educated American women
unable to break decisively with sex-role qualities which are
intellectually crippling: passivity, compliance, and diffidence;[72]
and these comments are far truer for Australian women. It's
literally only in the last year or so that I've come to head for
heaven on a hunch. For perhaps ten years a greyness had
smothered similar hunches: if it's mine, it's nothing . . . But
Australian economic statistician Frances Lovejoy suggests other
reasons why female academics generally fail to supply positive
role models for female students. More than half the positions
held by academic women in 1972, she shows, were untenured,
part-time tutorial staff, subject to annual renewal, while nearly
half of the female full-time teaching staff were junior staff whose
contracts might also be subject to annual renewal. Yet most
of the women Frances Lovejoy interviewed had at least an
honours, if not a master's or Ph.D. degree.[73]

Australian society's unusually low valuation of women,
accepted by women themselves, is reflected in the noisy silence,
the blank facelessness, of women in most of our decision-making
structures. As Frank Doczy, the Hungarian sociologist cited
earlier, comments: 'In a country which pioneered and won
early suffrage for women, it is amazing to find so few women
in public life as in Australia,'[74] though studies have shown
Australia is hardly unique in the poor showing of women in
politics.[75]

Baiba Irving has recently argued that while Australian women
'have rarely gained positions of political prominence in Australia,

they have not eschewed political involvement, either in their own organizations or in those controlled by men.' She then sketches a picture of that political involvement, showing 'the relevance of parliamentary politics to the general and specific needs of women'. This demonstrates that women have made important contributions to Australian politics: the Victorian Australian Women's National League, 1904–1945, had a membership varying between 10,000 and 40,000; the Queensland Women's Electoral League, 1903, reached a peak membership of 16,000 in 1928 – with only a handful left, however, by 1975; the N.S.W. Women's Liberal League, 1902–1923, had about 11,000 members in 1907. Irving also demonstrates substantial female participation in male-dominated parties. In the 1920s, a quarter of the N.S.W. National Federation's branches were female; in South Australia, urban branches of the Liberal Parties have typically attracted more women than men members. And 'on an average, women have constituted a quarter to a third of the membership of A.L.P. branches'.[76] But the crucial test of women's commitment to politics is not whether they will devote themselves essentially to 'servicing' 'real' political people – males. It is, rather, in Evelyne Sullerot's words, whether

there is an increase, however slight, in the percentage of women elected. It is only then that the female politician will see her prestige rise in society and that the political education of women voters, members of voluntary associations and local representatives will improve.[77]

The function, mood and personnel of present politics and parliamentary politics are geared to the needs of the 'pace-setting and boundary creating men', that is, to the requirements of a *particular kind* of men in patriarchal society. Indeed, the 'bodily' aspects of parliamentary politics in Australia are hostile to women and, in fact, to men seriously committed to family. A few years back a parliamentary friend showed me the one room where N.S.W. parliamentarians then had to sleep, sardine-style, in case of late-night sittings. Just as well there were no women parliamentarians* (the absence of lavatories kept women from sitting on N.S.W. juries till recently). The present bodily patterns of parliament are adapted to men who are willing to, or unconsciously need to, renounce family existence for a curious life-style which saves them from the strains of relating to everyday people, including their own families, in a routine way. Why then should we expect them to have any intuitive feel for the needs of such people, when their own life-style is antipathetic to them? Small wonder that, although the United Nations Convention on the Political Rights of Women was drawn up in 1953, Australia did not become a party to that convention till the Labor Government signed it on 10 December 1974.

Baiba Irving asks what is 'the relevance of parliamentary politics to the general and specific needs of women', and we could recast this to read: 'the general and specific needs of ordinary people'. The answer is tricky. On the one hand, parliamentary politics is relevant because it can involve great control over our lives. On the other hand, because parliamentary politics also enshrines an unnatural distance between the 'personal' and 'public' realms of living, it has a certain massive irrelevance. Yet that distance is diminishing as a new style of politician is starting to show up, and if we leave it to the power-lovers, the consequences are upon our own heads. And on our children's . . .

Women have been eligible to vote and stand for Federal Parliament since 1902, while all States except South Australia conferred the right to stand between 1915 and 1926 (South Australia did so in 1959): but women have made extraordinary little use of this right. In 1972, Don Aitkin, Professor of Politics

---

* In 1973, M.P. Lisa Mattson showed me similar arrangements in the Swedish Riksdag building. Each member has a quiet room with a comfortable bed and a loudspeaker system relaying chamber proceedings where required. But then, some 15 per cent of Riksdag members are women. Members of the Swedish women's movement are currently beginning to raise the demand that parliament sit at hours which are physically feasible for people who want to retain some normal family and community existence.

at Macquarie University wrote, in an article headed 'MP – for Male Pigs ?': 'In the Australian House of Representatives there is no woman member, and there have been only three since Federation (two of them wives of former members). Lumping all the Australian Parliaments together there were, in 1960, only 12 women out of 701 members, and there have been less than 40 since Federation. How many women have been Ministers of the Crown? Three.'[78] 'In 1972, [there were] sixteen women in a total of 728 [State and Federal] seats, i.e. 2.2 per cent.'[79] This is probably the lowest in the kin-communities spun off the body of England from about the seventeenth century. Women's participation is higher in the United States, though still less than 5 per cent. The Kennedy Commission on the status of women noted that the weakness of female participation in political life was 'a fact which astonishes the visitor from abroad on arrival in America'. How might such visitors feel about Australian women? Encel's claim that 'the situation is very similar in other countries', obscures differences that are rooted in history and worth noting. In the United States, many years ago President Franklin Delano Roosevelt appointed a considerable number of women to important government offices: as ministers (the rank directly below ambassador) for example, he appointed Ruth Bryan Owen, daughter of William Jennings Bryan, as minister to Denmark; Florence Jaffray Harriman (a railway magnate's widow) minister to Norway; he also appointed the first woman judge to the Circuit Court of Appeals (the court directly below the Supreme Court). And there are other examples.[80] While c. 1970, English women occupied less than 5 per cent of parliamentary seats, a disproportionate number of women held ministerial posts,[81] and women held 'a greater number of seats in local government than they do in the majority of other countries, excluding the People's Democracies'.[82] In Australia, there are still relatively few women at the local level of government. That level is a fertile training ground for women in many lands, but in Australia, addicted from its origins to relying heavily on central authority,[83] it is still, though decreasingly, not of major importance.

In 1972 N.S.W. Legislative Councillor Edna Roper attended the International Conference of Social-Democratic Women in Vienna. There she commented on the poor political showing of our women, claiming that 'discrimination against women in politics is very widespread in Australia'.[84] In January 1974, a Liberal Party woman expressed similar dissatisfaction: Mrs Joan Pilone, first Alderwoman on the Sydney County Council, declared she had reached an 'impasse' in her bid to enter Federal politics. 'There are', she said, 'seven and a half million electors in Australia, a little over half of them women. Half a dozen women, scattered throughout State Parliaments and the Senate . . . represent their interests. There is not one woman in the House of Representatives.'[85]

Following the Federal double dissolution in May 1974, five new women entered Federal Parliament, one, Mrs Joan Child, the fourth woman to win a seat in the House of Representatives and the first ever to represent the Labor Party. In reporting this event, an article in the *National Times*, written by a woman, was in itself an embarrassing testimony to the awkwardness Australians feel about women in parliament. For a start, there was the heading: 'Five Women in Parliament: and not a meek housewife among them'. Why should there have been? *Could* such words have appeared in a country where women were taken seriously as political beings? Joan Child – presumably because she has five children – 'has landed headlines like "The Lady of the House" and inevitably been asked to pose over the kitchen stove or hanging out the washing.' She claimed there had been a conscious effort to type her as a housewife. Yet even after May 1974 when Federal Parliament could boast all of five women members, some were still not satisfied. Anne Pengelly, federal secretary of the Young Labor Movement, one of a seven-member Labor and trade union team to visit certain Middle Eastern nations, announced in August 1974 that 'Syrian women enjoy greater parliamentary representation than women in Australia – and the Syrian Government wants to increase the number even further.'[86]

A quick sketch of the parliamentary participation of women in another small democratic nation, Finland, helps give some sense of the backwoods nature of the Australian position. As the national campaign for adult suffrage moved towards a peak c. 1905, Finnish women were organized in a multitude of bodies. In the first independent Finnish parliament (Siem) 1907, sixty women stood as candidates, and nineteen women, about 10 per cent of the total number of deputies, were elected; in the second election, 1908, twenty-five women were elected. By 1912 there were fourteen, some 7 per cent of the total, many of whom had by then been re-elected several times. In 1924 amongst the women elected were twelve socialists, while in 1926, Miina Sillanpää, former factory worker and domestic servant, became a Cabinet minister. In 1954 there were thirty women, that is, 16 per cent of the total, and two women Cabinet members, who constituted 14 per cent of Cabinet. In 1967, 17 per cent of parliamentarians were women, and in 1972, 21.5 per cent.[87]

How might we begin to explain the lamentable parliamentary performance of Australian women to date? Because we owe a good deal to Greek forms of political democracy, it might be worthwhile to ponder the possible implications of Carl Jung's remark that 'homosexuality was an important factor in the rise of the Greek *polis*'.[88] H. D. Lasswell speaks of 'the prominence of hate in politics', a notion that seems palpably true to me. If Lasswell is right, it isn't too surprising that women are not over eager to enter the top, most visible levels of an arena so much given over to psychic nights of the long knives. But that doesn't explain the *differential* performance between Australian and, say, American, English, Finnish or Swedish women. The differential performance of Australian women is directly related to the peculiarly crippled cultural definition of female-ness Australian history has bequeathed us.

After surveying women's participation in politics across many countries, Evelyne Sullerot concludes that 'a very important variable determining the level of female representation is the nature of the political regime';[89] that broadly speaking, regimes dominated by the left allow women greater political opportunity than those dominated by the right. With regard to Australia, this is certainly true. In 1967, for example, the

United Nations published a Declaration on the Elimination of Discrimination against Women[90] and in parallel with this, the Drafting Committee of the United Nations Commission on the Status of Women began to draw up a preamble embodying key principles concerning women's position in member states. Australia, along with the United Kingdom, both then under anti-Labor governments, sought to minimize the commitment for government and employer regarding women's return to work after child-raising.[91] In 1969 the same Australian Government endorsed the principle of equal pay, but refused to sign Convention 100 of the International Labour Organization, which binds signatories to implementing this principle, justifying the refusal by saying that wage-fixing fell into the province of the Commonwealth Conciliation and Arbitration Commission.[92] However, one of the first acts of the Labor Government elected in December 1972, was to move for immediate implementation of equal pay and this, along with Labor's subsequent actions, bears out Sullerot's point.

The new Labor administration's immediate actions and initiatives concerning women were impressive and presaged good things for the future. Recognizing 'that many women are the victims of subtle forms of prejudice and hostility', Labor reviewed and began to alter employment conditions in the pattern-setting Australian Public Service, allocated increased funds for training and retraining schemes for women, and launched a study on the feasibility of creating permanent part-time employment and trial schemes of flexible working hours. The new Government also extended maternity leave provisions for government employees, introduced 'the supporting mother's benefit' payable to mothers without supporting males, whether the mothers were married or not. Children were thus no longer the victims of patriarchal determination to banish them from the ranks of humanity unless legally labelled in terms of a specific male. The 'luxury' sales tax on oral contraceptives was abolished, grants were allocated for family planning, large-scale child-care and pre-school projects were given serious attention. The Government appointed Ms

Elizabeth Reid as the Prime Minister's full time adviser 'on issues relating to the welfare of women'.*

Also significant, though, is the fact that all the top decision-making bodies of the Labor Party, as for the other main parties, remain overwhelmingly, sometimes totally, male in composition. In the 1975 Federal A.L.P. conference, for example, the only female State delegate, Mrs Grace Vaughan, came from Western Australia. The Australian Young Labor delegation appointed a woman as a proxy delegate 'to take part when the real male delegate had to leave the room ... The Victorian left-wing delegation's proxy woman delegate wasn't given a go in the voting seat up to Thursday.'[93] At this same conference women in the audience were often noticed to be agitated and wanting to have a say. But A.L.P. top conferences are very much still 'Melanesian men's house' affairs, much like R.S.L. clubs in this way, and the drug-alcohol debate furnished a good example of the boorishness and gross injustice the community suffers from overwhelming male domination (in a constituency with so many females!). Minister for Health Dr Everingham argued that

... you cannot ban glamourous ... advertising on cigarettes and analgesics, and leave out alcohol ... he was citing statistics for the number of hospital beds ... occupied by people with alcohol-related illnesses. Meanwhile Mick Young had walked to the back of the delegates where he sat in disgust, quietly jeering at the wowser Doc Everingham with all his mates ... It was almost too much for many women in the audience. They started to voice their protests so loudly that a member of the press had to ask them to quieten down so the delegates could be heard. These women [not of course delegates]

---

* However the Swedish and Finnish examples might have been followed more profitably. Formal responsibility for 'equality' was handed over not to one individual but to a committee. In Sweden, this was 'The Council to Advise the Prime Minister on Equality Between Men and Women', with Anna Greta Leijon as Head-Secretary. (See 'Directives issued to the Council to Advise the Prime Minister on Equality Between Men and Women', roneoed statement given to author by Anna Greta Leijon, Head-Secretary. See too Anna Greta Leijon, *Swedish Women—Swedish Men*, The Swedish

felt that they had another angle to view the problems of alcohol, which was related to the high occurrences of drunken bashings of their own sex and of children. They wanted the amendment to be considered seriously, but it was easily defeated and the men quickly became excited as the 5.30 closing time came round.[94]

This was followed 'by a quick exit of delegates to the pool, and beers all round'.[95] Hence the excitement, no doubt.

The obliteration of women from top level decision-making structures has a kind of relentless mood-logic of its own. Thus, again deciding priorities under economic pressure, in August 1974 Federal Cabinet at one point decided to cut back child-care expenditure, though Prime Minister Whitlam had publicly pointed out some three months earlier that 'one in four of the nation's 1.3 million under-fives . . . had no parent at home during working hours [and] only one in ten attended a child-care centre.' Yvonne Preston describes the Cabinet discussion over what expenditures were to be cut back:

But while Cabinet has ministers prepared to battle to the death for the retention of repatriation perks and numerous pet ministerial projects, it fields not one battler in the cause of disadvantaged small children; not a single woman who might begin to understand the burden of working and worrying about infants at the same time . . .[96]

While some argue that there is a 'strong leavening of male authority within the [Australian] family situation',[97] others tend to think the mother is emotionally dominant in the family, which has been called a 'matriduxy'.[98] (Nobody appears to discuss whether she has any notable financial independence,

---

Institute, Sweden, 1968.) Following discussions dating from 1966, in 1971 the Finnish Government set up the Committee on the Position of Women. (See *Report of the Committee on the Position of Women in Finnish Society*, Helsinki, 1973, given to the author by two committee members, Leila Räsänen and Eeva-Elisa Tuominen.) Even better, as in France with Madame Giroud, a ministry should have been set up to look after 'issues relating to the welfare of women', the 51 per cent minority of Australia.

but perhaps the question is above such mundane matters.) In a fifty-page submission to the Royal Commission on Human Relationships, the Sydney Anglican Diocese agrees that many central family concerns are 'left to the woman' but continues:

Unfortunately . . . this is not because of the male's greater respect for his partner but because of his own laziness and unwillingness to accept responsibility. *The female isn't given pride of place in the relationship, it's just that if she doesn't do it no one else will* . . . in many cases she is used merely as an object of sexual gratification. [My emphasis][99]

The whole thing needs more airing, but for the sake of argument let's assume Mum *is* emotional ruler of the home. Two points need to be made. Our assumption of Mum's emotional dominance should not be taken to mean that 'Mum' has the same standing as the American 'Mom'. Family life as such, I suspect, has a higher status in the United States, having entered America in the seventeenth century with the Founding Fathers. In Australia, at least outside South Australia, concubinage, consensual arrangements and 'pairings' (we don't know how stable) were widespread during 'formative' decades. Stable family life, then, got off to a late start, but more serious, I suspect it never acquired the degree of legitimacy it possessed in less mateship-oriented milieus of the New World, let alone in the Old World. So if we assume for the sake of argument that 'Mum' is ruler of the home, perhaps the value placed on the home as an emotional arena is lower because it is shared here with more demanding rivals than in cousin communities: namely pub, football, workplace and mates. The second point: Australians still haven't made much headway in supplanting the polarities 'mothering' and 'fathering' by 'nurturant parenting'. So let us assume Mum *is* a 'matriduchess', and face up to the dark consequences of such an assumption. Denied access to the public arena of society at large except in a largely derivative, manipulative and thus demeaned way, Mum therefore exercises power the more formidably, within the private arena of the family. R. V. Sampson explores this as he elaborates on aspects of Mill and *The Subjection of Women*:

When healthy and sound emotions are denied a valid outlet . . . they seek to find substitute expression through whatever outlets are available. As Mill correctly sees, the female who is denied by birth the normal freedom permitted to persons born as males will seek power as a surrogate . . . In other words, women, denied the rewards of psychic freedom, develop a strong interest in preserving such opportunities for psychic power as they have been able to forge for themselves.[100]

Mum thus falls within the category of 'victim', and victims may wield great, and damaging, powers. But however destructive 'victims' are, victim and ruler are not equally potent *causal agents*. People denied access to power in public decision-making structures

have less control over their own destinies and the destinies of others than do those who hold the power. Powerless groups transmit culture, but they do not create it . . . Whether life lessons are taught by women or men, fathers or mothers, . . . as long as *machismo* is the dominant culture, we are doomed to repeat our violent history. The only hope is . . . the ambition to prove, not our manhood but our humanity . . . [Culture] has been primarily *man*-made, and . . . women have been inheritors rather than inventors of its values . . .[101]

And does it *really* benefit Australian men that Australian women are amongst the least confident and autonomous in the Western world? Even if our men were to think only in terms of international male rivalry, must it not be keeping them back to receive no astringent perspectives on themselves from women, whose mental universe is 'marginal' to men's and so holds formidable critical potential. In self interest, should Australian men not think about John Stuart Mill's question: 'Is it imagined that all this does not pervert the whole manner of the man, both as an individual and as a social being?'[102] Australian male friends of mine bewail the dullness of their male compatriots (a sure sign in itself that things are changing), while foreign male friends have done this for years. My Australian men friends say how hard it is to talk about 'inward' matters with their fellows (men students report far less difficulty, by the way). But inability to contact inwardness and feelings saps us *intellectually*, as is pretty well known. A major cause of this is that Australian males tend to be reinforced in their flatness by Australian women. A man looks into the eyes of a woman. If she were a robust and autonomous being, she would tend to look back with the measured and steady gaze of an independent existent, whose universe was in some ways fruitfully different (even if in other ways complementary). But what the Australian woman actually does, for the most part, is compliantly reflect back at the man his too-often taupe-coloured and boxed-in mental universe, leaving him lonely and as colourless as before. No wonder they don't have much to say to each other . . .

Notes

1.   S. Encel, N. MacKenzie and M. Tebbutt, *Women and Society: An Australian Study*, Cheshire, Melbourne, 1974, p. 146.

2.   Philip Slater, *The Pursuit of Loneliness*, Beacon Press, Boston, 1970, p. 72.

3.   Lewis Mumford, *The Myth of the Machine*, Secker and Warburg, London, 1967, p. 148.

4.   H. Marcuse, *Eros and Civilisation*, Sphere Books, London, 1969 (1955), pp. 50, 44.

5.   Erik Allardt's term in 'Culture, Structure and Revolutionary Ideologies', *International Journal of Comparative Sociology*, vol. 12, no. 1, March 1971.

6.   Henrik Ibsen, quoted in Leo Lowenthal, *Literature and the Image of Man: Sociological Studies of the European Drama and Novel, 1600–1900*, Beacon Press, Boston, 1957, p. 183.

7.   Sidney Abbott and Barbara Love, *Sappho was a Right-On Woman*, Stein and Day, New York, 1973, p. 140.

8.   Ronald Sampson, *The Psychology of Power*, Pantheon Books, New York, p. 13.

9.   H. C. Coombs, *A. N. U. News*, July 1974, p. 5.

10.   Russel Ward, *The Australian Legend*, Oxford University Press, Melbourne, 1958, p. 99.

11.   R. Conway, *The Great Australian Stupor*, Sun Books, Melbourne, 1971, p. 144.

12.   P. Chesler, *Women and Madness*, Allen Lane, London, 1975, p. 189.

13. N. MacKenzie, *Women in Australia*, Cheshire, Melbourne, 1962, p. xi.

14. ibid., p.81.

15. S. Encel, N. MacKenzie and M. Tebbutt, op. cit., p. 146.

16. C. McGregor, *Profile of Australia*, Penguin Books, London, 1966, pp. 61, 64.

17. Helen Ware, 'Methodological Issues: Investigation of Body Notions, Communication Patterns, and Ideas About Tampering with Nature', Australian Family Survey, 1971, Technical Data and Working Papers, vol. 15, Department of Demography, R.S.S.S., Australian National University, Canberra.

18. McGregor, op. cit., p. 66.

19. F. C. Folkard, *The Remarkable Australians*, Murray, Sydney, n.d. (c. 1964), p. 132.

20. E. Huxley, *Sun-Herald*, 14 May 1967.

21. *Playboy*, vol. 16, no. 9, September 1969, p. 229.

22. Kevon Kemp, *National Times*, 14–19 June 1971.

23. Drama critic Katharine Brisbane, *Australian*, 21 November 1972.

24. Xavier Herbert, *Australian*, 29 July 1974.

25. Al Grassby, *Australian*, 9 November 1974.

26. John Tittensor, *Nation Review*, 21–28 December 1973, p. 328.

27. *Pol*, vol. 2, no. 9.

28. *National Times*, 30 August – 4 September 1971, p. 14.

29. Helen Violaris, *Australian*, December 1967.

30. Dennis Brogan, *Harper's*, June 1958, p. 67.

31. F. Doczy, *Australian Women: A condensed study based on comparative analysis*, edited by Dr G. Todoroff, Sydney, n.d. (1949?), p. 4.

32. V. Buckley, 'Australia: myth versus reality', *Prospect*, no. 2, 1959, p. 20.

33. R. Conway, op. cit., pp. 124–5.

34. Jenny Ham, loc. cit.

35. C. M. H. Clark, *Australian*, 12 April 1973.

36. *Australian*, 12 April 1973.

37. Barry Argyle, *An Introduction to the Australian Novel 1830–1930*, Clarendon Press, Oxford, 1972, pp. 199, 206.

38. Jill Roe, ' "The Scope of Women's Thought is Necessarily Less": The Case of Ada Cambridge', *Australian Literary Studies*, October 1972, p. 388.

39. J. MacKenzie, *Australian Paradox*, MacGibbon and Kee, Melbourne, 1961.

40. Max Harris, *The Angry Eye*, Pergamon Press Australia, Sydney, 1973, p. 41.

41. S. Encel and M. Tebbutt, op. cit., p. 115.

42. ibid., p. 59.

43. ibid., p.60.

44. ibid., p. 36.

45. ibid., p. 135.

46. R. Taft, 'The Myth and the Migrants' in Peter Coleman, ed., *Australian Civilization*, Cheshire, Melbourne, 1962, p. 195.

47. John Kenneth Galbraith, *Economics and the Public Purpose*, Houghton Mifflin, Boston, 1973, p. 33.

48. Cf. Galbraith, loc. cit.: . . . 'the labor of women to facilitate consumption is not valued in national income or product. This is of some importance for its disguise; what is not counted is often not noticed. For this reason and aided by the conventional pedagogy as presently observed, it becomes possible for women to study economics without becoming aware of their precise role in the economy. This, in turn, facilitates their acceptance of their role. Were their economic function more explicitly delineated in the current pedagogy, it might invite inconvenient rejection.'

49. Prime Minister Whitlam, Statements to the House of Representatives in December 1973 and December 1974; 'excerpts [concerning] action the Australian Government has taken to improve the status of women within the community'. Australian Labor Party, New South Wales branch, January 1975, p. 1.

50. Peter Riach, 'Equal Pay and Equal Opportunity', *Journal of Industrial Relations*, vol. 11, no. 2, July 1969, pp. 99–110.

51. Jean Martin, *Sydney Morning Herald*, 4 July 1970.

52. Alice Cook, *Financial Review*, 11 December 1973.

53. Women's Bureau, Department of Labour, *The Role of Women in the Economy*, O.E.C.D. Study, Women and Work no. 12, Canberra, 1974, p. 176.

54. Geoffrey Gorer, 'Fifty Years After', *Observer*, 13 August 1961; cited in Hannah Gavron, *The Captive Wife*, Penguin Books, 1973 (1966), p. 17.

55. Lyndsay Connors, 'Hooting Mr Cameron does nothing for women suffering wage injustice', *National Times*, 7–12 January 1974, p. 13.

56. Prime Minister Whitlam, Statements to the House of Representatives, op. cit., p. 3.

57. Clyde Cameron, 'The Case for Equal Pay, Equal Employment Opportunity and the Minimum Wage for all Workers', address given to a forum on Women in the Workforce on 14 December 1973, Dept of Labour, F. & B. 2817 AA, Melbourne, Victoria 3001; Australian Government Publishing Service, Canberra, 1974.

58. Women's Bureau, Department of Labour, op. cit., p. 174.

59. M. Power, 'The Wages of Sex', *Australian Quarterly*, vol. 46, no. 1, March 1974.

60. Alice Clark, *Working Life of Women in the Seventeenth Century*, Routledge, London, 1919; Cass, New York, 1968.

61. Ivy Pinchbeck, *Women Workers and the Industrial Revolution*, Routledge, 1930; Cass, New York, 1969.

62. Coral Lansbury, 'The Feminine Frontier: Women's Suffrage and Economic Reality', *Meanjin*, September 1972, p. 291.

63. Gerda Lerner, *The Woman in American History*, Addison Wesley, Menlo Park, California, 1971, p. 134.

64. William L. O'Neill, *The Woman Movement: Feminism in the United States and England*, Allen and Unwin, London, 1969, p. 64.

65. Quoted in Philip Foner, *History of the Labor Movement in the United States*, vol. 3, International Publishers, New York, 1964.

66. G. Myrdal, *An American Dilemma*, Harper and Brothers, New York, 1944, p. 1077.

67. *Memoirs of Alice Henry*, ed. with postscript by Nettie Palmer, Melbourne, 1944; see too Alice Henry, *The Trade Union Woman*, Appleton, New York, 1915, and *Women and the Labor Movement*, Macmillan, New York, 1923.

68. S. Encel, N. MacKenzie and M. Tebbutt, op. cit., p. 115.

69. Don Edgar, in 'Women's Electoral Lobby Broadsheet', no. 9, October 1972.

70. H. C. Coombs, loc. cit.

71. Bettina Cass, 'Women in the Academic Profession: A Study of their Socialization Experiences', presented to section 27, Sociology, of the Forty-sixth ANZAAS Congress, Canberra, Australia, January 1975. Statistics adapted from Table 3, page 8, *University Statistics*, 1972, Commonwealth Bureau of Census and Statistics.

72. J. Bernard, *Academic Women*, Pennsylvania State University Press, University Park, 1964.

73. Frances H. Lovejoy, 'Career Opportunities in Australian Universities for female academics', paper presented to the Women in Tertiary Education Seminar, 18–19 May 1974.

74. F. Doczy, op. cit., p. 13.

75. Maurice Duverger, *The Political Role of Women*, UNESCO, Paris, 1955; E. Sullerot, *Woman, Society and Change*, World University Library, London, 1971. See too Stein Rokkan and A. H. Birch, 'Citizen participation in political life', *International Social Science Journal*, formerly *Bulletin*, UNESCO, Paris, vol. XII, no. 1, 1960. This deals with New Zealand, the United Kingdom, Finland, France, Norway and the United States.

76. B. Irving, 'Women in Australian Politics; A Look at the Past', *Refractory Girl*, Summer 1974–1975, pp. 27–8.

77. E. Sullerot, op. cit., p. 230.

78. Don Aitkin, *Sun-Herald*, 27 August 1972.

79. S. Encel, N. MacKenzie and M. Tebbutt, op. cit., p. 245.

80. Lois W. Banner, *Women in Modern America: A Brief History*. The Harbrace History of the United States, Harcourt Brace Jovanovich, New York, 1974, pp. 178–9.

81. Melville E. Currell, *Political Woman*, Croom Helm, London, 1974, pp. 70–71.

82. E. Sullerot, op. cit., p. 222.

83. See S. Encel, N. MacKenzie and M. Tebbutt: '. . . many functions carried out by local authorities in Britain are undertaken in Australia by the State or State agencies . . .' (op. cit., p. 273).

84. Edna Roper, 'So few women in Parliament', *Modern Unionist*, vol. 1, no. 12, October-December 1972, p. 9.

85. Joan Pilone, *Australian*, 12 January 1974.

86. Anne Pengelly, *Age*, 10 August 1974.

87. *National Council of Women of Finland*, Women of Finland, Helsinki, 1954, p. 11 and pp. 23–31; V. Palen-Kordes, 'Finland's Women Deputies and their Work', *Contemporary Review*, vol. 102, July-December 1912, p. 105; Alice Zimmern, *Woman's Suffrage in Many Lands*, Woman Citizen Publishing Society, London, 1909, pp. 68–9; Dr Tekla Hultin, M.P., 'Where Women have the Vote and More', *Review of Reviews*, vol. 47, January-June 1913, pp. 156–7; *La Femme Socialiste*, serie 4, 12, June-July 1924; John W. Wuorinen, *A History of Finland*, New York, 1965, p. 324.

88. C. Jung, *Civilization in Transition*, Bollingen Foundation, New York, 1964, p. 99.

89. E. Sullerot, op. cit., pp. 230–31.

90. *Yearbook of the United Nations*, 1967, pp. 521–2, resolution 2263 (xxii).

91. United Nations, Twentieth Session, 13 February – 6 March 1967, *Report of the Commission on the Status of Women*, p. 38.

92. Peter Riach, *Journal of Industrial Relations*, vol. II, no. 2, July 1969.

93. Margaret Smith, *National Times*, 10–15 February 1975.

94. ibid.

95. ibid.

96. Yvonne Preston, *National Times*, 29 July – 3 August 1974, p. 1. See too Paul Kelly, *Australian*, 2 August 1974.

97. P. Herbst and H. J. Fallding, quoted in 'Husband and Wife Interaction', in Jan Mercer ed., *The Other Half: Women in Australian Society*, Penguin Books, 1975, p. 217.

98. R. Conway, op. cit., and D. Adler, 'Matriduxy in the Australian Family', in A. F. Davies and S. Encel, eds, *Australian Society: A Sociological Introduction*, Cheshire, Melbourne, 1965.

99. *Australian*, 17 May 1975.

100. Ronald V. Sampson, op. cit., pp. 101–2.

101. Letty Cottin Pogrebin, 'Do Women Make Men Violent?', *MS*, vol. 3, no. 5, November 1974, p. 80, p. 52.

102. J. S. Mill, *The Subjection of Women*, 1869, World's Classics, Oxford, 1912, p. 150 (pagination of 1869 edition).

Chapter 2

Theories and Beginnings

'The entire woman is, so to speak, to be seen in the cradle of the child.'

(ALEXIS DE TOCQUEVILLE – with apologies)

Now the case is stated, we can turn to the main theories and hypotheses this book uses to explore the concept of woman in Australia's national identity. Our ancestors stalk us as we walk through the days, invisible and relentless ghosts whose power may be exorcised only when we start to recognize it: the past lives on in the present. So my work is 'past-into-present' history. Unhappily the concept of woman has to be virtually uncovered, disinterred, inferred, teased out, from the received versions of our national identity.

Despite their differences, those versions of our history share a crippling central characteristic: almost without exception, they are written by males about males, yet claim to tell us about *national* characteristics. In 1961, for example, Charles S. Blackton wrote an article entitled 'Australian Nationality and Nationalism, 1850–1900'.[1] To this day, no one has pointed out, in reference to his article, that women are part of our nation. In 1969, during a fifteen page article 'Australian Historians in Quest of a Theme', Geoffrey Bolton devoted six lines (on page 19) to women:

One can readily think of even bigger questions to occupy the sociologically inclined historian. Take, for instance, the history of women in Australia. Everyone has an incidental theory [so incidental as to be pretty well invisible] to account for their standing in Australia . . . Nobody has yet treated the subject centrally. Take another example: would it not be interesting for someone to write a trade union history – preferably a waterfront union – tackled from a sociological angle . . .[2]

Here, Bolton reflects the traditions of the historian's craft in Australia, for his personal empathy with women is considerable. But those craft traditions are so *Australian*, that first of all, he doesn't say what women's 'standing' is, though the passage loses its point without this. And then, look at the juxtapositions: women, about fifty-one per cent of our community, receive six lines, preceded by an earlier reference to Australian Rules football and followed by an exhortation to study watersiders.*

Geoffrey Blainey's *The Tyranny of Distance*[3] purports to be an inquiry into *Australian* customs, not Australian *male* customs: between pages 170 and 172, in a work of 339 pages, he devotes several passages to women. K. S. Inglis's *The Australian Colonists: An exploration of social history*, was published in 1974, after the women's movement was under way. There is no notable reflection of this historical breakthrough in Inglis's work. It claims to be about 'Australian Colonists'. It claims to be 'an exploration of *social* history'. But its comprehension and treatment of women is slight enough to justify our asking for a re-titling: 'The Australian Male Colonists: An exploration of social history as experienced by males 1788–1870'. Similarly, Ian Turner's *The Australian Dream*[4] should be re-titled 'The Australian Male Dream'. We would then know what sort of book we were buying, and semantics would not be outraged. And Russel Ward's seminal work *The Australian Legend* would more accurately be titled 'The Australian Legend as Envisioned by Males', or 'a Male'.

The only extenuating circumstance one can advance for all this, is perhaps that the single most striking feature of our national identity is a womanlessness that amounts in some senses to her obliteration; and the males who articulate and, implicitly, celebrate that identity (and themselves in the process) are being *more* authentic Australians in the very act of being *less* competent analysts, on any acceptable definition, of an alleged 'national' character, 'social' history, etc. All this is substantially true of the

* My uncle was a wharfie and my Master's thesis dealt with the 1928 all-ports waterfront strike, in case the reader suspects I'm unaware that this is a rich historical subject.

main participants in the long discourse on national identity from, say, Vance Palmer, Russel Ward, Michael Roe, Ian Turner, Geoffrey Serle, to Geoffrey Blainey and Humphrey McQueen.

To gather first approximations about the overall standing of women in any group in patriarchal society, one should begin by searching for a sense of how males feel about themselves. For example, it's common to begin exploring the self-concept of American Negro women by noting that centuries of slavery have diminished the self-assurance of Negro men. Centuries of British colonialism likewise threatened Irish male identity. Males in both cases, I propose, have used the unconscious mending device of trying to ensure 'their' women felt even more demeaned than they felt, and often (as in the case of the Irish) this seems to have worked. Why were Quebec French-Canadian women last in Canada to receive the vote?

The French-Canadian élites of the post-1837 generation tried to compensate for their economic and social impotence . . . by insisting on their uniqueness as a race. As time passed, this became a conviction. The early decades of the twentieth century were to see the apogee of traditional nationalism, with the development of such themes as the 'revenge of the cradle' . . .[5]

Central to my conceptual scaffolding are aspects of Louis Hartz's theory.[6] Hartz pictures Australia as a fragment 'spun off' the body of industrializing Western Europe at a moment when the 'lower orders' were beginning to influence communities in a way, and on a scale, never before seen in history. To Hartz, we are a bit of working class Western Europe, a freak fragment of Europe 'charged with the proletarian turmoil of the Industrial Revolution',[7] a community truncated at birth and during formative decades of an aristocracy, and of the upper and some of the middle reaches of the bourgeoisie. Established as a penal colony in 1788, Australia lacked an aristocracy and even a middle class of much solidity or national pride. For a long time, as Russel Ward points out, national pride was left to the 'lower orders',[8] and on the whole was considered a mark of their natural inferiority. Ward's key concepts fall within a

Hartzian framework, and I agree with both that the 'lower orders', partly through the relative weakness of higher strata, had an unusual, and, for the nineteenth century, unique influence on our national *mores*. We are renowned throughout the world for this fact. We are also more well known than we imagine for the curiously low standing of our women. I submit that the two are causally related. In large part *because* the 'lower orders' have bulked large in shaping national identity, the vision of woman in that identity is, for a western nation, unusually impoverished. The psychosocial mechanism I see as mediating this impoverishment is captured in these words from John Stuart Mill's *The Subjection of Women*:

And how many thousands are there among the lowest classes in every country, who . . . because in every other quarter their aggressions meet with resistance, indulge the utmost habitual excesses of bodily violence towards the unhappy wife, who alone . . . can neither repel nor escape from their brutality [and whose dependence makes them believe] that the law has delivered her to them as their thing, to be used at their pleasure, and that they are not expected to practise the consideration towards her which is required from them towards everybody else.[9]

Not for one moment am I arguing that Australian working class males, or Australians, are *physically* brutal to women: I'm trying to get at the psychology involved. Women's overall standing tends to be lowest amongst males whose own social standing is closest to the bottom rungs of the status hierarchy. Such males demeaned (and demean) 'their' women as a largely unconscious device to make up for the (usually unacknowledged) anguish they experienced as a result of their own demeaned position on the status ladder. In patricentric-acquisitive societies, personal self-evaluation finally stems from one's location on that ladder, and no consciously-held ideologies, even the most radical, even the most passionately and elaborately protested, can save men from this relentless and ugly fact. The women of males on the lowest rungs of the ladder internalized the proffered definition of female worth and they *became* what 'their' males needed them to become. In all States except

South Australia, such males contributed during formative times to the overall value structure in a way probably unparalleled in other communities of the western tradition (though 1 don't know how accurate it is to see us in terms of that tradition alone). So whatever influence these males exerted in shaping the standing of women, had a spin-off for the entire moral economy.

It's assumed throughout this book that 'formative' experiences, early experiences in a community's growth, are stubbornly 'imprinted'. They certainly can change, but only if strong countervailing forces are put into operation. 'Formative' experiences hold the aces, much as do the first five years of a child's life. The concept 'formative' has a fairly wide currency among historians. For example, a leading historian of the American women's movement, William L. O'Neill, refers to 'frontier circumstances . . . [which] improved the status of women' as 'part of the *ancestral experience* [my emphasis] of most Americans . . .'[10] Writing of 'The Irish in Victoria, 1851–91 . . .', Oliver MacDonagh uses phrases like 'formative stages' and 'infancy and first childhood', with an implication, it seems, that these were unusually strong in setting patterns.[11] But more precisely, what do such phrases mean, and how might they 'work'? Robert Waelder's account serves the purpose nicely.

There is a specific historical hypothesis that has been formulated by Freud. In short, it says that just as childhood experiences have a great impact on the organism and make a disproportionate contribution to character . . . so do experiences in the childhood of a nation, its formative period, lastingly and indelibly influence national character and outlook. . . . What we mean then by the childhood of a nation . . . is *the time during which the group was formed and stabilized* [emphasis in original] – in which the ethos common to the group came into being and was accepted and the mutual identifications established.

National or other groups, may have more than one formative period, more than one childhood.

Such periods, according to the Freudian hypothesis, are particularly sensitive periods, and experiences of these times have a lasting imprint on the future life of the group . . . because it is the period in which the group is formed and stabilized it is also a time of success in terms of the group values. The behaviour and the methods of the time have thus 'worked' and become deeply engrained in the people's memory . . . They are transmitted as memories from generation to generation; they are also re-enacted in countless social situations from earliest childhood on and their efficacy is thus proved in what amounts to self-fulfilling prophecies. It is hardly possible for later adverse experience to dislodge convictions so deeply rooted . . .[12]

Hartz's 'fragment' theory implies a peculiar sensitivity about the 'moment of birth' and/or 'formative decades' of a new 'fragment' spun off the body of an old nation. Frederick Jackson Turner's hypothesis regarding the American frontier relies on some analogous mechanism, and so does that of Ward. He begins his book with a quote from De Tocqueville which implies psychohistorical mechanisms similar in rough outline to a Freudian approach:

The entire man is, so to speak, to be seen in the cradle of the child. The growth of nations presents something analogous to this; they all bear some marks of their origin; and the circumstances which accompanied their birth and contributed to their rise, affect the whole term of their being.[13]

If we take the notion of 'formative' experiences seriously, then to probe its implications for women's standing we must consider the fact that we were an offshoot of *nineteenth century* England, a time when capitalism entered an especially malevolent stage. That century marked a new level of obsession with profit, status and domination. It demanded that the bourgeois male delineate himself as achiever and producer with new clarity, and persuaded males to turn their backs on their own sexuality with a harshness never before experienced on such a vast and sustained scale. Individuals were carrying out a gigantic historical task behind their own backs. The widening of 'relational' as well as social 'distance'* between sexes involved

* Human beings may be physically close to each other, perhaps even sharing the same house, but far apart 'relationally'. They do not feel at ease together,

in this process is suggested by Evelyne Sullerot when she writes that pre-medieval

collectivism had integrated women into the community [whereas] the reign of private ownership and the beginning of early capitalism after the end of the Middle Ages gradually increased the distance between the position of men and women . . .[14]

According to Marx's analysis, as capitalism extended the area of commodity-fetishism, it tended to replace the pre-industrial, direct relationship between producers (who were as likely to be women as men) with 'material relationships between persons and social relationships between things'.[15] (In making this point about relational and social 'distance' I am not denying the brutality of precapitalist-and-precontraceptive society. That brutality touched women, children and old people most acutely.)

With the development of capitalism, a related psychohistorical dynamic operated to diminish the personhood of woman. It derived from the need of the rising bourgeoisie to conquer and yet imitate the aristocrat. Bourgeois men, especially those either in reality or, in their own eyes, still in the process of 'making it', had to feel certain 'their' women were as decorative as those of the aristocracy, as 'incapable of useful effort' and thus they were to constitute a badge of 'vicarious leisure', 'to be supported in idleness by [an] owner'.[16] The main reason for the spread of contraception among middle class families was this desire of males to preserve decorative wives.[17] Later, of course, when producer capitalism began to give way to consumer capitalism, the working class tried to ape the bourgeoisie: 'no bloody wife of *mine* is going to work.'* Thus within the western patriarchal tradition, the nineteenth century played a decisive part in

don't have much in the way of shared feelings, interests and activities. In Australia, I suspect the relational distance between the sexes is, by and large, stretched thinner than in comparable communities. Because I think our history has helped make this so, my book aims to shrink the relational distance by showing how events and processes in the past, dead ghosts, have impoverished our present. Exorcism to the rescue!

* A nice example of De Tocqueville's 'principle of stratified diffusion'.

spreading that definition of the female we call 'feminine', far beyond its original historical home in the aristocracy. And so by the mid-twentieth century, one anthropological observer of English folkways could conclude a study of 'differences' in England with these words:

As far as differences in values and attitudes are concerned, the greatest contrast between groups of English people is not that between different social classes or between different regions but between men and women.[18]

Our 'formative experiences' took place in crucial early stages of industrial capitalism in England. Some writers found the English of this period unusually tinctured by cruelty, a harbinger, perhaps, of the civilized viciousness which universalizing twentieth century capitalism has brought. Eighteenth century English audiences were 'considered to be inordinately fond' of 'the realistic portrayal of crime and violence' which both reflected and encouraged 'sadism in the audience'. Leo Lowenthal quotes Addison, who was 'rather tolerant of the excesses of the opera and stage':

But among all our Methods of moving Pity or Terror, there is none so absurd and barbarous, and what exposes us to the Contempt and Ridicule of our Neighbours, than that dreadful butchering of one another which is so very frequent upon the *English* [emphasis in original] stage.

'He sympathizes', Lowenthal continues, 'with French critics who had pointed to the sight of "Men stabbed, poisoned, racked or impaled" on the English stage as "the Sign of a cruel Temper" in the English national character.'[19] We should note, by the way, that French capitalism was far less developed than English when Addison wrote. Steven Marcus believes there was:

a characteristic Victorian tone . . . resonant of danger, doom, and disaster . . . [which] tells us of a world hedged in with difficulty and pain, a world of harsh efforts and iron consequences. In such a world reality is conceived of as identical with pain and negative conscience is the ruling principle.[20]

Then there is Alexis de Tocqueville's shocked feeling in 1840 that 'the English seem disposed carefully to retain the bloody traces of the dark ages in their penal legislation'.

The élite strata of early industrial England seem to have been peculiarly, if piously, cruel. Theodore Roszak suggests that 'alienation' might be more severe among capitalist élite strata. 'It may even be the case', he writes

that alienation, properly understood, has been more heavily concentrated in the upper levels of capitalist society than in its long-suffering lower depths. How otherwise is one to account on Freudian grounds for the monomaniacal acquisitiveness and ascetic self-discipline of the typical robber baron, except to see such grotesque behaviour as a fierce perversion of the life instincts into anal-sadistic aggressiveness?[21]

Norman O. Brown more explicitly delineates the pathology of early nineteenth century capitalist strata, I think:

... psychoanalysis has accepted as a demonstrated theorem that a definite type of ethical character, exhibiting a combination of three traits – orderliness, parsimony, and obstinacy – is constructed by the sublimation of a special concentration of libido in the anal zone, and it is therefore labelled the anal character ... [There is a direct connection] between Freud's anal character – with its orderliness, parsimony and obstinacy – and the sociological type of the capitalist as delineated by Sombart and Max Weber.[22]

However neither Roszak nor Brown relates this to women, and any failure to relate overall analyses of the human condition to the concept and standing of women is fatal. Erich Fromm's work *The Anatomy of Human Destructiveness* surpasses them in this respect and reveals their essential male-centredness. But Marcuse, more than anyone else, grasps the fact that analyses of the human predicament are futile unless they treat as central the so-called 'woman question'; and since women have been conditioned to believe themselves peripheral to that predicament, its full comprehension is being held back tragically. Finally, only women can express women's experience of the so-called human condition, and it is only now that women, to use Jill

Conway's words, are 'achieving the capacity to confront, analyse and articulate another kind of experience which commands no place in the institutions which are the guardians of the dominant culture'.[23] The loftiest investigations into the human condition usually treat woman as marginal if they consider her at all: thus they are semantically inaccurate and misleading (we'll ignore their arrogance). In fact they concern the *male* condition. By contrast, Marcuse understands the central importance of woman to any basic change in patriarchal society. He explains that patriarchal society has defined certain human attributes as 'feminine' and thereby diminished them.[24] Patriarchal society has taken one group of human qualities – tenderness, nurturance, compassion, inwardness – pushed them down one end of a sexually-structured value spectrum, labelled them 'feminine', and thereby, to varying degrees depending on the specific type of patriarchal society – downgraded their value or standing. By this procedure (unconsciously carried out, it seems, in the service of building abiding social structures, thus in service to the species), male human beings have been able to turn their backs on qualities which are possibly attributes as authentic of males as they are of females. I suspect they defined them as 'feminine', indeed, in order to be *able* to turn their backs on these qualities within themselves. As part of the same long evolutionary process, males have defined another group of human qualities – initiative, adventurousness, endurance, courage, aggression, knowledge-as-domination, the capacity for sustained abstract knowledge – as 'masculine'. The process has enhanced the social standing and dominance of males, and deprived females of their right to call upon this group of human attributes within themselves. The mutual stunting has been appalling. But capitalist society achieved new extremes in this polarization. The 'anal-character' stands for those new extremes, and those extremes are, I propose, the key source of what Roszak described as the 'monomaniacal acquisitiveness and ascetic self-discipline . . . the grotesque behaviour' of members of the 'upper levels of capitalist society'.

The fact that Australia was born at a time when British élite strata – and consequently our own – were in one way and another concerned with entering the stage of industrial capitalism, has had, I suggest, grim implications for the standing of women. Thus Ronald Conway aptly draws our attention to a matter of central importance for Australian 'formative experiences': the fact that 'the high-tide mark for a woman-depreciating puritan type of British patrism [held sway] between 1800 and 1840'.[25] A fine example of woman-depreciating puritanism can be found in the treatment of 221 Irish orphan girls who left Plymouth for Port Adelaide on board the *Roman Emperor*, 17 July 1848: I don't know that there is a deeper way of expressing contempt for woman than by denying her bodilyness. On the voyage more than half of the girls started to menstruate for the first time, perhaps because of the relatively good food. 'Not a single extra piece of cloth or linen had been provided for the shipload of adolescent girls. The surgeon had difficulty with all [sic] washing and hanging out of clothes and linen, "these important duties interfering somewhat with seamen's notions of clean decks, and trim rigging" . . .'[26]

The stage capitalism reached in the nineteenth century was marked by an increasingly constricted inner climate in the nuclear family. That family structure, long pre-dating the nineteenth century in western communities, probably always denied an adequate outlet to woman's healthy and sound emotions by the extent to which it accentuated her subordinate social status. The increased constriction of inner-family climate brought by nineteenth century capitalism affected men quite as much as women; though in different ways. For one thing, it affected the little boy as he grew up. In seeking psychic compensation for a diminished social dignity and emotional mutuality with her husband, woman gained increased power over the child as a surrogate. This meant women made a heavier investment of Oedipally-tinged ambition in children.[27] Part of the effect on the little boy was to prepare him the better for a savagely competitive and emotionally bleak society, and, taking the family as the little society which grooms the child for the big society ahead, there's not much doubt that such preparation impoverished the entire social fabric.

If there is anything in the idea of 'imprinting', the particular ambience English upper class marriage had evolved by the mid-nineteenth century is of central importance for Australian sexuality, man-woman relations and identity. In an effort to convey something of how I sense that ambience* at present, I offer passages from the diary of a twenty-four-year-old migrant to Van Diemen's Land, Kezia Elizabeth Hayter. Kezia Hayter was a protegée of Elizabeth Fry, though evidently not herself a Quaker, and was the only agent of Mrs Fry's 'Ladies Committee' to migrate in order to help Tasmanian women convicts. She landed on 19 July 1841. Her diaries suggest a woman obsessed with a morbidly guilt-stricken vision of religion, which she pretty clearly associated with her expectations about the marriage she planned with Captain Charles Ferguson, a future Chief Harbour Master in Victoria. As his wife she would bear five children. Living at Government House for a time, she mixed socially in governing circles. Here is a long excerpt from Kezia Hayter's diary between 2 February 1842 and 21 July 1842:

I am very discontented with myself . . . alas what a daily warfare a Christian's life is . . . [Reflecting on] the importance and the responsibilities of a woman's duties . . . I became much more convinced that I have much to learn to subdue in myself before I shall be worthy to be the most obedient and gentle wife to you I desire to be . . . [She is often exhausted by her] arduous duties at the [Female Convict] Factory but I come away each time with increasing encouragement and hopes that I have been useful. [She looks forward, however, to the time when she is duty bound and happy] to use all my powers of usefulness for your comfort and to throw all my energies into the quiet . . . of woman's province Home oh how I love you. [She often feels unwell, though specifies no symptoms.] Yesterday . . . was a day of such extreme bodily weakness and mental suffering to me. [On one occasion she evidently catches an infection, which she sees as] . . . contracted that I might be chastened with severe sorrows rather than forget my God and his very chastening is proof of love oh may it work the purpose for which it is sent may it make me more fitted to

---

* R. V. Sampson's studies of the climate in the families of Elizabeth Barrett Browning, John Stuart Mill and Samuel Butler capture this ambience with devastating impact.

be your own dear wife and companion . . . Oh there is no sin in loving you as I do you are a boon from God . . . [sic].[28]

Marriage in English upper circles at that time was associated not only with loss of legal status but with *feelings* of inferiority, manifested even by quite outstanding women. One such was the beautiful and courageous Sheridan grand-daughter, Mrs Caroline Norton, through whose tireless efforts the Infant Custody Bill became law in 1839:

I . . . believe in the natural superiority of man, as I do in the existence of a God. The natural position of woman is inferiority to man. Amen! That is a thing of God's appointing, not of man's devising. I believe it sincerely, as a part of my religion.[29]

Taken as human qualities, most attributes of eighteenth and nineteenth century 'femininity' were pretty thin: sexual frigidity, a stunted capacity for will, initiative, autonomy. Therefore part of the price of increased bourgeois social weight in modernizing England was a style of being female ('The Perfect Lady') which embodied a formidably impoverished personhood. In updated form, the style is represented in today's 'crypto-servant', universal dolly-bird, with her stunted, de-eroticized sexuality. By comparison, the nineteenth century's social definition of male-ness seems more inviting. Though his sexuality was sharply split and thus seriously impaired, the 'masculine' male scores well on will, autonomy, initiative and courage, those stars in Erikson's table of human virtues.[30] Yet he scores unevenly on other attributes: appallingly on 'intimacy', ambivalently on 'integrity', badly on inwardness, insightfulness and compassion.

But if this is a fruitful way of seeing one major sociosexual configuration developed by the nineteenth century, alongside it we can pick up a wider spread of that ancient social concept of male and female which involved a greater shared humanity, a blunted sociosexual differentiation, and a rich overall personhood. So while capitalism enlarged the relational and social 'distance' between man and woman just as it did between aspects of the personality of man himself, there also appeared signs of fellowship on a scale and perhaps a quality either not known in the west before, or submerged for some time. Thus in the nineteenth century, within the patriarchal, nuclear family, though apparently only for a small number of men and women, patterns emerged which pointed towards a more promising future.[31] These patterns were most likely to be found amongst professional, bourgeois, aristocratic and upper working class strata; and in cultures where the weight of aristocracy and bourgeoisie as identity sources was strong.

Being born of the nineteenth century, Australian sociosexual patterns were heir to both these configurations. They were both 'in the air', saturating the thought-world of the developing child as he and she absorbed attitudes to the body, authority and work which would equip them to take their respective places in the antipodean universe. But the former configuration predominated and proved a more powerful source of models for identity formation.

For any historian seeking to use identity theory, there is a further issue central to the status of woman in democracies,[32] and especially relevant to a democracy like Australia, 'charged with the *proletarian* turmoil of the Industrial Revolution' [my emphasis].[33] Calvin Hernton and others confirm one's feeling that sex and race are intimately related. Bodily differences seem to encourage us to define a given group as 'the other', and this allows us the more easily to project on such a group a complex range of unconscious feelings which otherwise would tend to remain painfully internalized. Human differences or polarities do not have to be handled in terms of antagonism. In societies such as those Erich Fromm designates as life-affirmative, they are not handled that way.[34] But in most forms of patriarchal society, differences have been and increasingly are being handled in terms of antagonism and destructiveness. Democratic capitalism is certainly one such form of patriarchal society, and Hartzian theory suggests that feudal cultures, which *explicitly* accept superior and inferior statuses, can manage race relations better than egalitarian societies.[35] Where, as with Brazil, one of Hartz's European 'fragments' has held on to certain feudal values, the race problem is the more easily handled as one of *defined statuses*. Where a feudal tradition is absent, such as in the United States or in Australia, the question of race – essentially a question of *body* difference – is more awkward and bitter. Hence the White Australia Policy and the United States 'Negro problem'. Gunnar Myrdal correctly remarked that the 'Negro problem' is actually a 'white problem', and similarly, the 'woman problem' is actually a 'man problem'. Democratic societies – therefore above all *very* democratic societies like Australia, in which working class strata have bulked large in forming hegemonic values, are possibly in some ways at a relative disadvantage in managing sexual relations since they explicitly deny the 'rightness' of differences. In some senses, as far as women are concerned, egalitarian society males seem (like Professor Higgins) to be saying 'Why can't a woman be like *me*'? Lee Rainwater suggests this is almost exactly what many working class males feel about female patterns of sexual response.[36] And to deny the validity of 'differences' in this area is to deny them at the deepest level. (That the differences are ultimately 'complementary' differences doesn't, I think, alter the main point.)

Much that was admirable came out of our formative decades, but much that helps explain Australian woman's not-quite-western low status also came out of them: violence, brutality, widespread prostitution and a concomitant generalized contempt for women;* male addiction to the company of males and heavy drinking; and a reverence for muscle-over-mind, which masked envy and manifested hostility towards the intellect. And no catharsis, no blood-letting on the scale of the American War of Independence erupted to seriously modify early patterns in Australia's development. Indeed, later experiences and processes – the goldrushes, for example – often also served to etch some early lines deeper.

Of the gold rushes in Victoria, where their impact was greatest, Geoffrey Serle notes that the gold migrants as a group were 'magnificent economic material with educational qualifications and professional and industrial skills superior to any other group of migrants to Australia, at least in the nineteenth

* See p. 134

century'.[37] On the following page however, he shows that a widespread shared motivation amongst these migrants, might well have been what Slater calls 'a lack of success in confronting the social conditions obtaining in their mother country'.[38] Serle writes:

The one scholar who noticed the matter at the time affirmed that this was 'a much more select body than has ever before left our shores'. He singled out members of the professional classes facing too much competition, younger sons of squires and Scottish lairds, small farmers feeling the pinch of foreign competition, Cornish miners, and handicraftsmen from quiet country towns.[39]

Sailing to Queensland on board the *Queen of the South* in 1863, Charles H. Eden, 'a gentleman', was accompanied by 'farmers' sons with small capital . . . and farmers' sons without any capital at all [as well as] military men . . .' Generalizing about his reasons for emigrating, Eden underlines Serle's picture:

Every profession and calling in England being already overcrowded, and those unfortunate beings, younger sons, continuing to be born, there can be no doubt that these and other portionless individuals must direct their attention to the only outlet left open, viz. our Colonies.[40]

Here is Philip Slater's comment on psychic 'losers' in relation to the United States:

This nation was settled and continuously repopulated by people who were not personally successful in confronting the social conditions obtaining in their mother country, but fled those conditions in the hope of a better life. This series of choices (reproduced in the west-ward movement) provided a complex selection process – populating America disproportionately with a certain kind of person.[41]

Should one expect that such driven and self-doubting folk could provide *effective countervailing strata* to offset existing patterns influenced by earlier convict 'born losers', and by élites with no really robust sense of identity? Both contributed to male uncertainty, and in their own uncertainty, males of our formative times were generally unwilling to countenance robust confidence among 'their' women. Hence the gold rushes could scarcely have solidly dented some of the stubborn patterns laid down in earlier decades.

The fact of our birth and formative decades in the nineteenth century, then, must be taken into account in any attempt to tease out the sources of woman's low standing in Australia. Australian historians tend to stress aspects of that century other than those I pointed up. For most historians, it was pre-eminently the era of the French Revolution, of individualism, liberalism and nascent democracy. And of course these must find a central place in any balanced appraisal of woman's situation. But it will not necessarily be as glowing a place as orthodox history suggests because it sees these processes too strongly in terms of enhanced human wellbeing. Their darker sides deserve more attention, if women are to be considered as serious historical subjects. Democracy entered modern history with capitalism, so if my hypothesis that capitalism involved the psychic diminution of woman is valid, it must enter any balanced historical assessment of nineteenth century western achievement. Men and women, after all, are not discrete entities. They are, in the final sense, two complementary aspects of one entity called 'the human being'.

We turn now to parameters within which to catch lines of our national identity. Australians tend to think of New South Wales in formative times as 'western', in the sense of belonging to the western tradition, but that is not altogether so. We need to comprehend our national identity along several historical dimensions or continua. To start, we should see our 'formative' selves partly as members of a pre-modern society. There are two reasons for this. Firstly, there is the important, some might say central, role of the Irish in shaping basic folkways: attitudes to the body, sexuality, and women; to time, work, play and authority; to eating and drinking. Secondly, there is the formative impact of convictism, best seen as a pre-capitalist, thus pre-modern institution, akin perhaps to slavery, even though thrown up by the early phases of capitalist development.

We also need to comprehend our national identity in terms of the range of *colonial* societies. Colonial élite males generally have a good deal of difficulty with self-definition and self-confidence. The Americans gained some clarity through the War of Independence. I don't think we have ever gained a great deal – one small sign being that we protest too much . . .

We need, next, also to comprehend our national identity in terms of a genocidally-inclined racist group.[42] Our treatment of Aborigines has left us with a lot of guilt. And if there is any meaning in the idea of formative experiences, then early (and continuing) Australian male experiences with Aboriginal women – that luxurious phrase 'black velvet' is certainly suggestive – have contributed an early layer to the general low esteem in which women are held in our country. We also feel guilt at our prosperity in an ocean of very poor non-Europeans.

Just as it is misleading to think of early New South Wales as basically, or only, an ordinary western community, it is also misleading to implicitly treat our early élite strata in terms of western European aristocratic, bourgeois and professional layers. We might get closer to the thinness of that early élite, its derivative quality, by thinking of Marx's notion of a 'compradore bourgeoisie', or Rosa Luxemburg's and Trotsky's picture of colonial ruling strata as congenital weaklings, puny specimens of the genre. These argue that the mother country is not concerned to build a robust replica of its own social structure in a colony, but distorts it to fit the needs of the mother economy. We took England's refuse, and guarded it as well as administrators of integrity could, given that they were kept on a financial shoestring. We supplied England with wool. Overall, in meshing with imperial England's needs, early New South Wales developed, as Manning Clark reported – into a 'broken, cold and unnatural' form of society. Because our élites have always been so uncertain of who they are, they have always been ill at ease over issues of authority, and their uncertainty contributes to what some have seen as an unusual degree of *authoritarianism* in Australia.[43] But feelings about authority are central to identity, and the strange unease Australians experience over authority questions is reflected in their general uncertainty about who they are. In this, our élites recall the strident but fragile élites of many post-1945 emergent nations.

So much by way of sketching a broad grid through which we can think about finer-meshed aspects of our national identity as we go further.

Such is the standing of women in Australia that one of our most interesting historical controversies, the great debate on national identity, virtually ignores women. In that debate, Vance Palmer's *The Legend of the Nineties* (1954) and Russel Ward's *The Australian Legend* (1958) have played a central part. The most arresting challenge to date has been made by a young radical, Humphrey McQueen. In reading the page proofs of *A New Britannia*, McQueen was struck by 'five major weaknesses' in his work, the third being that 'the role of women [was] ignored'. Despite his 'androgynous spirit', however, he decided to leave women out of his 'argument concerning the social origins of Australian radicalism and nationalism'.[44] In the interests of accuracy, then, and without wishing to offend McQueen's 'androgynous spirit'*, we must rephrase that subtitle to read 'argument concerning the male origins of Australian radicalism and nationalism'. But the debate has ranged more widely than my selection of the names of Ward and McQueen suggests.[45] In 1966 Michael Roe staked a central claim for the role of middle-strata urban groups in moulding national identity.[46] Ward partly embraced this argument in a 1970 paper, 'Two Kinds of Australian Patriotism'.[47] Douglas Pike threw up a

---

* McQueen writes: '. . . despite my androgynous spirit the task of reshaping history to include women must be left to one of their number.' This, he evidently feels, excuses his ignoring 'the role of women'. However my being a woman did not excuse me from the task of studying, teaching and writing history which very largely concerned males though it purported to concern community, while *Lang is Greater than Lenin*, my first book, concerned one of the bleakest male universes imaginable. And does McQueen really imagine the 'role of women' is *not* his business as historian and radical, quite as much as it is a woman's? What mid-Victorian archness is this? Women are not just one half of the human race: one half of every man, in a very real sense, is a woman. Even if McQueen did not *claim* to have an 'androgynous spirit', he has one, though evidently well locked, as Theodore Roszak puts it, in the dungeons of his psyche.

central problem by showing the overlap in folkways between poor farmers ('smallholders') and rural workers.[48] The one woman who has centrally intervened so far, Coral Lansbury (not at that time influenced by the women's movement), followed the Australian male lead by largely ignoring the role of women. (One writer who does not do this is the Englishman Barry Argyle, in *An Introduction to the Australian Novel, 1830 – 1930*.)

Women, then are virtually ignored in serious discussions of Australian national identity. This itself, of course, reflects their curiously low standing. In the United States, where women's standing is somewhat higher, male historians more often pay explicit attention to the role of women in analysing national identity.[49] Historians are as much part of their culture as anyone else, and Australian historians – overwhelmingly male – honestly don't *see* women as serious historical subjects. We have suggested that, in celebrating male achievement in the past (and that, generally speaking, is the stuff of history) historians are helping affirm male identity in the present. In effect however, they deny this to women, while accepting their taxes, and claiming (implicitly or explicitly) to engage in research and teaching of *national* relevance (women are more than half that nation). Regarding the university undergraduate level, male historians seem unaware of the implications of the fact that they teach their male-oriented courses to a high percentage of female students. Only about twelve to fourteen per cent of faculty staff are female. Young women therefore fail to see women as respected authority figures and worthwhile role models, just as they are denied what is given by males to males: the right to see their faces in the past as worthwhile builders of the present. Virginia Woolf points out that women must reach back through the mother:[50] to be denied a sense of past generations, as Australian women are, except in at best a token, or at worst an impoverished way, is to be demeaned and mutilated in the present.

Two important contributors to our thinking on the role of women in the Australian national identity have been outside the ranks of those officially participating in the debate, and they have been women. One is Judith Wright who says:

The 'mateship' ingredient in Australian tradition was always and necessarily one-sided; it left out of account the whole relationship with woman.[51]

Male literary critics acclaim her poetry widely, but male historians largely ignore a basic point she makes on national identity when it threatens their male-centred conceptualization of our history. A similar treatment was accorded Barbara Baynton when she illuminated the crippled side of the mateship ethos burgeoning (at least in the minds of leading writers) in the late nineteenth century. In 1903 a contributor to the *Bulletin* wrote:

Her studies of some Australian people and scenes are realistic beyond anything of the kind yet written here – beyond Lawson, even beyond Miles Franklin. Nothing could be closer to life. For minute fidelity there has been no writer anywhere to surpass this writer. Four of the sketches are in all essentials perfect so far as they go.[52]

And the Brisbane *Evening Observer* in the same year carried this report:

A note of tragic intensity is struck which shows that Barbara Baynton has dug deeper than any Australian writer who has preceded her.[53]

A. G. Stephens conceded her to be outstanding, as do Vance Palmer[54] and A. A. Phillips. But 'the world she presents is one of callousness, stupidity, laziness, insensitivity and insolence: a world where fear not friendliness is the main motivating element.' And so, like A. G. Stephens, while Palmer and A. A. Phillips 'recognize her exceptional power . . . in their major works [they] disregard her because she runs counter to the scheme they establish'.[55] Baynton's reward for her acclaimed literary excellence has been something pretty close to literary oblivion. She threw a particularly dark light on mateship, and just as Judith Wright's comments on this basic Australian male-bonding institution have been largely ignored by male analysts and celebrants alike of our national identity, so too has Baynton's illumination of it.

Since in explicit terms woman has been pretty well left out of the national identity debate, to a large extent one has to *sense* her part in the formation of that identity, moving partly by inference. Two questions of central concern to male participants in the debate have been and are these: did 'up-country' *mores* carry greater weight than urban?; was there an early 'working class' and if there was, to what extent did it shape early patterns? For our purpose, however, the best approach is to cut across these questions to a certain degree, by emphasizing the fact that one central configuration in our identity was shaped by what the nineteenth century called 'the lower orders'.

Is there a more satisfactory word we could use for the early nineteenth century 'lower orders'? Humphrey McQueen offers the term 'lumpenproletariat'. Marx and Engels reserved the harshest bits of their formidable vocabulary for the interstitial folk embraced in this term ('dangerous class . . . social scum . . . that passively rotting mass') but as Peter Worsley has remarked, the word 'lumpenproletariat' is also more of an insult than a concept. It is often used in relation to early industrializing societies, such as late eighteenth century England, and we can thus view men and women from these strata as in the process of falling under the sway of the individualist-achievement ethos. So, as with the eighteenth century characters of *The Beggars' Opera*, it is clear such folk had begun to move a fair way towards assimilating the values of patricentric-acquisitive society. In long historical perspective, we may, in the words of Robert Endleman, view the 'scions of the lumpenproletariat' here as elsewhere, as trying to climb the 'ladder of individualistic success-achievement struggle'.[56] But that process took time, often more than one generation, and while the process was taking place, early folk patterns were being etched more deeply into an emergent community. Upwards-mobility is very slow to budge some of these.

I propose we call the late eighteenth and early nineteenth century 'lower orders' by a term coined by Gareth Stedman-Jones: the 'casual poor'.[57] We can see them as pre- or proto-working class, 'vegetating', as Engels put it, 'in the borderland

between working class and lumpenproletariat'. The casual poor
tended to accept their self-evaluation in terms of the hegemonic
status hierarchy. Too many historians have failed to see this
acceptance because the casual poor often assumed defiant attitudes and vehemently denounced 'swells', 'toffs', etc. At the
same time, like today's 'Hell's Angels', they set up their own
élitist universe. It was marked by a highly restricted code (in
Basil Bernstein's sense, a 'grammar of motive'),[58] by intolerance
and brutality. Nowhere was – and is – that brutality clearer than
in their treatment of women and children. Woe betide these
should they fail to enact the special deference rituals towards
males enjoined by that ugly universe. The casual poor adopted
what Erikson calls 'negative identities'. Top they wanted to be,
and their situation was such that they could only be 'top at the
bottom', the Ned Kelly syndrome; or, as card players put it,
'going *misère*'. But one is just as much a prisoner of the status
hierarchy by replicating it in forms appropriate to the lowest
rungs of the ladder, as in trying to ascend to its higher rungs. And
one is equally under its sway in adopting a 'negative identity'
designed to defy it, as in affirming it: the emotional cathexis
carries the same voltage either way. To escape the values of the
status hierarchy, you have to cool the whole thing, dissolving
affect on the question.

Since the value structure enveloping the early casual poor was
contoured basically by those on the top rungs of the status
hierarchy, accepting hierarchy meant, for the casual poor,
accepting a demeaned version of their human worth. All the
brave defiance, all the triumphalist ideologies in the world
couldn't and can't ultimately shake this core acceptance. One
last consolation, however, was left to the casual poor and
naturally enough they tended to clutch at it: their women could
be more demeaned, more lowly, than they. In this, too, for the
most part they were imitating their betters.

In relation to the standing of women in early New South
Wales, the question as to whether certain key formative values
derived from 'up-country' or 'urban' strata, then, is secondary
to the fact that the earliest manifestations of those values were
associated with the casual poor; later influences reinforced

early influences, but these were in large part associated with
working class rather than early sub-working class strata. The
configuration of values within our national identity whose
earliest face was associated with the casual poor is of course
only one of the configurations making up that identity. Russel
Ward suggests there are two main such configurations.[59] There
may indeed be more. I accept Erikson's view: 'a nation's
identity is derived from the ways in which history has, as it
were, counterpointed certain opposite potentialities . . .'[60] But
the abiding influence of the casual poor in our 'formative'
times has, I think, to be kept in mind if we want to comprehend
the unusually diminished quality of woman in our folkways.
No doubt nineteenth century observers exaggerated, but their
impressions, on which Ward draws a good deal, have much to
offer. Australia, said one observer in 1849, is 'essentially the
country of the poor', while in 1853 another added: 'It is, as is
proudly and emphatically asserted, "the poor man's land".'[61]
Yes indeed: the poor *man's* land. But what might this mean
for poor *women*? And what has it meant for *women in general*?

Democracies, historically, have been open to the major
influences of quite different social classes. The United States
has been most influenced by its bourgeois beginnings in the
seventeenth century. English and Swedish democracy bears the
mark of an aristocracy and upper bourgeoisie, Finland, of a
lesser gentry and peasantry. In all cases, it goes without saying
that the modern industrial proletariat has also been of crucial
importance. But Australia's form of democracy has virtually
lacked the influence of layers above a middle or lower bourgeois
order, and farmers and working class layers.* Where, as in
Australia, during formative times higher status layers have been
of dubious or minor weight as countervailing influences to
'the lower orders', the situation of woman is least hopeful.
Encel and Tebbutt write: 'In aristocratic and caste societies,

* The ethnic contribution of the Irish coexists with considerations of class
and colonialism, both important in shaping the value structure and folkways of a given democracy, but that ethnic contribution may also be analytically separate.

women can attain positions of influence and authority',[62] but in a democracy contoured as ours is, males seem to take special care to keep such options closed to women. Their care has understandable psychodynamic roots. But the effect has been to keep the range of models for female identity formation sadly constricted for Australian women.*

Australia is internationally renowned as a proud democracy to which one of the world's strongest trade union movements has made crucial contributions. Widely (if hazily) linked in many minds with the strength of our democracy and our unionism is 'mateship'. Mateship is an informal male-bonding institution involving powerful sublimated homosexuality. Indeed some of its most ardent intellectual celebrants are slowly coming to see that mateship is deeply antipathetic to women – even though a major Australian female style is to try and be what I define as 'a matey woman', 'one of the boys'. Notwithstanding these valiant efforts, there is some gut sense in which a woman is not wanted. Back off, don't crowd me, love. You aren't really necessary. You aren't really there . . . (so I tiptoe in my heart). In an A.B.C. broadcast given in 1971, Professor Sol Encel said:

Mateship . . . automatically excludes women because it is based on the idea of men as workmates and companions, [while] the most important form of enduring relationship between the sexes is marriage, which conflicts directly with all-male relations. There is a sexual element involved here as well, since there are obvious affinities between mateship as a social relationship and homosexuality as a sexual relationship.[63]

The aura of antipathy that engulfs a woman in an R.S.L. club, or an all-male pub (they still exist in Dublin and working class north England too!) hurts, it actually hurts. The emanation from groups of young men at swimming pools and beaches is toxic.

*Discussing my projected course on women in Australian history, several students expressed this neatly: 'But you can't teach a whole year about Caroline Chisholm.'

There is a sense in which much of the male universe in Australia withholds shared humanity from females on a scale one doesn't meet with as intensely and constantly in other western countries.

Cross-cultural male domination of institutions and male hegemony of cultural parameters in patriarchal society make it nonsense to claim that the standing of Australian women is unique. Yet the curious impoverishment of her situation surely commands the historian's attention, because Australia has so long been internationally renowned for its proud commitment to economic justice and egalitarianism. Indeed the *extent* of that commitment is often claimed as the key feature of Australia's variant of democracy. Therefore the fact that woman is implicitly defined out of such a commitment faces the historian with a major problem about *democracy itself*. In no form of democracy is the sociocultural 'weight' or influence of the working class greater than in Australia; in no form perhaps is it less than in Sweden, where aristocratic and upper bourgeois strata have had a deep 'imprinting' effect on national values.[64] The civic standing of woman is higher by far in Sweden than in Australia. Some might argue that the greater the social weight of aristocrat and upper bourgeois, the less 'democratic', by definition, the moral economy of a community. So if historians, political philosophers and political scientists were to begin to consider the situation of women with any intellectual seriousness, they might then have to recast some basic conceptual structures. If they were to include women, as a first approximation, one might have to begin with an apparently paradoxical formulation: the greater the degree of democracy, the greater the misogyny. If women were to be defined as relevant to political philosophy, one might have to conclude that such a democracy was profoundly undemocratic. 'Demos' means 'people'. A more accurate term would clearly be 'androcracy'. The key terms of discourse will have to be re-thought now that we are beginning to confront the fact that, as George Simmel pointed out long ago, the very standards by which mankind has estimated the fundamentals of our civilization are 'not neutral . . . but in themselves essentially masculine'. He continues:

The requirements of art, patriotism, morality in general and social ideas in particular, correctness in practical judgement and objectivity in theoretical knowledge . . . all these are categories which belong as it were in their form and claims to humanity in general, but in their actual configuration they are masculine throughout.[65]

Notes

1.   C. S. Blackton, *Historical Studies*, vol. 9, no. 36, May 1961, pp. 351–67.

2.   G. Bolton, 'Australian Historians in Quest of a Theme', *Teaching History*, September 1969, pp. 5–20.

3.   G. Blainey, *The Tyranny of Distance*, Sun Books, Melbourne, 1966.

4.   I. Turner, *The Australian Dream: A Collection of Anticipations about Australia from Captain Cook to the present day*, Sun Books, Melbourne, 1968.

5.   Jennifer Stoddart, 'The Woman Suffrage Bill in Quebec', in Marylee Stephenson, ed., *Women in Canada*, New Press, Toronto, 1973, p. 91.

6.   L. Hartz, *The Founding of New Societies*, Harcourt Brace & World, New York, 1964.

7.   ibid, p. 3.

8.   R. Ward, *The Australian Legend*, Oxford University Press, Melbourne, 1958, and 'Two Kinds of Australian Patriotism', *Victorian Historical Magazine*, vol. 41, no. 1, February 1970, pp. 225–43.

9.   J. S. Mill, *The Subjection of Women*, 1869, World Classics, Oxford, 1912, pp. 467–8.

10.   W. L. O'Neill, op. cit., p. 18. See too Philip Toynbee's comment (*Observer*) on Gore Vidal's *Burr*: 'The most enthralling and plausible account of the Formative Years that I have read . . .' (Panther edition, St. Albans, Herts., 1974).

11.   Oliver MacDonagh, 'The Irish in Victoria, 1851–91: A Demographic Essay', *Historical Studies, papers read before the Irish Conference of Historians*, vol. 8, T. Williamns, ed., Gill and Macmillan, Dublin, 1971.

12.   Robert Waelder, 'Psychoanalysis and History: Application of Psycho-analysis to Historiography', in Benjamin B. Wolman, ed., *The Psycho-analytic Interpretation of History*, Basic Books, New York and London, 1971, p. 24.

13.   Cited in Russel Ward, *The Australian Legend*, op. cit.

14. E. Sullerot, *Woman, Society and Change*, World University Library, London, 1971, pp. 34–5.

15. K. Marx, *Capital*, vol. 1, Modern Library edition, pp. 89–90.

16. Thorstein Veblen, *The Theory of the Leisure Class*, Mentor, (1899, 1912), New York, 1957, pp. 106–7.

17. J. A. and Olive Banks, *Feminism and Family Planning in Victorian England*, Liverpool University Press, 1964.

18. Geoffrey Gorer, *Exploring English Character*, Cresset Press, London, 1955, p. 303.

19. Leo Lowenthal, *Literature, Popular Culture and Society*, Pacific Books, Palo Alto, California, 1961, pp. 82–3.

20. S. Marcus, *The Other Victorians: A Study of Sexuality and Pornography in Mid-Nineteenth Century England*, Corgi Books, London, 1970, p. 17.

21. T. Roszak, *The Making of a Counter Culture*, Faber & Faber, London, 1970, p. 96.

22. N. O. Brown, *Life Against Death: The Psychoanalytic Meaning of History*, Routledge & Kegan Paul, London, 1959, p. 203. This, significantly, is taken from Chapter 14, 'The Protestant Era'.

23. J. K. Conway, 'Coeducation and women's studies: Two Approaches to the Question of Women's Place in the Contemporary University', *Daedalus*, 1974, p. 241.

24. Herbert Marcuse, 'Feminist Socialism: The hard core of the dream', loc. cit.

25. R. Conway, op. cit., p. 120.

26. C. W. Parkin, 'Irish Female Immigration to South Australia During the Great Famine', B. A. honours thesis, Department of History, University of Adelaide, 1964, p. 27.

27. Philip Slater, op. cit., p. 69.

28. Kezia Elizabeth Hayter, 'Diary of Kezia Elizabeth Hayter', Tasmanian State Archives.

29. Cited in Ronald Sampson, op. cit., p. 54. Sampson is quoting from Jane Grey Perkins, *The Life of Mrs Norton*, 1909, pp. 149–50.

30. E. Erikson, *Childhood and Society*, Penguin Books, 1965. They are perhaps more closely related to patricentric-acquisitive virtues than to 'human' virtues as such.

31. It goes without saying that emerging patterns arose alongside, and sometimes out of the matrix of, existing similar residual patterns. As Erikson

puts it in *Young Man Luther:* In all times, there are 'islands . . . where sensible people manage to live relatively lusty and decent lives: as moral as they must be, as free as they may be, and as masterly as they can be'. (Faber and Faber, London, 1958, p. 71).

32.   New categories are being born as we try to comprehend the situation of women. The old categories – class, caste, oppressed minority, etc., have a certain mileage but finally run out of puff. Not surprising, as they were evolved to fit males. Women are only beginning to weigh in seriously in the construction of social reality and its conceptualization. But works I've found helped me include: Kirsten Amundsen, *The Silenced Majority: Women and American Democracy*, Prentice-Hall, Englewood Cliffs, N.J., 1971; Gerald D. Berreman, 'The Concept of Caste', *International Encyclopedia of the Social Sciences*, vol. 2, Crowell Collier MacMillan, U.S.A., 1968, pp. 333–9; Gunnar Myrdal, op. cit.; Gale Rubin, 'Woman as Nigger', *Argus*, reprinted in Betty and Theodore Roszak, eds., op. cit.

33.   Louis Hartz, op. cit., p. 3.

34.   E. Fromm, op. cit., p. 168ff.

35.   Louis Dumont's thesis is not without relevance here: the Indian caste system reflects a stubborn tendency towards hierarchy, Dumont says. Suppress that tendency in one form, and it will find another way of manifesting itself. See *Homo Hierarchicus: The Caste System and its Implications*, Paladin, St. Albans, 1972.

36.   L. Rainwater, *And the Poor Get Children: Sex, Contraception and Family Planning in the Working Class*, Quadrangle Books, Chicago, 1960.

37.   G. Serle, *The Golden Age*, Melbourne University Press, Melbourne, 1968 (1963), p. 47.

38.   P. Slater, op. cit., pp. 13–14.

39.   G. Serle, op. cit., p. 48.

40.   Charles H. Eden, *My Wife and I in Queensland*, etc., Longmans Green and Co., London, 1872, p. 5.

41.   P. Slater, op. cit., pp. 13–14.

42.   Yet as racists go, we are not especially outstanding. Humphrey McQueen (*A New Britannia*, Penguin, 1970, and elsewhere) exhausts his stock of racist adjectives on us. If he ever situated Australia in an *international* perspective, what words has he got left to describe German Nazis, Americans in the Deep South or Vietnam (think of My Lai)?

43.   See, for example, D. S. Anderson in *Australian Journal of Psychology*,

December 1970; D. K. Wheeler, 'Edwards Personal Preference Schedule and National Characteristics', *Australian Journal of Sociology*, April 1969, pp. 40–7.

44. H. McQueen, op. cit., pp. 13–14.

45. Here is a select guide to recent contributors.

Allan Ashbolt, 'Myth and Reality', *Meanjin Quarterly*, December 1966;

John Barrett, 'Melbourne and the Bush; Some Urban Dwellers' Connections with the Country', History Department, La Trobe University, 1972 (roneoed paper);

Coral Lansbury, 'The Miner's Right to Mateship', *Meanjin Quarterly*, December 1966, and *Arcady in Australia: the Evocation of Australia in Nineteenth Century English Literature*, Melbourne University Press, Melbourne, 1970;

Ronald Lawson, 'The "Bush Ethos" and Brisbane in the 1890's', *Historical Studies Australia and New Zealand*, vol. 16, no. 58, April 1972, and *Brisbane in the 1890's: A Study of an Australian Urban Society*, University of Queensland Press, St. Lucia 1973;

H. McQueen, op. cit., and 'Reply to Russel Ward', *Overland*, 48, Winter 1971;

Michael Roe, 'The Australian Legend', *Meanjin Quarterly*, vol. 21, no. 3, September 1962;

Ian Turner, 'The Retreat from Reason', *Meanjin Quarterly*, June 1966, and 'Review of *New Britannia* by Humphrey McQueen', *Historical Studies Australia and New Zealand*, vol. 16, no. 56, April 1971, pp. 634–7;

Russel Ward, 'Review of *Arcady in Australia*, by Coral Lansbury', *Historical Studies Australia and New Zealand*, vol. 15, no. 58, April 1972, pp. 292–5, 'Britannia Australis', *Overland*, 47, Autumn 1971, pp. 47–9, and 'Reply to Humphrey McQueen', *Overland*, 50/51, Autumn 1972, pp. 79–80;

Owen Webster, 'The Need for Intransigence', *Meanjin Quarterly*, September 1966;

Douglas Pike, 'The Smallholders' Place in the Australian Tradition', Tasmanian Historical Research Association, *Papers and Proceedings*, vol. 10, December 1962, p. 32.

46. Michael Roe, 'The Australian Legend', loc. cit.

47. R. Ward, 'Two Kinds of Australian Patriotism', loc. cit.

48. D. Pike, 'The Smallholders' Place in the Australian Tradition', loc. cit.

49. See, for example, David Potter, 'American Women and the American Character', *Stetson University Bulletin*, vol. 62, no. 1, January 1962.

50. Virginia Woolf, *A Room of One's Own*, Penguin Books, 1965.

51. Judith Wright, *Preoccupations in Australian Poetry*, Oxford University Press, Melbourne, 1966, pp. 132–4.

52. *Bulletin*, 14 February 1903.

53. *Evening Observer*, 14 February 1903.

54. Vance Palmer, ed., *A. G. Stephens: His Life and Work*, Robertson and Mullens, Melbourne, 1941. See, for example, pp. 110–11.

55. June E. Lee, 'Barbara Baynton: A Study of her Writing', combined English-History honours thesis, Melbourne University, 1966.

56. R. Endleman, *Personality and Social Life*, Random House, New York, 1967, p. 205.

57. G. Stedman-Jones, *Outcast London*, Clarendon Press, Oxford, 1971.

58. B. Bernstein, *Class, Codes and Control*, vol. 1, Paladin, St. Albans, 1973.

59. R. Ward, 'Two Kinds of Australian Patriotism', loc. cit.

60. E. Erikson, *Childhood and Society*, op. cit., p. 277.

61. A Resident of Twelve Years, *New South Wales, its Past, Present and Future Condition*, etc., London, 1849, p. 20; G. B. Earp, *What We Did in Australia: Being the Practical Experience of Three Clerks*, etc., London, 1853, p. 115.

62. S. Encel, N. MacKenzie and M. Tebbutt, op cit., p. 299.

63. S. Encel, 'The Inequality of Women', Australian Broadcasting Commission *Fact and Opinion. A Nation Changes*. Part 5.

64. Irene Scobbie, *Sweden: Nation of the Modern World*, Ernest Benn, London, 1972, p. 162. Consider the case of the Swedish Prime Minister, Olof Palme, whose attitude to women is extremely enlightened. He comes from aristocratic and substantial bourgeois families. His father, Gunnar Palme, is from a 'comfortable upper middle class family'; his mother, Elisabeth von Knieriem, an aristocrat. In Finland, a lesser landed gentry and peasantry have contributed to a very sturdy democracy where, some say, the position of women is superior to that in Sweden.

65. George Simmel quoted in Karen Horney, 'The Flight from Womanhood: The Masculinity Complex as Viewed by Men and by Women . . .', in Jean Baker Miller, ed., *Psychoanalysis and Women*, Penguin Books, 1973, pp. 6–7

Chapter 3

Women among the Casual Poor

'. . . the slave of slaves . . .'

(LENIN)

Australian historians such as Manning Clark tentatively link the standing of women in Australia with convictism. But before we ask how convict women helped shape the concept of woman in our national identity, we should look at *free* women from the same social strata, 'the casual poor'.

If we agree that Russel Ward's Australian in *The Australian Legend* symbolizes an important component of our national identity, it's frightening to notice the overlap between his characteristics and those of the 'nomad races' of English poor, the casual poor Henry Mayhew described in the mid-nineteenth century. For example, common to all, Mayhew wrote, was 'use of a slang language . . . lax ideas of property . . . repugnance to continuous labour . . . their pugnacity – and their utter want of religion'.[1] Frightening: because the contempt of Mayhew's poor men for women was profound. The customs of the free casual poor formed a matrix, a seed bed, for those of convicts. Lloyd Robson, drawing on Mayhew regarding the 'young prostitute', suggests this by describing *free* casual poor women in a chapter called 'The Female Convicts':

Looseness of morality was a characteristic of some of the poorer parts of London, and licentiousness was fostered by the poor lodging-houses frequented by boys and girls, who rapidly formed attachments in these places of childish profligacy. A young prostitute spoke of coming up to London, falling in with three Irish girls and four men, and going haymaking with them: 'I had a fortnight of haymaking. I had a mate at haymaking and in a few days he ruined me. *He told the master that I belonged to him. He did not say I was his wife. They don't call us their wives.*' [My emphasis][2]

Mayhew felt that these 'low-lodging houses, where boys and girls are all huddled promiscuously together' suggested a 'system of barbarity, atrocity, and enormity, which certainly cannot be paralleled in any nation, however barbarous, nor in any age, however "dark" '.[3]

My main concern is to tease out the quality of personhood accorded to women by casual poor men, and consequently much of the self-concept of these women. The words underlined from Robson, above, suggest that the man had 'thingized' the woman ('He told the master that I belonged to him'), and in this respect, his feelings were those the wealthy middle-class author of *My Secret Life* expressed towards working women.[4] The 'objectivization' of human relations characterizing capitalism, and most vividly manifested by capitalist social strata, transformed women into 'something less than human beings'.[5] Perhaps particularly in its mid-nineteenth century form, the institution of marriage transmitted bourgeois values to many women in an acutely constricting way. But though marriage had not always reached the 'lower orders', bourgeois hegemonic values still reached them because they permeated all levels of the status hierarchy. Indeed such values were manifested in specific and often brutal, physical and psychic ways at its lowest reaches, one reason being that life was generally experienced with more anguish there.* The attitude capitalist hegemonic strata felt towards women thus came to be reflected, in varying ways, down the entire status ladder. So while the working class 'mate' who 'told the master that I belonged to him' expressed a working class attitude, a writer in the early twentieth century *Imperial Review* showed that attitude spanned the range of the whole status ladder from top to bottom: 'Half the wives, in every rank of life, are more or less invalids . . . Lord Nozoo, in the play, asks Hodge, "Well, how are your pigs, wife, ducks, children, and so forth?" ' . . . 'The average Working Man's wife is treated as a slave and a cow. She keeps on breeding in a miserable rabbit-hutch.'[7]

I want to go back to Mayhew's young London prostitute, because those emphasized words have more to tell us. For

---

* Wilhelm Reich remarks that 'the well-to-do citizen carries his neurosis with dignity or he lives it out in one way or another; in working class people, it shows itself as the grotesque tragedy it really is.'[6]

example, we might guess they imply the man wanted the woman to experience greater feelings of unworthiness than he did, and if so it was an aim widely achieved among the casual poor. This process, largely unconscious, operated (and operates) at all levels of the status ladder, for in a society where, to a large extent, the value structure took (and takes) shape round status, personal self-evaluation also tended to run to earth in some niche on the status-hierarchy. The origins and growth of contemporary civilization, inevitably deformed till yesterday by scarcity, have been dominated by 'the performance principle' under whose sway 'all civilization has been organized domination' and society, as we noted earlier, 'stratified according to the competitive economic performance of its members'.[8] In most times and places, men have come to want to do what, historically speaking, they have had to do to survive,[9] and in achieving this, repression from without has found an accomplice in repression from within: 'the unfree individual has embraced his own unfreedom by introjecting his masters and their commands into his own mental apparatus.' As Marcuse writes, 'No philosophy, no theory can undo the democratic introjection of the masters into their subjects . . .'[10]

Marxists and others show that the unfree may, with varying degrees of success, mount strategies to 'undo' such introjection. For example there is class struggle ideology.* However (as the history of Marxism shows) as a general rule neither this nor any other ideology can save lower class males from unconsciously experiencing very early, and therefore very strongly, feelings of acute unworthiness because they occupy the lowest rungs of a status hierarchy whose values they internalize while tiny.[12] And in any case the alternative social maps ideologies can furnish were usually not accessible to the casual poor who formed the majority of settlers in Australia's first five decades. The casual poor sub-culture of early New South Wales was organized around its own sort of élitist principles, involving what Erikson, discussing today's Hell's Angels and similar groups, calls

* Frank Parkin's illuminating thesis proposes class struggle ideology as one of four main models of the 'moral order' which workers tend to hold.[11]

'negative identities'.[13] If one cannot be top at the top, one may have no option but to try to be top at the bottom. But with early industrial sub-cultures, as with those of late capitalism, all the magic insignia of defiance failed (and fails) to convince males of their inner worth, and even before their social betters stumbled on the process of schooling society to build consensus essentially around the values of rulers, estimates of human worth, by and large, flowed from high to low. So we have the

'prosperous Victorian father . . . jingling in his pockets the profits of phossy-jaw or industrial phthisis . . . His shadowy features can be seen behind those of many upright, useful and gifted men, and *his principles and prejudices have a direct bearing on the whole character of the society in which he thrives, down to its lowermost strata.*' [My emphasis][14]

Because self-evaluation for a casual poor male turned largely upon his position in a dominance hierarchy, he tended to demand, by way of compensation, that his woman occupy a lower niche in that hierarchy; and he simply failed to experience her as sexually relevant, sexually on his wave-length, if she did not meet this status-requirement. So we may see the man who mistreated Mayhew's young prostitute as unconsciously trying to undo his own feelings of profound worthlessness and despair by ensuring that 'his' woman felt worse. This might ease his own pain, diluting it through passing it to another, and might help fill the abyss? A destructive magic, which intensifies the initial sadness, and a universal, not entirely unconscious, mechanism; most of us know a bit about it. It seems to have operated with special savagery among the lowest strata in those black early decades of industrializing England.

In his writing on mid-nineteenth century barrow street vendors, Kellow Chesney catches something of the self-estimate and social role of casual poor women in earlier decades, because these strata were slow to change their folkways.

Woman's subordinate place in coster society was very marked; she shouldered a great share of the labour but (if one excludes brawling) took little part in its recreations.[15]

Mayhew tells us that while coster women were 'rigidly faithful to their husbands or paramours, . . . the fidelity characterizing the women does not belong to the men'; though, 'in the worst pinch of poverty, a departure from this fidelity – if it provided a few meals and a fire – was not considered at all heinous.' Coster women were also often beaten and one old coster man told Mayhew 'they seem to like the men better for their beating.'[16] Elsewhere Chesney describes mid-nineteenth century port labourers and street traders, as well as workers in sections of the iron-working and construction industries, as 'semi-barbarous tribes whose social territories formed, as it were, the marches of the underworld'.[17]

To catch the life-texture of women in such groups it's necessary to go past Charles Dickens, to Arthur Morrison's books.[18] Morrison tells the story of a boy (largely himself) growing up in derelict 'marches of the underworld' in the 1870s; in the process of slipping out from history, Morrison's 'tribes' preserved archaic qualities which entitle us to (gingerly) contemplate them as sources of life patterns in earlier decades among the casual poor. In the marches of the underworld, inner anguish expressed itself in endemic physical violence. Here is Morrison's sketch of Sally Green:

Down the middle of Old Jago Street came Sally Green: red-faced, stripped to the waist, dancing, hoarse and triumphant. Nail-scores wide as the finger striped her back, her face and her throat, and she had a black eye: but in one great hand she dangled a long bunch of clotted hair . . . It was a trophy newly rent from the scalp of Norah Walsh, champion of the Rann womankind.[19]

Readers of the early New South Wales and Van Diemen's Land press can meet her sisters. For example in Hobart on 2 February 1840, 'Jane Tuthans, Norah Keefe, Elizabeth Brown, and Mary Morgan were charged by Constable Latham with having a regular battle royal in Watchorn-street'; while in Launceston on 9 August 1860 'Bridget Murphy was charged with smashing several panes of glass value 8s in the dwelling of Catherine Ward, of Wellington-street.' Two weeks later 'Mary Whatnell, alias Hogan, charged Margaret O'Brien with assaulting her';

and on 8 September, 'Eliza Gough charged Eliza McCarthy with assaulting her.'[20]

Casual poor women were held in as little esteem in Australia's formative decades as in Hogarthian London. What impact does the standing of women have on the general moral tone of a given group, class or community? Roger Thompson gives this answer:

The ingredients which go towards the concoction of the moral tone of a society are many and often of subtle flavour . . . Yet to accept [the notion of a] multiplicity of factors does not . . . invalidate our initial contentions that women may have a very marked impact on the moral tone of a society . . .[21]

'A very marked impact' understates the position. The standing and self-attitudes of women serve as a central cause, and most sensitive weathervane, of any society's general moral climate. The numbers of free casual poor women steadily increased in early New South Wales, and attitudes towards them overlapped with those displayed towards unfree (i.e. convict) casual poor women. So let us look at some examples of how free casual poor women were seen and how they saw themselves. In 1811 the *Sydney Gazette* reported this incident:

A PERSON (for A MAN I cannot call him) of the name of RALPH MALKIM, led his lawful wife into our streets on the 28th. ultimo, with a rope round her neck, and publicly exposed her for sale, and shameful to be told, another fellow, equally contemptible, called, THOMAS QUIRE, actually purchased and paid for her on the spot, sixteen pounds in money, and some yards of cloth. I am sorry to add that the woman herself was so devoid of feelings which are so justly deemed the most valuable in her sex, agreed to the base traffic, and went off with the purchaser . . .[22]

Peter Cunningham, Royal Navy Surgeon, writing in 1827, relates an incident concerning 'a rich and amorous Sydney youth, with the bloom of fifty-six summers on his cheeks, [who] was linked in love's dear bands with one of our pretty penitents, from whose eyes he first drank in the sweet infection while his "fairest of the fair" was performing public penance on a market day (with her gown-tail drawn over head) for dabbling too deeply in strong waters on the preceding evening.'[23] This woman seems to be a convict, but because the same method of punishment was also used for free casual poor women, we can look at it in this, just as well as the next, chapter ('Our Founding Mothers the Convicts'). That such women were 'beyond the pale' is suggested by the fact that at this time the bodies of middle class and other élite women were generally smothered in constricting clothing. Casual poor women did not wear underclothing. So this woman was forced to publicly expose her genitals. That exposure in a society dominated by puritan hegemonic values symbolizes the fact that, in a way, this woman was *outside* society; cast-out

Describing the often cruel treatment of women on board free migrant ships to the Australian colonies up to the 1840s, Michael Cannon underscores our point that the lower men were in the social scale, the more brutalized they were, and the more brutally they tended to treat women:

There may have been some chance of controlling these events, even on the long and monotonous voyage, if the officers and seamen had been disciplined and trained in the same traditions as the Royal Navy. But merchant seamen of the time were notorious for their everyday brutality and depravity. They included the riff-raff of every nation, who were treated like animals on board and on shore, made to work endlessly for low wages, flogged if necessary, tipped ashore to become the prey of waterfront crimps and boarding-house keepers, and shanghaied in their drunken and diseased state to begin the cycle all over again . . . To allow such men to spread disease among female emigrants was a crime of a particularly callous nature, even when the women were willing accomplices. Yet it happened often enough, largely because of the refusal of the British government to institute proper precautions against intercourse on board.[24]

But the higher ranks on board immigrant ships sometimes also mistreated poor women. An inquiry into the ship *Subraon* in 1848 indicted the Ship's Master and Chief Officer in regard to young Dorcas Newman, who died of miscarriage, and the Third Officer in the case of Martha Magee.[25]

Caroline Chisholm was so enraged by the cruelty and contempt she knew were widely shown towards girls migrating to New South Wales in the early 1840s, that she singled out a peculiarly unsavoury captain and surgeon in a test case over Margaret Bolton and the ship *Carthaginian*. Twenty-six-year-old Margaret Bolton, in the words of the 1842 Immigration Committee which later investigated the affair, was a 'correct, but peevish girl'. This, as Margaret Kiddle suggests, possibly explains her troubles: only a woman of position and substance could refuse overtures from higher-status males with impunity. Margaret Bolton accused the *Carthaginian*'s captain and surgeon of gross immorality, and so they found occasion to drag her up on deck, throw several buckets of water over her, and handcuff her hands behind her back. After shivering in wet clothes all night, she evidently caught some infection, as after that she was never well enough to work. Governor Gipps warned Caroline Chisholm 'that a government prosecution was a serious matter' (there's an undefinable similarity between his and the received current view of Chisholm – a do-gooder – but not really with it? In any case, a woman . . .). Caroline Chisholm would have been grateful for Gipps's warning, of course, because otherwise she'd never have understood the 'seriousness' of prosecution. However she did understand the seriousness of the insult to women, and due to that understanding, a lot was aired in the press about the abuse of immigrant women, Surgeon Nelson's 'habit' of 'throwing lime in the faces of the immigrants to stifle them' hit the headlines, and finally, the captain and surgeon were fined £50 each and imprisoned for six months.[26] I don't know what restitution was made to Margaret Bolton, not least for the fact that she was never able to work after the episode . . .

The upper ranks were hardly free of cruelty, on ships any more than in society at large. Still, I'd stick to my general proposition in both these domains: the lower the status of men in the nineteenth century, the more brutalized they were and the more brutal their attitude towards women. Their capacity to 'thingize' women matched that of their social betters, too:

take this fragment of a song sung by shantymen on home
bound ships about 'sailors' tarts':

> And when we get to the London docks
> There we shall see the cunt in flocks.

As a further evocation of the brutality brought by a brutal way
of life to its victims, male and female, I offer this case cited in
1849 by J. C. Symons, an experienced circuit barrister and
editor of the *Law Magazine*:

... in 1840 a publican found guilty of stealing a 'piece of honey comb-
tripe and a cow heel, worth ninepence', was not only jailed but as a
convicted felon, sentenced to forfeit his whole property. On the
other side there was the case of a man who so belaboured a girl that
he destroyed one of her eyes, broke her nose and induced concussion
of the brain, then, after violently kicking her prostrate body, seized
her legs and hurled her over a parapet to a ten-foot drop. His victim
survived and he was sentenced in the absence of any extenuating
circumstances to twelve months' hard labour. This happened 'near
Gloucester': in the heart of a slum area he would have been unlucky
not to escape prosecution.[27]

As an example of how shared humanity may be withheld from
women by men at the bottom of a status ladder in a society where
human values ultimately collapse back to status, here is a late-
nineteenth century instance described by Laurence Housman.
This is the one that hurt me most, probably because it recalls
to any woman her own vulnerability as childbirth approaches.
Housman saw this happen 'on the borders of one of our great
London parks':

A poor working woman, about to become a mother, was on her way
home when unexpectedly her pains overtook her, and she could go
no further. A policeman came to her aid, and went to find a convey-
ance; and while she waited a crowd gathered, men and boys; and as
they watched her they laughed and made jokes. She was a symbol to
them of what sex meant; some man had given her her lesson, and
now she was learning it; and to their minds it was a highly satisfactory spectacle.[28]

A 'successful' relationship between poor men and women is reflected in the words of a London 'working woman' of 1909:

One of the Suffragists has told us that a working woman, speaking of her husband in a London back street, said the other day: 'He's a saver, and he don't knock me about much, but somehow he never thinks as a woman counts'.[29]

Many labourers in steady enough work in early New South Wales moved up and out of the ranks of the English casual poor. But upward social mobility changes some things only slowly, sometimes only after many generations. Alexander Harris, whom Russel Ward uses as a source chiefly for positive human attributes within the Australian national identity, arrived in New South Wales in the 1820s and began to publish books on his antipodean experiences in the 1840s. Alongside Harris's accounts of mateship and anti-authoritarian attitudes, we find other qualities, just as understandable as the positive ones:

the labouring population are universally lost to all sense of moral duty and religious obedience ... Drunkenness, profanity and unchastity are the prevalent habits which the class has acquired. What else could be expected? The original stock is the very lowest: the blood-stained hand and ruthless heart from the most barbarian parts of Ireland; the professional depredator from the vilest haunts of London; the lowest slaves of profligacy, inebriation, violence and lust.[30]

For the most part, such men treated their women appallingly. And the women reflected their treatment. In 1843, James Backhouse described 'indigent' women at the Sydney Benevolent Asylum in these words: 'Several of them were very aged, and lamentably depraved. Strong drink has brought many of them, both young and old, to the state of destitution they are in . . .'[31] In this letter written in 1847 to his beloved Clarinda, Henry Parkes, a working class Londoner who was to become one of our leading politicians, gives a haunting description of Australian poor women:

I went down one of the gaps in the line of Maitland shops, to have a close look at the quiet stream . . . It was a scene of English looking quiet; but when I came back to the street, and gazed on the hard sunburnt unfeeling faces of the women and the dirt and slovenliness of the uncared-for children, I felt at once that I was still in N.S.W.[32]

Reminiscing about 'Old Sydney in the Forties', Mrs Eliza Walker recalled that 'the services of women were used in making the approaches to [an] old stone bridge' over the Tank Stream.[33]

In the 1850s, describing *A Lady's Visit to the Gold Diggings of Australia in 1852–1853*, Mrs Charles Clacy suggests a basic continuity in the attitude of the 'lower orders' to 'their' women in a passage which recalls the 'thingizing' attitude revealed in Mayhew's account of the young haymaking prostitute:

But night on the diggings is the characteristic time: murder here . . . revolvers cracking . . . a party of bacchanals chanting various ditties . . . Here is one man grumbling because he has brought his wife with him, another ditto because he has left his behind or sold her for an ounce of gold or a bottle of rum.[34]

But that 'thingizing' process embodied in selling another human being would have meshed in with earlier patterns: for the needle grinds more deeply into any groove time has already etched stubbornly into the historical record. The casual poor mental-universe of early nineteenth century London lived on in the antipodes. In 1859 one observer sketched areas in Melbourne and Sydney marked by 'riot and debauchery – sin in its bizarre and most lurid aspects . . . as vile as Whitechapel':

Serpent-like gutters, choked with filth, trail before the tottering tenements, and a decayed water-butt, filled with greasy-looking rain-catchings . . . stands and rots at the end of each court. Brazen women, hulking bullies, and grimy children, loll about the door-ways . . .[35]

From early in the nineteenth century, casual poor women and working class women often came to the Sydney Benevolent Asylum to have their babies.[36] In 1861 the Asylum's secretary, the Hon. George Allen, M. L. C., explained to a select committee that of the 'great many' women who came for the purpose of 'lying in',[37] most were not 'town-girls', that is, prostitutes, but servants 'seduced in service'.[38] Many such casual poor women displayed few motherly feelings. Here is Alderman J. G. Raphael addressing the 1861 select committee. The asylum, he said, was 'nothing but a pleasant domicile for the worst of characters'.[39] Describing 'single girls who come . . . to be confined with their bastard children', he claimed they were

continually making a practice of being confined there, and either of getting rid of their children, and then going back to be confined with another, or else of living on the institution. During the time I have been connected with the institution I have seen instances of the most brazen and hardhearted conduct on the part of these mothers. I have seen a woman who had been three different times in the institution to be confined; upon the last occasion she threw her child down upon the grass and went away, saying she should soon get another.[40]

The committee chairman asked Raphael a further question:

I believe some of them, or at least one of them, has been confined there three times within four years? 'Yes; and that one told me on the last occasion that we might do what we liked, – she would come in when she pleased, would go out when she pleased . . . and that she meant to have another, and would be in again shortly.'[41]

Attitudes towards mothering, as towards the body and sexuality, may be seen as linked with a lowly position in the dominance hierarchy and acceptance of a low self-concept. The tragedy of the Benevolent Asylum woman who 'threw her child down upon the grass and went away, saying she would soon get another', lies in the fact that her situation discouraged her from consciously experiencing feelings of motherly love. For most women in pre-contraceptive history, and perhaps especially for casual poor women, Evelyne Sullerot's words bear thinking about:

one cannot even talk of mothers' loving or not loving their infants; these words cannot even have today's meanings . . . what we mean by maternal love is a modern invention inseparable from mastery over survival.[42]

Many, if not most, mothers like these must have unconsciously handled grief at losing babies by denial and defiance, because inner collapse was a likely possible alternative. To have a baby, as a single casual poor woman, was to confront unbearable options. Here, for example, is what Rosamond and Florence Hill saw in the lying-in ward of the South Australian Destitute Asylum in 1875:

The greater number [of destitute mothers] enter service, chiefly as wet-nurses, their infants being boarded out, and the mother paying the cost. But in the Australian climate it is especially difficult to preserve the life of an infant when removed from its mother . . .[43]

In the early twentieth century casual poor women still remind one of an outcast group. In 1901, for example:

in our city lock-up, women are run in and detained during the night and no matron nor woman officer is in charge . . . the half-drunken, violent woman, sometimes almost nude, the disreputable, dirty female, drunken and shameless . . . It is the sorrow of decent women that sister women have sunk so low . . .[44]

From 1903 to 1905, Dr Charles Willis, later principal medical officer in the N.S.W. Department of Public Instruction, described male treatment of casual poor women in a Western Australian mining district, mateship territory *par excellence*. He spent a 'large portion' of his time treating venereal diseases contracted through 'so-called Japanese laundries', which extended round the north-west and operated 'more or less in conjunction with each other'.

Women were passed around the circuit from one laundry to another, so as to provide a greater attraction for the male residents.[45]

The rewards (or 'substitute gratifications') men gain from prostitution probably find their source in debasement of another human being as much as, if not more than, sexuality – if there exists such a thing as sexuality as a-thing-in-itself. Sexuality may fuse with gentleness and affection; equally, it may be compounded with humiliating another and so for the moment, trying to bury one's own feelings of nothingness. Dr Phyllis Chesler puts it well:

Prostitutes are degraded and punished by society; it is their *humiliation* through their *bodies* – as much as their *bodies* – which is being purchased.[46]

The same sense of casual poor women as outside the pale of humanity, comes through in the minutes of evidence given before the 1915 N.S.W. 'Select Committee on Prevalence [sic] of Venereal Diseases'. Prostitutes, 'the low dirty class of women', 'have syphilis' and 'get' innocent men. They should be 'douched out', 'cleaned up'. An Australian Labor Party parliamentarian, J. J. G. McGirr asked the committee: '. . . if a woman give a man syphilis – or gonorrhoea – can she be charged with inflicting grievous bodily harm on him?' Witnesses had already made it clear they thought men 'got' gonorrhoea from 'horrible prostitutes', then gave it to their wives.[47] And do David Ireland's working men at Puroil, in *The Unknown Industrial Prisoner*, 1971, have a much more human feeling towards the tragic women who act as prostitutes? Ireland displays deep compassion for the industrial working *men* – Knuckles, Sumpoil, the Two Pot Screamer. But what do he or his proletarian heroes feel, for example, about Sandpiper? She is called 'Sandpaper', 'in reference to the texture of a certain stretch of her anatomy', and the Two Pot Screamer watches her 'sprawled on the bed like a mongrel dog . . .'[48]

We can try to enter the thought-world of nineteenth century casual poor males in other ways. Lee Rainwater's study of contemporary working men and women's sexuality in another Anglo-Saxon community, the United States,[49] can be of use in considering what he describes as 'lower-lower' working class people in earlier England and Australia, because, like the aristocracy to some extent, the lower reaches of the working classes were slow to adopt those bourgeois folkways which began to permeate society between, say, the mid-to-late-eighteenth century and the early twentieth. Rainwater says:

Like their wives, working class husbands find the world around them confusing and chaotic; they do not feel that they understand it, and they feel that what goes on is essentially unpredictable, up to fate. Women are, of course, part of that world and characterized by the

same unpredictableness and confusing qualities as the rest of it . . .
Working class men, *even more than men in general*, [my emphasis]
tend to think of women as temperamental, emotional, demanding and
irrational. Many of these find their wives' demands for affection
irritating and threatening . . .[50]

Towards the end of the nineteenth century, unskilled males in
Australia were rapidly improving working conditions through
trade union organization and strike action. But their women, by
and large, shared very little in this. Their lack of self confidence
and self belief was too mutilating, and to a large extent the
direct source of this lack lay in the psychological needs of
unskilled males to compensate for their own feelings. It is thus
hardly surprising that the early trade unions – how different
is it now? – did little to help unskilled women better their
conditions. Yet as Beverley Kingston shows in her book *My
Wife, My Daughter and Poor Mary Ann*,[51] unskilled women
(domestic servants, workers in pickle factories, laundries)
desperately needed that help.

If the casual poor universe, an important matrix of some
central Australian folkways, was a dark one for women, how did
children experience it? How much *mothering* were women, held
in such low esteem and holding themselves in such low esteem,
able to give their children? Mothering takes a great deal of
psychic and physical energy; self-hate, however, drains such
energies enormously. It's hard to say much about how children
were treated inside homes, let alone how they felt, for as Lord
Shaftesbury explained, cruelties to children 'are of so private,
internal and domestic a character as to be beyond the reach of
legislation'[52] – and public scrutiny.* But a few mid-century
observers thought New South Wales, and Sydney particularly,
constituted an especially damaging *milieu* for children. For
example in 1859 in New South Wales a select committee

---

* This helps make sense of the fact that while the Royal Society for Prevention of Cruelty to Animals was set up in England on 16 June 1824, it was
not until 1881 that the National Society for Prevention of Cruelty to Children
was established.

inquired into 'The Condition of the Working Classes of the Metropolis'. One witness, J. H. Palmer, said:

In no part of the world I have visited have I ever heard language so obscene and profane as from the children in this city. 'And you have heard this so frequently as to give you an impression that it is habitual?' Yes; and I think the habitual use of such language may be considered as a sure indication of low moral feeling.[53]

In 1859 Frank Fowler pointed to Sydney boys of ten years and upwards before whom 'your London gamin pales into utter respectability'.[54] Palmer, before the 1859 select committee, also noted the 'early association of sexes'[55] in Sydney, and we recall Mayhew and the author of *My Secret Life* both show this as typical of London casual poor children. However in the antipodes prostitution was apparently widespread among quite young girls. Fowler, for example, commented on the number of very young prostitutes. 'So openly was this social plague contaminating the streets of Melbourne and Sydney when I left, that public meetings were daily held to help tackle it . . .' A witness before the 1859 select committee ('an intelligent officer of the Metropolitan Police') thought a substantial number of the much-increased number of Sydney prostitutes in 1859 were 'children . . . scarcely above the age of infancy'.[56] J. R. Clayton, rates collector, claimed he saw girls not over twelve years 'on the town'.[57] Inspector C. E. Harrison thought about one-third of Sydney prostitutes were young children, while he noted, too, a 'very large amount of juvenile vagrancy in the city among the girls especially . . .'[58] And those who doubted such views in a sense partly validated them. Mr Windeyer said, 'I have seen very young girls following the calling of a prostitute . . . but not so young as to make it a worse sin than common. If by female child you mean a girl of fourteen or fifteen, yes, many, but for that purpose she is no longer a child.'[59] (However, J. M. McLerie, the Inspector General of police, would only go so far as to say the number of prostitutes was increasing and that 'more than half the prostitutes of Sydney are under 20'.[60])

The Report of the select committee suggested the gold rushes had intensified the plight of casual poor women and their children. For example one witness said:

. . . since the discovery of gold, the unsettled courses of many working men, and their frequent absences from home . . . have left numbers of women and families in Sydney without protection or any regular means of subsistence.[61]

J. R. Clayton endorsed this view: 'I find there is a great amount of destitution among females in consequence of their husbands leaving them and going to the diggings.'[62] The Very Reverend W. M. Cooper, Dean of Sydney, held a similar opinion.[63]

Psychologically, the gold rushes could have had something of the effect of warfare in promoting uprootedness and anomie. Philip Slater calls war 'the most absurd and vicious of all the games that men play', but it is nevertheless one of their most revered activities. Perhaps, as with mateship, a similar male-bonding sentiment about the gold rushes has prevented male intellectuals from giving a balanced appraisal of its effects on the moral economy. At any rate, writers have hardly concerned themselves in any central way with the impact of the gold rushes on stability, community, women and children. Robin Walker has pointed the way by asking whether later bush-rangers were influenced by a disturbed goldfields' childhood, and we also ask whether in this and other ways, prostitution was one of gold's short- and medium-term legacies. We can only ask (and also ask why, with so much work now being published on the glamour of gold, the question has not seriously been asked before . . .). Whatever the answers, by 1875, the chief warder at Sydney's Darlinghurst gaol told Rosamond and Florence Hill: 'This is the worst city in the world for young females. I am an old soldier, and have been in the West Indies and many other places, but I never knew any so bad as this.'[64] The relatively unusual prosperity of Australian colonies is often noted, so at first sight it's surprising to find the Reverend S. W. Brooks saying in 1878: '. . . if there is one work which, beyond all others, society has a direct interest in doing, it is to care for the wild brood of the streets, the shoeless, shaggy-haired waifs of both sexes . . .'[65] There are many reasons why children should be neglected here, just as they were in all patriarchal societies in the nineteenth century,[66] but Geoffrey Blainey suggests one that might be specific to Australia:

The dearth of women persisted for so long that it must have flavoured society in countless ways. In the years when it was most marked, the material standard of living was unusually high because most men only had to support themselves instead of a wife and children. Much of that higher standard of personal spending went into alcohol . . . In a society dominated by men, a *different set of values reigned*. [My emphasis][67]

So far I've outlined a theory that suggests an unconscious psychosocial tendency which causes males in patricentric-acquisitive society to need, and bring about, a situation where 'their' females experience a more impoverished selfhood than the relevant group of males. The more robust the personhood of the male, the more robust that of the female. I know this is a most imperfect approximation: for example, I suspect the degree of autonomy of female sub-culture amongst Finns has given Finnish women a greater degree of immunity from this tendency than most Australian women. But here is how, at this stage of my work, I would set out that imperfect approximation.

In the first instance females tend to take their identity from the males on whom they are *directly* dependent for physical and psychosexual sustenance. (It is only now that, on any appreciable scale, women are beginning to decide they will take their *own* need-priorities as the starting point and *then* begin the process of relating to men. That way women may relate to men as existents in a mutuality which – amongst other things – can sustain a surprisingly rich and enduring sexuality!) The males on whom a given group of females are directly dependent tend to take *their* self-definition from males next highest in rank on the status ladder.

Back to Australian free casual poor 'founding mothers'. This 'tendency' involves the 'complicity' of women. Satchmo was right: it takes two to tango. Women 'fit' the tendency by internalizing the required male definition (institutional transmission belts include family, church, economic structure). Casual poor women consequently tended to act out the definition casual poor males held of them, in accordance with our rough formula: the male in a given group needs 'his' female to feel more demeaned, inadequate, or uncertain in identity, than he himself feels. Here are a few examples of women meeting this requirement. In 1833 Governor Bourke refused bounty payments to shipping agents for one Emma Langenhand, 'a very riotous inmate of St. Mary le Bone Workhouse . . . [who] after a long continuance of violent and refractory conduct on board Ship, ultimately threw herself overboard . . . and . . . was drowned.'[68] In August 1848 Mr F. Wilkinson lodged complaints about certain women under his charge on the *Fairlie*. Regarding the young woman Hannah Lawrence, for example, Wilkinson

had to find fault with her behaviour, her gross and low language, which compelled me to order her on the poop for a number of hours as a disgrace . . . She is indolent, lazy, and consequently dirty . . . never washed one of her own clothes, but actually threw her chemises overboard, when too filthy to wear . . . [There is also] Mary Sutton, a married woman, a dreadful creature, the most abusive, violent and illtempered being in the Ship . . . a constant source of trouble to me from their gross misbehaviour, associating chiefly and constantly alone with the Ship's crew . . . particularly at night, which led in some instances to serious disturbance and fights.[69]

During an inquiry into the conduct of Irish orphan girls aboard ship for New South Wales, Dr H. Douglas, M. D., surgeon superintendent of the immigrant ship *Earl Grey*, told the Orphan Immigration Committee on 12 October 1848 that, of some forty to fifty orphans, some 'openly charged each other with being public women', some that 'they have given disease to various persons', and they frequently charged each other with having children. Over such issues they were found lethally fighting. These women probably lacked much alternative to being 'public', and that brought the disease and children. Yet *they*, the women, assumed the guilt for these 'crimes' and charged each other with them, just as the ruling strata of men who made such 'crimes' worthwhile and therefore feasible, decreed that they should. In 1852 Mrs Charles Clacy describes a sly-grog shop woman on the Australian gold fields:

Whilst her husband was at work farther down the gully, she kept a sort of sly-grog shop, and passed the day in selling and drinking spirits, swearing, and smoking a short tobacco-pipe at the door of her tent. She was a most repulsive looking object. A dirty gaudy-coloured dress hung unfastened about her shoulders, coarse black hair unbrushed, uncombed, dangled about her face, over which her evil habits had spread a genuine bacchanalian glow, while in a loud masculine voice she uttered the most awful words that ever disgraced the mouth of man – ten thousand times more awful when proceeding from a woman's lips.[70]

The sly-grog woman had internalized a definition of her humanity satisfactory to the loudly-protested and fragile identity of males in her social class. Arthur Morrison describes the casual poor London women he grew up amongst in the 1860s and 1870s:

horrible draggled women [pawing] . . . sailors over for whatever their pockets might yield . . . big, coarse women, with flaring clothes, and hair that shone with grease [and a woman who was] no beauty [with] coarse features, dull eyes, and tousled hair, [a] thick voice and . . . rusty finery.[71]

Discussing working class young people in 'Some Aspects of Pack Rape in Sydney', in 1969, G. D. Woods writes of the girl-members of basically male gangs:

. . . the numbers of girls likely to be involved in gangs are much fewer than the numbers of boys, but the girls who *are* involved are almost invariably more delinquent, more emotionally disturbed and more difficult to handle than the boys.[72]

The boys' attitude to sexuality is dehumanized in the extreme. Their own sexuality, and consequently the sexuality of the girls, they feel is split off from the total person. Thus they live out the days impoverished and starved, but, to be fair, they do need a stunted vision of themselves if they are to fit into the slot society prepared for them from wayback. Sexuality experienced as split off from the total person, is experienced in conjunction with a demeaned and debased vision of woman. In such cases we are dealing with status (or status-caste ?) and debasement, rather than with sexuality as honest lust in the context of a total liking. The former is central to my definition of 'pornographic' sex as distinct from 'erotic' sex.* This all fits the pack rape boys' attitude to sexuality. The girls' behaviour

is such that it accustoms the boys to accept sexual intercourse almost as a right, and certainly as something common, casual and freely available; almost as, in the works of Wayland Young, 'a sneeze in the loins'.[73]

The cluster of attitudes thus encapsulated comes across in the *Guardian*'s report of a Hell's Angels' gang-bang-cum-pack-rape in 1973 – and in the attitudes of this enlightened newspaper and the trial judge. After a seventeen-year-old girl was 'actively engaged in intercourse' with seven Hell's Angels for over an hour, she was found 'rambling and sobbing' and had to be half-carried to a couch for medical examination at a police station. The *Guardian*'s headline: 'Was girl "hungry for sex" – Judge.' The *Guardian* illustrated the news item with a photo of the Hell's Angels planning a gang-bang for the following day, to celebrate their acquittal by the Judge.[74]

Perhaps it all collapses back to some vision of sex as punishment, the vision hovering over Laurence Housman's picture of that 'crowd of men and boys' who laughed as they watched 'a poor working woman' having labour pains in a late-nineteenth century London park. Punishment, though, for what? Punishment for the pain working class males must endure in work that is an insult and in a status that is worse: bearable, perhaps, only because 'their' women may fulfil the function of scapegoat. Thus while society is arranged so that men are forced to define their humanity in terms of a position on a status-achievement ladder, how far can women really hope to achieve a richer personhood?

* Marcuse refers to a general 'de-eroticized' sexuality in the setting of repressively de-sublimated sexuality.

Notes

1. H. Mayhew, *London Labour and the London Poor*, 1861–62 ed., Frank Cass, London, 1967, p. 2.
2. L. Robson, *The Convict Settlers of Australia*, Melbourne University Press, Melbourne, 1965 (1970), p. 75.
3. H. Mayhew, *London Labour and the London Poor*, 3 vols., vol. 3, London, 1864, p. 412.
4. Steven Marcus, *The Other Victorians*, pp. 196–7.
5. ibid., pp. 134–7.
6. Reich's psychiatric work brought him into close contact with 'working class' as well as 'well-to-do' people.
7. *Imperial Review*, 1904–1909, Mitchell Library.
8. H. Marcuse, *Eros and Civilisation*, op. cit., pp. 50, 44.
9. Erich Fromm, 'The Application of Humanist Psychoanalysis to Marx's Theory', in *Socialist Humanism: An International Symposium*, E. Fromm, ed., Doubleday, New York, 1966, p. 233.
10. H. Marcuse, *Eros and Civilisation*, p. 14.
11. F. Parkin, *Class, Inequality and Political Order*, Paladin, St. Albans, 1972.
12. Miriam Dixson, '*Lang is Greater than Lenin': Lang and Labour 1916–1932*, Melbourne Political Science Monographs, 1976. Chapter 7, 'Theories', (B), 'How Might Ideology operate in the Personality?'
13. E. Erikson, *Identity. Youth and Crisis*, W. W. Norton, New York, 1968.
14. Kellow Chesney, *The Victorian Underworld*, Pelican, 1972, pp. 13–14.
15. ibid., pp. 51–2.
16. H. Mayhew, op. cit., Frank Cass edition, p. 20.
17. Kellow Chesney, op. cit, p. 33.
18. A. Morrison, *Tales of Mean Streets*, Methuen, London, 1894; *A Child of the Jago*, London, 1896, McGibbon and Kee reprint, 1969; *The Hole in the Wall*, London, 1902, Tom Stacey Reprints, London, 1972. (My thanks to Professor Ron Neale for introducing me to Arthur Morrison.)
19. A. Morrison, *A Child of the Jago*, p. 64.
20. *Colonial Times*, 25 February 1840; *Launceston Examiner*, 9 August 1860, 23 August 1860, 8 September 1860. See too Martha Brown and Mary Anne Jarvis, *Colonial Times*, 3 March 1840; Sarah Jacobs, *Colonial Times*, 31 March 1840; Esther Holmes ('a very old and regular attendant [who] was sent to the house of correction for three months, for riotous conduct in

the public street' – *Colonial Times*, 21 April 1840). In the *Hobart Town Courier and Van Diemen's Land Gazette*, 24 January 1840, one may meet Mary Welch and Elizabeth Humphreys, and on 7 February 1840, Margaret Mason. See too *Hobart Town Daily Mercury*, 3 January, 10 January 1860.

21. R. Thompson, *Women in Stuart England and America. A Comparative Study*, Routledge and Kegan Paul, London and Boston, 1974, p. 252.

22. *Sydney Gazette*, 14 September 1811.

23. P. Cunningham, *Two Years in New South Wales: A Series of Letters comprising Sketches of the Actual State of Society in That Colony, etc.*, 2 vols., vol. 1, H. Colburn, London, 1827, pp. 290–91.

24. M. Cannon, *Who's Master? Who's Man?*, Nelson, Melbourne, 1971, p. 141.

25. Report by the Immigration Board of Inquiry re immigrant ship *Subraon*, Fitzroy to Greig, 14 November 1848, *H.R.A.*, series 1, vol. 31, p. 683.

26. Margaret Kiddle, *Caroline Chisholm*, Melbourne University Press, Melbourne, 1950, pp. 51–3.

27. J. C. Symons, cited in Kellow Chesney, op. cit., p. 101.

28. L. Housman, cited in Constance Rover, *Love, Morals and the Feminists*, Routledge & Kegan Paul, London, 1970.

29. *Tracts on Women's Suffrage 1907–1917*, British Museum, London, n.d., but the tract occurs in an article reprinted in the *English Review*, October 1909.

30. A. Harris, *Settlers and Convicts*, London, 1847, Melbourne University Press reprint, Melbourne, 1964, p. 230.

31. J. Backhouse, *A Narrative of a Visit to the Australian Colonies*, Hamilton, Adams, London, 1843, p. 458.

32. H. Parkes to C. Parkes, 27 September 1847, PC A1044, cited in A. W. Martin, 'Henry Parkes; Man and Politician', in E. L. French, ed., *Melbourne Studies in Education 1960–1961*, Melbourne University Press, Melbourne, 1962, p. 14.

33. Mrs Eliza Walker, 'Old Sydney in the Forties', Royal Australian Historical Society, *Journal and Proceedings*, 1930, vol. 16, p. 312.

34. Mrs Charles Clacy, *A Lady's Visit to the Gold Diggings of Australia, in 1852–1853*, ('Written on the Spot'), Hurstand Blackett, London, 1853, p. 95.

35. F. Fowler, *Southern Lights and Shadows*, London, 1859, pp. 43–4.

36. J. Backhouse, op. cit., p. 458.

37. 'Minutes of Evidence Taken before the Select Committee on the

Sydney Benevolent Asylum', New South Wales Legislative Assembly, *Votes & Proceedings*, 1861–2, 2, p. 924.

38. ibid., p. 937.

39. ibid., p. 1028.

40. ibid., p. 1029.

41. loc. cit.

42. E. Sullerot, *Woman, Society and Change*, p. 63.

43. R. and F. Hill, *What We Saw in Australia*, Macmillan, London, 1875, p. 141.

44. Evelyne Gough, *Non-Represented ... Female Labour*, Spectator, Melbourne, 1901, p. 16.

45. Select Committee on Prevalence of Venereal Diseases, New South Wales Legislative Assembly, *Second Progress Report*, Government Printer, Sydney, 1916 (hereafter N.S.W. Select Committee on Venereal Diseases, 1915).

46. P. Chesler, *Women and Madness*, p. 100.

47. N.S.W. Select Committee on Venereal Diseases, 1915, pp. 45, 46, 55, 117, 121.

48. D. Ireland, *The Unknown Industrial Prisoner*, Angus and Robertson, Sydney, 1971, p. 55 and p. 48.

49. L. Rainwater, *And the Poor Get Children*, Quadrangle Books, Chicago, 1960.

50. ibid., p. 77.

51. Beverley Kingston, *My Wife, My Daughter and Poor Mary Ann*, Nelson, Melbourne, 1975.

52. A. F. Young and E. T. Ashton, *British Social Work in the Nineteenth Century*, Routledge & Kegan Paul, London, 1956, p. 149.

53. 'Select Committee on the Condition of the Working Classes of the Metropolis', New South Wales Legislative Assembly, *Votes and Proceedings*, 1859–60, vol. 4, questions 1248 and 1249, p. 1352, 20 December 1859 (hereafter N.S.W. Select Committee on the Working Classes 1859–60).

54. F. Fowler, op. cit., p. 23.

55. N.S.W. Select Committee on the Working Classes 1859–60, question 1255, p.1352, 20 December 1859.

56. ibid., p. 1272.

57. ibid., question 255, p. 1296.

58. ibid., questions 347 and 349, p. 1301.

59. ibid., question 583, p. 1312.

60. ibid., question 127, p. 1290.

61. ibid., p. 1268.

62. ibid., question 240, p. 1295.

63. ibid., question 1524, p. 1385.

64. R. and F. Hill, op. cit., p. 276.

65. S. W. Brooks, *Charity and Philanthropy: A Prize Essay (Historical, Statistical and General) on the Institutions in Sydney which aim at the Diminution of Vice, or the Alleviation of Misery* . . ., F. Cunningham, Sydney, 1878, pp. 12–13.

66. Philip Slater, op. cit., pp. 73–4 and p. 67, seems to suggest we do worse by children in the twentieth. The 'technological social-structural juggernaut' 'men' have created, he claims, 'is essentially child-antagonistic or at least, child-alien'. Men certainly *kill* children more through war. Lionel Tiger points out that 'organized hurtful aggressiveness in the form of war is not a human problem but a male problem. Almost exclusively, it is males who create and staff the more or less elaborate social mechanisms for applying force and weaponry to human interactions.' 'Understanding Aggression', *International Social Science Journal*, vol. 23, no. 1, 1971, UNESCO, Paris, pp. 10–11.

67. G. Blainey, *The Tyranny of Distance*, p. 171.

68. Messrs Buckles, Bagster and Buckle to Under Secretary Hay, Hay to Bourke, 29 April 1833, *H.R.A.*, series 1, vol. 17, p. 91.

69. Mr F. Wilkinson to Mr F. L. S. Mereweather, 25 August 1848, *H.R.A.*, series 1, vol. 26, 1848, p. 648.

70. Mrs Charles Clacy, op. cit., p. 106.

71. A. Morrison, *The Hole in the Wall*, pp. 26, 34, 27.

72. G. D. Woods, *Australian and New Zealand Journal of Criminology*, vol. 2, no. 2, June 1969, p. 114.

73. ibid., p. 115. (Two Germans, Volkmar Sigusch and Gunter Schmidt, insist that the picture of 'thingized' sexuality painted in part by these incidents and by Lee Rainwater is true of Anglo-Saxon working class people, but not to the same extent of German workers. A 'de-emotionalizing of sexuality [is] . . . typical of the American lower classes', they say. Broad cultural traditions, they argue, cut deeply into class patterns; Wilhelm Reich would take issue with them, at least for the 1920s!) ('Lower-Class Sexuality: Some Emotional and Social Aspects in West German Males and Females', *Archives of Sexual Behaviour*, 1, 1971, pp. 29–44.)

74. *Guardian*, 22 March 1973.

Chapter 4

Our Founding Mothers the Convicts

A 'broken, cold and unnatural form of society . . .'

(cited by MANNING CLARK)

The central question in this book is 'why do Australian women have a much lower overall standing than women in other democracies?' One important reason lies with our 'founding mothers', the convict women.

For a long time, Australian historians have addressed themselves to details of convict existence, but there has been little serious concern with the *overall* impact of convictism on community.[1] P. R. Eldershaw writes: 'Surely it is overdue for someone . . . to appraise the social significance of such a large body of felonry within a free population.'[2] Since Australian historians have had little to say about the overall impact of convictism on our moral economy and because they've never been much concerned with women, it makes sense that so far they've failed to ask: 'What overall impact on our social *mores* might *convict women* have had?'. But the failure becomes increasingly hard to justify as we begin to grasp the importance of the formative experiences of child-rearing, 'socialization' and mothering. In *Convicts and the Colonies*, A. G. L. Shaw describes convict women as 'the mothers of the first generation of native born Australians', later quoting part of a letter from Mrs Elizabeth Leake to Mrs Taylor: it was 'almost impossible for those families who study the quiet and morality of their children to endure Female Convicts'.[3] *Early* mothers might have constituted enduring models for female identity-formation, for we know children may grow up to be helpless transmitters of attitudes acquired in their hypervulnerable preverbal stages. If this did happen early in our history, we have to question Shaw's

own verdict on the overall impact of convictism, for he concludes that 'socially it did no great harm'.[4]

In 1838 Archbishop Ullathorne designated a convict 'a
slave', and it's clear contemporaries sensed the connections
between slavery and convictism better than we do. For example
Colonel Arthur, a witness before the 1838 Molesworth Committee (British House of Commons Select Committee on
Transportation) was asked: 'Then the condition of the convict
in no respect differs from that of a slave?' Answer: 'No, except
that his master cannot apply corporal punishment with his own
hand, or by his own orders.'[5] Given Lenin's famous description
of women as 'the slave of slaves', one might have expected
more historical curiosity about women convicts; after all
Marxism is now quite fashionable among academics. But here
again the authentic Australian-ness of our historians seems to
be blocking their professional sensibility.

Though they don't seem to have grasped the central role of
women convicts any more than modern historians, many
nineteenth century observers registered reactions which, taken
overall, raise the possibility that convictism had a stunting
impact on the moral economy. In 1838 Ullathorne claimed that
among convicts one found 'obscene mouthed monsters',[6] with
a 'slovenly putting on . . . tawny, stagnant features, sluggish
eye, and drowsy ox-like movement of feet and shoulders, and
downward head . . .'[7] Addressing the House of Commons in
March 1838, Sir William Molesworth spoke of the 'moral
horrors' of transportation[8] and in 1840, Henry Parkes obviously
alluded in part to convictism when he wrote that he was 'dis-
appointed' in all his expectations about Australia 'except as to
its wickedness'.[9] Manning Clark sums up the view of Alexander
Maconochie in the 1840s. Maconochie

came to the conclusion that the fretfulness of temper which so
peculiarly characterized the intercourse of society in the penal
colonies was to be attributed to the convict system. Degraded servants
made suspicious masters: masters suspected their equals and superiors
as well as their inferiors.[10]

Even if this view were only partly true, it has devastating implications for the moral economy of any community 'imprinted' with convictism. If it is untrue, we historians should spend more time than we've done in showing how and why.

In 1863, Commissioners inquiring into the operation of Acts relating to transportation and penal servitude, recommended that Western Australia should be used for 'extended transportation' of those sentenced to penal servitude. As part of the ensuing outcry from the other Australian colonies came an 'Address from the Women of Ballarat and Ballarat East . . . to the Women of England'. Help us avert 'a terrible calamity . . . lest we be steeped to the lips in the polluted stream of convictism'. 'Victoria', they added, was 'already deeply tinctured with the convict stain.'[11] Degradation, contamination, pollution, stain . . . quaint words, archaic, uptight sentiments? Or has the historian's sense of the meaning of moral climate been blunted by contemporary historical forces? For example, contemporary mass culture is shot through with currents of insult, denigration and muted hatred for women, and if a fraction of such feelings were directed at Jews or Blacks, we'd realize we lived in a morally-blighted and dangerously-ill community. But to judge from our noisy silence on the matter, we historians have little understanding of its historical significance, so we can hardly expect to be notably sensitive to moral climate in the past. However, to contemporaries the reality of moral climate was experienced only too vividly: and it frightened them.

In the 1870s J. F. Archibald expressed anguish at the contaminating aura of convictism. Sydney in the 1870s, he said

was a cant-ridden community. Cant – the horrible offensive cant of the badly reformed sinner – reigned everywhere. There was no health in the public spirit – socially and politically . . . and over all brooded, in law-courts, press and Parliament, the desolating cruelty inherited from the System.[12]

In 1893, when Francis Adams said 'the native Australians . . . have in their underside the taint of cruelty',[13] could one imagine that sensitive man had failed to pick up what was apparent to

Archibald? Manning Clark's picture suggests few of the redeeming qualities Russel Ward ascribed to convicts:

When these men and women spoke for themselves before their judges, they seemed to be liars, drunkards and cheats, flash and vulgar in dress, cheeky in addressing their gaolers when on top, but quick to cringe and whine when retribution struck. With hearts and minds unsustained by any of the great hopes of mankind, driven on by the terror of detection, strangers to loyalty, parasites preying on society . . . they were men and women who roused their contemporaries to disgust and to apprehension, but rarely to compassion, and never to hope.[14]

Patrick O'Farrell wrote of convictism: '. . . those origins left deep and disfiguring scars.'[15] Douglas Pike judged the convicts 'by and large, . . . a worthless lot',[16] but an English literary historian, Barry Argyle, offers a more devastating overall appraisal. Convictism, combined with a shortage of women, has had a pervasive influence on the moral climate, he argues, and is linked with 'cruelty and isolation', the two themes of his analysis of the Australian novel 1830–1930.

To escape [women], or simply as substitutes, men took mates. Naturally, imprisonment encouraged this, as it inevitably encouraged *le vice anglais*. Australian history and fiction contribute to the well-documented belief that algolagnia and necrophilia have been more attractive to the English-speaking peoples than to others . . . Such pursuit of joy through pain goes some way to explaining De Tocqueville's civilized shock that in 1840 'the English seem disposed carefully to retain the bloody traces of the dark ages in their penal legislation.'[17]

In 1971 Michael Cannon, one of the few Australian historians with a poet's feel for community mood and climate, argued that convictism 'helped to give Australia twisted features which were markedly different from development elsewhere',[18] and, as if to bear him out, one of our leading novelists, Xavier Herbert, recently told the *Australian*

There is a tradition of bastardry in Australia. We are a cruel people. It comes from bearing the chains, in every State except South Australia.[19]

K. M. Dallas situates convictism in a British imperial matrix which, historically, helps fuse convictism with slavery: 'That there are degrees of slavery does not alter the basic point', he says.[20] Dallas shows some awareness of the psychological inadequacy of Russel Ward's observation that the poor identified with Australia because, even as convicts, they enjoyed a higher living standard than poor free English labourers:

Nor need we concern ourselves with the proposition that the slave was enjoying a higher living standard than he had previously known. This, like the discipline and industrial training, was an essential condition of the efficiency of any slave system. Like horses, convicts were improved by being 'broken in' (as James Macarthur said of his servants) and by being fed well and regularly . . .[21]

Dallas's article also sheds additional light on the baffling lack of commitment to community of so much of the Australian élite strata: 'the slave-minded ruling class', he observes at one point – referring to formative times. Like American slave masters, many raped the soil and moved on to a repeat-scenario. But Dallas remains a true Australian in some ways. His focus on women is very slight.

We turn now to some aspects of early demography. By and large I accept Manning Clark's reference to our early colonies as a 'broken, cold and unnatural form of society'. The pattern of early demography did much to shape that brokenness, and I think the pattern found its final source in the psychic structure of the contemporary British élite, in a curious pious cruelty which characterized it during early phases of the Industrial Revolution.

The total numbers of convicts sent to New South Wales and Van Diemen's Land, according to Robson's survey, were 122,620 males and 24,960 females:[22] that is, 15 per cent were women[23] (and half went to Van Diemen's land). The 1812 British Select Committee on Transportation said that while the most serious male offenders were chosen for transportation, 'it has been customary to send, without any exception, all [females] whose state of health will admit of it, and whose age does not exceed 45 years.'[24] If we add the 9,688 men sent to

Western Australia between 1850 and 1868, 1,173 sent to New South Wales as 'exiles' in 1849, and about 4,580 sent directly to Port Phillip, Moreton Bay and Norfolk Island, the final total comes to 163,021. But the total number of females remains 24,960. The consequences of populating communities without women or with few women were known at the time, of course, and this omission eloquently testifies to the cruelty of those who structured us in this way.

Of the sample of women convicts Robson used in his study, 55 per cent were tried in England (though not necessarily born there), and of these, 71 per cent were in the age range of fifteen to thirty-four years, 34 per cent were listed as married or 'widowed'; 29 per cent were Protestant, 28 per cent Roman Catholic, and almost all were classified as domestic servants. We can get a rough idea as to other occupations from the itemization of women on the First Fleet's *Lady Penrhyn*. While 65 per cent were domestic servants, there were also milliners, hawkers, mantua-makers, lace-weavers, silk-weavers, needleworkers and dealers. There was, too, a glove-maker, an artificial flower maker, a tambour-worker, a clog-maker, a chapwoman, a barrow-woman, a maker of child-bed linen and a nurse.[25] Ward and Clark as well as Robson report that the 'vast majority' of convicts were unskilled or semi-skilled urban dwellers.[26] Eighty-three per cent of Robson's sample had committed offences against property, only one per cent against the person.[27] As to the place of birth of women convicts, 43 per cent were English, 47 per cent Irish, and 9 per cent Scottish. However before 1840 in New South Wales, the concentration of Irishwomen was more marked than that of the men, since until that time, no woman tried in Ireland was sent directly to Van Diemen's Land; while 5,040 were sent to Sydney.[28] In New South Wales as in Van Diemen's Land, the sex ratio among convicts was much higher than for free settlers. In 1820, there were 11.69 per cent male convicts for every female, but if one takes the free into account, the sex ratio becomes 3·93.*

---

* While by 1830 in Van Diemen's Land there were 18,228 free men and 6,276 free women, there were 9,000 convict men to 1,500 convict women.[29]

In 1829 the sex ratio was 9.36 per cent for convicts, 4.09 with free taken into account; 1833, 8.10 per cent and 3.51 per cent; 1836, 9.80 and 3.32 per cent; 1841, 7.61 and 2.60 per cent; 1846, 10.82 and 1.93 per cent; 1851, 29.95 and 1.55 per cent.[30] If convicts have been at all important as 'imprinters', such a grotesque imbalance will have contributed something to women's low standing.

Our founding mothers, the convict women, had a deeply crippled self vision. If Max Harris is right, that vision must be of no little importance in accounting for the diminished self vision, as well as the low social profile of Australian women to this very day. Harris writes:

The effect of our convict origins has been consistently underwritten by our historians because it was rapidly bred out of the nation during the goldfields era. *But if implanted attitudes are not changed by an influx of population but rather absorbed by the newcomers, then convictism is the prime source of Australian character.* [My emphasis][31]

In explaining why convict women had so lowly a view of themselves, we could simply point to manifest aspects of *society*'s view of them and leave it at that. In the first place, for example, their social status in their places of origin, as we have noted, was abysmally low, and second, their economic usefulness in early eastern Australia was deemed to be negligible. Despite nascent colonial capitalism, which included commercial capitalism and minor industries, the key industries were single-male staffed: whaling, sealing, pastoralism. R. Connell and T. H. Irving, the authors of 'Class Structure in Australian History', rightly see the pastoralists, who drew extensively on convict labour, as 'an arm of the state, a vast outdoor department of penal supervision', and conclude: 'For half a century, in effect, imprisonment was the colonies' main industry.'[32]

It is true that some convict women played an economic role that was noted. In Rosetta Terry, Molly Morgan and Mary Reibey,[33] for example, we see the kind of independent business women more prominent in seventeenth and eighteenth century England and colonial America. They did well, but 'this was rare; most independent business by women was certainly on a small scale and more reliant on a craft than on capital.'[34] Historically, such women must be seen as a kind of survival from the pre-industrializing era, and they were quite minor and fast diminishing. Another example is Ester Johnson, convict *de facto* wife of George Johnson, who managed his pastoral interests during his court martial after Governor Bligh's deposition. Yet even adding free landed women of substance such as Elizabeth Macarthur, Ann Drysdale and Caroline Newcomb,[35] there is no tenable case for suggesting that either convict women, or free women, were regarded* as anything other than of trivial economic importance during formative decades in eastern Australia. Women in our formative times, then, to an extreme and unusual extent, were defined as economically irrelevant and, to a similar extent, clustered into low-status, demeaning occupations: 'Of about 190 jobs advertised in the *Sydney Gazette* in 1810, only 7 were for women.'[36] Further, it's pretty clear that the English élite thought of convict women – to the extent they did think about them – mainly as a kind of sexual servicing outcast group. Convict, free casual poor and later, to a certain extent, working class males, followed élite hegemonic values in this, as in a wide range of issues relating to the moral economy, as the following lines from 'Class Structure in Australian History' show:

The idea of a gentleman seems to have been held as a basic social category by convicts and by immigrant workmen . . . The convicts may have scoffed at propaganda about the 'sanctity of property', but their chronic thieving was an adaptation to the property system rather than a rejection of it.[37]

We may well think no more needs to be said by way of explanation of the crippled self vision of our founding mothers, the convict women. Yet there are less tangible, and complementary, influences shaping their impoverished sense of self, and we

---

* I stress the words 'were regarded'. Clearly, women were and always have been of central importance in the economy. For one thing they produce, and often sustain, the 'direct' producers. However male conceptualization of social reality refuses to 'count' this, and having defined women as economically invisible, devoutly believes and follows through this logic.

can get at these through Allport's concept of the 'victim'. Let us then consider convict women as a kind of 'victim'. Allport proposes that the 'traits due to victimization' fall into two main groups: 'intropunitive' and 'extropunitive'.[38] If the victim handles the master's contempt and the anguish it evokes extropunitively, he/she turns the pain outwards, away from the self. Included in the category of extropunitive traits are aggressiveness and revolt (stealing is one form of this), slyness and cunning. Crucial to understanding the low self-image of convict women, their victimhood and the mechanisms by which they handled it, was their treatment by convict men, the male group most relevant to them. Now some key male convict attitudes about women arose from casual poor *free* males, and the view casual poor males held of themselves ultimately derived from their position in a dominance hierarchy. From this flowed a casual poor male's need for his woman to be lower in standing and poorer in self-estimate than he was. But listing sources of *convict* pain and ugliness, Alexander Harris concludes: 'infinitely worse than all is the sense of the iron dominion exercised over them by the masters.'[39] So it follows that when, with convictism, the issue of 'dominion', that is, of *dominance*, came to bulk larger and eat more deeply into personality than it did among the free casual poor, a convict would tend to need his woman to be just *that* much more wretched than did the male of the free casual poor.

Convicts, whether male or female, evoked widespread revulsion, and we should never imagine that only the well-shod felt horror and fear about them. In 1831, a Bill introduced in the British Parliament by Lord Howick to finance emigration from the poor rates, was 'interpreted even by London labourers as one intended to enforce compulsory transportation . . . [and so] they petitioned Parliament against what they feared would be enforced exile'.[40] In the colonies, popular revulsion about the 'convict stain' was slow to disappear. As late as 1875, Rosamond and Florence Hill noted the 'suspicion with which most of the other colonies regard new arrivals of the male sex from Western Australia lest they prove to be escaped prisoners or ex-convicts'.[41] However convict *women* were the victims of victims, and, I propose, also functioned as a kind of universal outcast group for most classes in penal society. Language gives the clue here. In describing convict *women*, the articulate of the day testified to a special quality of ugliness, despair and demoralization far beyond that of convict men. True, we have to be on guard for hyperbole: men in most patriarchal societies have rarely been able to bear or comprehend the forms in which women manifest anguish, and our witnesses tend to be men from higher social strata than the convict women. The gulf of sex added to class, seems to have ruled out any fellow feeling which could have brought some softening of attitude or treatment, and therefore of the language used to describe the women's despair. Thus in 1787, for example, Surgeon Bowes on the First Fleet transport *Lady Penrhyn* said:

I believe . . . I may venture to say there was never a more abandoned set of wretches collected in one place at any one period than are now to be met with in this Ship.[42]

In the language used to describe women convicts, we get a hint of the fact that they were treated as outcasts of a sort, and also that many convict women reacted to that treatment by 'extropunitive' mechanisms, turning the master's hatred away from the self. Thus in 1796 Governor Hunter told the Duke of Portland that the women convicts were 'generally found to be worse characters than the men'.[43] In 1799 came an official reference to 'complaints . . . daily made to the Governor of the refractory and disobedient conduct of the convict women . . . those troublesome characters . . .'[44] Barely a month later Hunter complained that the 'convict women . . . to the disgrace of their sex, are far worse than the men, and are generally found at the bottom of every infamous transaction committed in this colony . . . they have grown disorderly beyond all suffering.'[45] In November Hunter gave instructions that 'the Women who have been and continue to be by their general Conduct a disgrace to their Sex be strictly directed to attend to the dutys [sic] of the Sabbath day . . .'[46] On 1 March 1802 Governor King described 'most' female convicts as 'of the worst description, and totally irreclaimable, being generally the refuse of

London, very few of them . . . useful'.[47] In 1820, Assistant Surgeon Owen was examined on aspects of convict behaviour at George Town:

Are the women very profligate ? They are. Do they change the men that they cohabit with ? They do. I impute this to their fondness of liquor, and they will leave a person with whom they have lived for a short time in order to obtain liquor from another.[48]

In 1822, Commissioner John Bigge, whose report, for the most part, was couched in judicious language, spoke of the 'disordered, unruly and licentious appearance of the women'[49] at the Parramatta Female Convict Factory. (English authorities often seem more scandalized and moved by the women's plight than were members of the New South Wales establishment, habituated into accepting an 'outcast' definition of convict women.) In 1827 Cunningham found the women 'more quarrelsome and more difficult to control than the men [and] . . . certainly more abandoned in their expressions, too, when excited.'[50] In 1833, Alick Osborne, Royal Navy Surgeon, described female convicts as possessed of 'loose, idle habits',[51] while in 1837 W.B. Ullathorne asked: 'What shall I say of the female convict, acknowledged to be worse, and far more difficult of reformation, than the man ? Her general character is immodesty, drunkenness, and the most horrible language.'[52] Charles Darwin, too, found the women 'much worse' than the men,[53] and the magistrate Thomas Macqueen wrote: 'I have been daily called upon to sentence from 20 to 60 of the most disgusting objects that ever disgraced the female form.'[54] All witnesses testifying before the Molesworth Committee believed women convicts were 'worse' than the men[55] and this view has endured well into our own period. Of convict women in Van Diemen's Land, B. P. Andrews writes that 'prisoner women servants were of lower grade than the men',[56] while in 1963 R. C. Hutchinson wrote 'Most female convicts were of the lowest type and behaved accordingly.'[57]

We have a good deal of evidence to suggest that poor women in pre-industrial societies, and in industrializing England, accepted female aggressiveness and directed it outwards, while women from higher social strata tended to deny it, turn it inwards, or manipulatively direct it towards their children. For example, women took an active part in the late eighteenth century French revolutionary movements and English bread riots,[58] while in the early nineteenth century, female factory operatives at Lowell in Massachusetts, went on strike.

Allport's second group of 'traits due to victimization' is the 'intropunitive' category. Here the victim accepts and turns back upon him/herself the master's definition of him/her. The victim also transforms the master's contempt for him into *self*-contempt and *self*-hate. That self-hate gives rise to a need to express aggression, but the 'intropunitive' victim turns such aggression back upon himself. As a result the victim may manifest traits such as passivity and withdrawal, denying membership of his/her own group, self-hate, and clowning. Nineteenth century Australian commentators, however, tended to emphasize the occasions on which our founding mothers were seen to adopt the 'extropunitive' category. But we noted earlier that only one per cent of women convicts had committed crimes against the person, 83 per cent against property. Externalizing violence fits with both categories, but fits better with 'crimes against the person'. Might the emphasis observers placed on externalized violence among Australian convict women be explained partly by increased violence among women because of their brutalized treatment here? However it's by no means clear that all or most convict women did handle their sadness and anger by diverting it outwards, or 'externalizing' it by 'extropunitive' behaviour. The articulate observers of the day might well not have bothered to comment on the broken, passive, 'well-adjusted' women convicts who directed violence inwards upon themselves. To a certain extent, the received view that convict women were 'refractory' has to be explained in terms of the outlook of nineteenth century commentators, most of whom came from highly 'character-armoured' élite groups for whom any authentic display of emotion was threatening enough to cause notice. That convict women who chose to be 'refractory' drew more public attention than the quite large group who responded passively (and doubtless more self-destructively), is suggested by a recent study. Sampling the conduct of 150 convict women, H. S. Payne found 54·1 per cent responsible for 95 per cent of offences by women in Van Diemen's Land, and so he concluded:

The frequent newspaper reports reflecting on the vice in the colony, while substantially true, neglect to account for about a third of these women who did not have any sentences recorded against them.[59]

We certainly cannot deny the words of Roger Therry, N.S.W. Attorney-General from 1841 to 1843, when he said of Parramatta Female Factory women: 'Their violence at times was excessive . . . They destroyed often the furniture of their cells, broke plates and dishes, and threw everything provided even for their own convenience over the walls of their prison-yard'[60] (the last words show that even in turning violence outwards, the women were simultaneously being self-damaging). But we should also pay attention to Alexander Marjoribanks describing the Parramatta women in 1847. They

are kept so very strict, that I do not well see how they could evince any of their evil spirit . . . The women are not allowed to talk . . . The children are very well educated, and the women are remarkably clean, and neatly dressed. They have their hair closely cut when they first enter the factory . . . They are kept always busy sewing and washing . . .[61]

And where Marjoribanks praised orderliness, a French visitor, De M. Laplace, commented on a broken sadness that came to the surface when violence ceased to mask it:

Laplace's picture is perhaps the saddest and most sombre painted by any visitor to the factory, for while he made no attempt to whitewash the character of any of the inhabitants, he did indirectly attack the organization itself by exhibiting his own reactions, for he was oppressed by the atmosphere and felt, as he said, that the prison bruised his soul and broke his heart.[62]

In 1851, Lieutenant G. C. Munday visited the Hobart Female Factory. His description recalls that of Laplace:

As we passed down the ranks the poor creatures saluted us with a running fire of curtseys and a dead silence was everywhere observed.[63]

And this view is endorsed by a comment about the Hobart Female House of Correction (Female Factory) in a recent study: 'With the exception of some of the worst characters . . . the women were generally orderly and quiet although, when not being watched, they frequently used bad language and sang improper songs.'[64]

Thus women convicts responded to their victimhood 'extropunitively' (turning aggression outwards) or 'intropunitively' (turning it inwards). But whichever mechanism they adopted, the treatment they received produced in them a degree of desperation and often disintegration which in some ways differed in kind and intensity from that of males.

The women's response fits that of a group which, as we said earlier, seems to have functioned as a kind of universal outcast group. A surprising range of people, men and women, in that 'broken, cold and unnatural form of society' appear to have wreaked an unknowing psychic and physical revenge on convict women. Even early Governors, who were unusually compassionate men for their day, seem to have been caught up in this eerie process. Defined as outcast, the women became outcast, and their consequent ugliness put them further beyond the reach of kindness, further beyond the pale. As early as 1791, for example, Governor Phillip had built over 100 huts at Parramatta but those he set aside for women were built of unlimed bricks and quickly fell into disrepair.[65] 'If', said Governor Hunter of the convict women, 'we estimate their merits by the charming children with which they have filled the colony . . . they well deserve our care.'[66] If he meant this, it did not prompt him to stipulate among the public buildings he requested in 1796, any for women,[67] and until the Reverend Samuel Marsden persuaded Governor King to build women a room over the men's gaol at Parramatta, there was no official accommodation for them.[68] This room was built in 1804, to house sixty; but there were seldom fewer than 200 women and children there during the day. Commissioner Bigge described it thus:

The factory . . . consists of one long room that is immediately above the gaol, having two windows . . . Its dimensions . . . are 60 feet by 20; and at one end are store-rooms, where the wool, yarn and cloth are kept. There is one fireplace, at which all the provisions are cooked. The women have no other beds than those they can make from the wool in its dirty state; and they sleep upon it at night . . . No attempt has been made to preserve cleanliness in this room, as the boards had shrunk so much, that when they were washed, the water fell through them into the prison rooms below.[69]

Marion Phillips writes of Governor Lachlan Macquarie (1809–1817): 'With all his humanity Macquarie never displayed genuine interest nor care for these women.'[70] Samuel Marsden claimed he presented two memorials in 1808 to the British Colonial Office on the plight of female convicts, and left England in 1809 'assured by his Majesty's Government that instructions had been given to Governor Macquarie to erect a suitable building for the women convicts.'[71] The instructions were probably those Castlereagh dispatched to Macquarie on 14 May 1809, instructing him to stop women being chosen on board the transports (as Marsden had alleged they were), and to be more careful when arranging assignment for female convicts:

The female convict, it is stated, is seldom apprenticed and she lives indiscriminately, first in one family, then in another. This general license [sic] and want of restraint seems to have the worst tendencies.[72]

Marsden's treatment of convict women suggests that basically (there are exceptions[73]) he shared the general view of them. For example on 5 July 1817 he sentenced 'Elizabeth Bayley, Convict . . . to be Confined on Bread and Water for Two Months. No Mitigation.' Her crime? 'Refusing to Work';[74] and his treatment of the beautiful Anne Rumsby shows great cruelty.[75] Yet for whatever reasons, he drew invaluable attention to the outrages officialdom perpetrated against convict women. Here he is in 1815 on the Parramatta Female Convict Factory:

. . . instead of the Government factory being a house of correction for the abandoned females, and a benefit to the colonists and other inhabitants, as a check upon public vices, it becomes a grand source of all moral corruption, insubordination and disease, and spreads its pestilential influence through the most remote part of the colony.[76]

It is true that Marsden was a personal enemy of Governor Macquarie, and Macquarie tried to rebut several of Marsden's allegations through *A Letter to the Rt. Hon. Viscount Sidmouth in Refutation of Statements made by the Hon. Grey Bennet, M.P., etc.* However a recent writer has aptly described Macquarie's denial of Parramatta's moral degeneracy as 'lengthy, violent, and one might say, forced',[77] and Macquarie was clearly ill at ease on the matter. He *did* behave deplorably towards convict women, this man who often acted generously towards convict men, and one wonders how much, if any, spontaneous human concern he felt for the women. For example, building-prone though he was, Macquarie failed to provide elementary protection for convict women. Lieutenant-General Sorell in Van Diemen's Land repeatedly pressed him on this. In 1818 we find Sorell referring, one feels with concern, to Macquarie's 'desire that the erection of a Factory for Female prisoners here should not at present be undertaken . . .'[78], and in December 1820 Sorell 'assured Macquarie that unless some building was erected, there was no alternative but to allow the mass of females to go at large'.[79] When Commissioner Bigge told Sorell that employment and housing for female convicts was much needed, 'Sorell referred him to Macquarie's former despatches'.[80] In 1822 Bigge personally reproached Macquarie over the Parramatta Factory, not accepting Macquarie's protest that he had failed to build alternative accommodation for female convicts because he'd sought official approval which was slow in coming. Bigge pointed out that Macquarie

had undertaken several buildings of much less urgent necessity than the factory at Parramatta, without waiting for any such indispensable authority . . . I cannot help regarding, therefore, the want of authority alleged by Governor Macquarie as a feeble and unsafe justification for the delay . . . [Macquarie in fact had at hand enough money to build] good accommodation at a very moderate rate of expense [because] an expensive building, or any architectural ornament [was not needed].[81]

Macquarie, who became Governor of New South Wales in 1809, began to build a new Female Factory in July 1818 but did not finish till 1821.[82] Later, Governor Bourke removed the weaving loom at the factory for ' "reasons of economy " so those at the factory remained idle, but he did little else',[83] while of Van Diemen's Land women convicts, Kathleen Fitzpatrick writes:

It had always been considered that female convicts were more difficult to manage than males, but when the probation system was adopted no provision was made for them at all beyond the giving of an order that the only existing discipline for them, assignment to domestic service, was to cease.[84]

Macquarie was well aware of what happened to convict women – his dispatches show this beyond any doubt. Nevertheless he handed out tickets of leave to women when captains or surgeons of their ships recommended them – an 'indulgence', the Principal Superintendent of the Parramatta Factory told Bigge, which often led to women 'cohabitating'.[85] Constant pregnancy was the outcome, and it scarcely escaped official notice. Indeed as early as 1796 Hunter said 'we generally find those of a certain age taken up in the indispensable duties of nursing an infant.'[86] In 1836 James Backhouse noted that the seventy-one women convicts at the 'Penitentiary for Female prisoners were "employed in washing, needle-work, picking oakum, and nursing" '.[87] Thus the vulnerability of convict women was perfectly well known, yet in 1838 the Molesworth select committee on transportation noted that 'out of 590 females in the Factory at Parramatta in 1836, 108 were nursing children.'[88]

The anthropologist Mary Douglas stresses that caste is intimately linked with the body: bodily function, bodily differences. We recollect that in the early nineteenth century, the 'lower orders' exhibited startling bodily differences. They spoke differently, their faces looked 'different', their clothing was distinctive, their bodies smelled strongly at a time when anal-obsessive cleanliness was beginning to emerge as a mark of the upwardly-mobile. Caste is pivoted around 'purity and impurity', Mary Douglas explains. Questions touched by considerations of purity and impurity often ultimately concern the body and include: who shall eat with whom ? Who smokes with whom, drinks what, with whom ?[89] Who shall speak to whom and who may joke with whom, follow closely. The treatment of the bodily needs of women convicts, and of their babies' bodily needs, underlines my feeling that convict women fulfilled the psychic function of an 'outcast' group for that 'broken, cold and unnatural' society. Malnutrition, long periods between meals (for example, at times, no food between twelve mid-day and eight the next morning) were common. In 1841 the *Austral-Asiatic Review* commented on toilet and living arrangements in the Hobart Female Factory:

The capacity of the building is so unequal to the number of the wretched inmates, that their working rooms resemble the hold of a slave ship; what their sleeping-rooms must be, shut up during the whole night . . . must be obvious to all. So foetid, so wholly unfitting for the human being is the atmosphere after the night's inhalations, that if we are correctly informed, the turnkey's [sic] when they open the doors in the morning, make their escape from the passages . . . to avoid semi-suffocation.[90]

It would almost seem that the babies of convict women were deemed to have 'inherited' their mothers' stigma. At any rate the best way I can make sense of the way the babies were treated is to assume an unconscious 'caste' approach to their mothers. One is 'born into' the caste system, and it is possible that the modern western class and status system slowly grew out of, and bore the marks of, a kind of caste gulf.[91] For a start, the infant mortality rate in the Hobart Female Factory was 'unbelievably high'.[92] After a baby was weaned, mothers were punished for the crime of having become pregnant by being placed in the Factory's 'crime' class. So according to James Backhouse, mothers were tempted 'to keep their infants in a weakly state, that the time, apparently necessary to nurse them at the breast, may be delayed'. The *True Colonist* described the way babies were fed after weaning:

... What but death or worse than death, an emaciated existence during the whole period which that life may be continued, can result from the weaning a number of children, several by one woman, the food given to all of them at one time, (for it cannot otherwise be provided in a warm condition) so that their little heads are stretched forth towards the feeding spoon which is offered to them in succession. If they are asleep at 'the feeding time', they must be awakened, and if so, what parent is there who knows not the unwillingness with which an infant is disturbed in its repose – wretched indeed must it be – will receive food, especially when to obtain it at all, must be an effort of which even the healthiest of infants are either unwilling or incapable, they must either be awakened to receive their passing share of food, or they must remain without food until the next feeding time, some hours onwards. [sic][93]

A recent writer denies charges made by local newspapers that the Factory's Matron, Mrs Mary Hutchinson, was to be blamed 'for the emaciated condition of the weaned infants and the large infant mortality rate', and suggests she was 'probably deeply concerned about the high infant mortality rate, although she may have been too proud publicly to demonstrate her concern'.[94] She herself had twelve children, and six died during infancy. I don't find this altogether convincing. An alternative theory is that, like too many privileged or élite women in early colonial days, Mrs Hutchinson lacked fellow-feeling for convict women, following men in defining them as outcast. In New South Wales, too, one senses something of a wish to see an inherited stigma attached to convict women's children – their female children, in this case. Governor King wrote in 1800:

Soon after my arrival in this colony I had frequent opportunities of observing the numerous children of both sexes going about the streets in a most neglected manner ... [he noted] the early abuses the female part suffered, not only from the unprotected state they were in, but also from the abandoned examples of their parents ...[95]

In the tiny early community of our founding mothers, prostitution was rife. Did widespread prostitution lower the overall self-esteem, self-belief, dignity and social standing of early women *in general*? Did that pattern 'set'? Did a low esteem for women, and the woman, as Theodore Roszak puts it, 'locked up in the dungeons'[96] of man's psyche, become a kind of cultural 'gene', handed down in families to children in their pre-verbal stages? Does the past still haunt us in the present, enshrined (as Ibsen said) in 'all sorts of old dead ideas . . . ghosts all over the country'?

Writing of *Women in Stuart England and America*, Roger Thompson posits that widespread prostitution has a profound overall impact on the standing of women in a community, and I agree with him:

The existence of widespread prostitution . . . is most likely to occur in societies with an unbalanced sex ratio. It arises from a sense of the inequality of the sexes, and is often a logical accompaniment of a patriarchal society. The male who patronises prostitutes *tends to develop a depreciating attitude towards women and an exaggerated sense of self-importance.* [My emphasis][97]

Widespread prostitution, perhaps especially in formative times for a small community, diminishes all women, because, as Thompson implies, men tend to generalize their contempt for prostitutes so that it falls on all women. Phyllis Chesler, as we noted earlier, points out that money is paid for the humiliation of prostitutes as much as for their bodies.[98]

We were a 'frontier' community in those times. Does the 'frontier' explain the extent of prostitution? Prostitution certainly flourished in America's nineteenth century wild west! 'Newer western communities in particular found prostitutes flaunting their attractions abroad, to the distress of the conservative and moral.'[99] But in seventeenth and early eighteenth century Massachusetts and Virginia, *also* frontier communities, Thompson was 'able to find hardly any evidence of the existence of prostitution'.[100] So let's suspend judgement on whether *all* frontiers must have widespread prostitution.

In 1820, the Honourable H. H. Grey Bennet, M.P., said there existed in New South Wales a 'system of general prostitution'. How widespread *was* prostitution among our founding mothers in those formative decades? Marsden was one of Bennet's informants, and an important source of evidence on the decayed moral climate of the time. What Marsden meant by morality was rather too sharply focused on sexuality, largely divorced from its social surround, thus setting him free to indulge his own more wide-ranging brands of immorality. In addition, since Marsden's own attitude to sexuality was curiously cramped, he is, in all, a suspect witness. Yet many others also testified to the fact that prostitution was widespread, and Bennet's reference constitutes only one in a long series ranging to 1924. In August 1799, for example, the Reverend William Henry wrote to the London Missionary Society, 'It is as common and in fact more thought of here for a man to keep a prostitute and have a number of children by her than it is for a man to have a wife and children in England.'[101] Again, however, we have to be careful about Henry as a witness. Of the many unions which took place outside marriage in New South Wales deep into the nineteenth century and beyond, we don't know how many were stable, or more or less stable. This is what really matters so far as the quality of companionship and child-rearing is concerned, and some writers think – though not on the basis of much hard data – that a 'large proportion' of such unions 'may have been stable unions'.[102] An analysis of 150 women convicts between 1843 and 1853 finds that only 24 per cent were 'designated prostitutes'. Yet contemporary voices are insistent, and demand further attention. In 1812 the House of Commons Select Committee on Transportation reported that convict women were 'indiscriminately given to such of the inhabitants as demanded them, and were in general received rather as prostitutes than as servants'.[103] In 1816 Nicholas Bayly wrote to Sir H. E. Bunbury: 'The Women, bad as they are, are really to be pitied': there were not sufficient lodgings for them, or occupations, and they were forced into prostitution for these reasons.[104] In 1817 Earl Bathurst protested to Governor Macquarie over 'representations' reaching him on 'the State of Prostitution . . . the Female Convicts during their voyage to the Colony are permitted to live with the Officers and Seamen of the Ships.'* On 3 March 1818, commenting on prostitution on board the ship *Friendship* (hardly a friendly milieu for the women, then!), Governor Macquarie wished there were some system by which to guard against this. Several of the convict women

are Young and when Embarked it is to be hoped Not altogether abandoned [but are] too frequently Exposed to such scenes of Debauchery during the Passage, as to leave but little Hope of their being Speedily reclaimed after their arrival here.[106]

In 1818 the Reverend Vale wrote to Earl Bathurst:

I understand there is no place of separate confinement for females sentenced to Sydney Jail: but this I certainly know, that so contracted is the provision for the accommodation of female convicts in general, that the greater part are compelled to prostitute themselves in order to find a place for their nightly shelter . . .[107]

The 1838 Molesworth Committee claimed of convict women 'they are all of them, with scarcely an exception, drunken and abandoned prostitutes.'[108] When assigned, to defend herself against 'constant pursuit and solicitation', a convict woman tended to choose one male. She seldom remained long at one place, because often she committed an offence or became pregnant, and in either case she was returned to the Government. Later 'she is reassigned, and again goes through the same course; such is too generally the career of convict women, *even in respectable families*'. [My emphasis] Referring to experiences before 1846, T. H. Braim wrote: 'It is a revolting fact, that individuals were found, who did not disdain to receive

* In the United States, Kate Waller Barrett insisted that the roots of prostitution must be found in the trans-Atlantic voyage, and stressed the need for preventive measures on board immigrant ships. Kate Barrett was one of the many women who militantly publicized the widespread prostitution in late nineteenth and early twentieth century America, especially among immigrants. One of the puzzles for Australian historians is why privileged women in early New South Wales concerned themselves so little with the manifest tragedy of poor women who were partly or entirely prostitutes.[105]

the wages of prostitution, earned by female assigned servants; yet these wretches were neither pilloried nor hooted from the colony.'[109]

But the 'ghosts' of convict prostitution seem to have outlived the institution of convictism: there's the rub. In 1859, for example, Frank Fowler threw retrospective light on the casual-poor-into-convict-into-prostitute syndrome. 'Slumming' along with friends, he noted

the awful old women who turn out of the alleys at night to beg and rob . . . sublime in their Repulsiveness. You can read a history of the blackest crime, commenced in the old world and culminated in the new, in the bleared face of every one of them. 'How came you out here?' I asked of one who solicited alms of me as, in the company of half-a-dozen friends, I passed through the place on a tour of inspection. 'I was picked up by a scamp when I was a girl: he deserted me: I made away with his child: I was sent out here for life thirty years ago. *And now what are you going to give me?*'[110]

Can we imagine this poor woman would not have turned to prostitution once here? In 1860, if we can believe police inspector John McLerie, convict women continued to have a demoralizing effect on free poor women. Giving evidence to a select committee on the Condition of the Working Classes, McLerie said:

I attribute a great deal of the misconduct of juvenile females to another cause; we have in the city a great deal of the old female convict element, a large proportion of women who are scarcely a day out of gaol or the custody of the police; they live in those low neighbourhoods when out of gaol, and their example has a pernicious effect on the growing-up female children . . . in fact, imprisonment of these degraded females has so little deterring effect upon them that children growing up among them have no fear of committing crime.[111]

The fact that women convicts could still be seen as late as this comes as a shock, perhaps because we've tacitly agreed to ignore the deeper implications of convictism, especially where it concerns women. Yet the woman who wrote *Girl Life in Australia*, published in 1876 but drawing on experiences in the 1850s (and

6os), referred to 'old convict women' in 'huts' and also to 'two haggard-looking convict women', as if these were not especially surprising to her.[112] We noted earlier that Ballarat women in the 1860s were frightened by the moral corruption which convictism threatened: 'Mothers, Sisters and Women of England': help us 'lest we be steeped to the lips in the polluted stream of convictism . . . from famaliarity [sic] with evil alone can spring indifference to its loathesomeness and horror . . .'* From our last chapter we recall what the Hill sisters reported in 1875: the chief warder at Darlinghurst Gaol described Sydney as 'the worst city in the world for young females'.[114] Convictism and prostitution lend credibility to his claim, even though it is exaggerated. In 1883, R. E. N. Twopeny found prostitution rife in Australia.[115] In June 1891, Lady Windeyer, wife of the New South Wales Chief Justice and a leading figure in the state's emerging women's movement, was reported to say 'women had been looked upon somewhat as chattels, men being so to speak their owners.'[116] In November of that year, J. W. Hill said that the moment she married, woman became man's 'bond woman – a semi-slave'.[117] Of course these remarks could have been made in many places, but *they were actually made* in New South Wales, where, in the 1870s, if we accept Archibald's view, convictism ('the system') still saturated the climate ('brooded' over institutions). So in reaching for the vocabulary of bondhood, did Lady Windeyer catch echoes of an institution which still hung heavily over the man-woman relation – that is, over the very heart of our folkways? In 1924, just as Twopeny had done in 1883, G. Meudell observed that prostitution was 'rife'.[118] We can, if we want, simply put this down to frontier crudeness and incipient industrialization. But can we really afford to neglect convictism to the extent we have?

While most of our founding mothers and early poor women

* In the 1850s Mrs Sophia Phillips of Culham, Western Australia, recorded concern over 'female convicts'. Here is part of her diary entry for 21 June 1857: 'Sunday: Steere Tom and Pritchard getting signatures against having female convicts . . .' And for 1 July 1857: 'Sam obliged to go to York with the memorial against Female convicts . . .'[113]

were forced into prostitution for material reasons, as the century wore on other motives begin to demand attention. In 1858 Dr Sanger, the resident physician at the women's prison on Blackwell's Island in the United States, arranged for 2,000 prostitutes to be interviewed. He estimated that, through physical mistreatment, liquor and disease, the average professional life of a prostitute was four years, but concluded that a good half entered prostitution because they were attracted by the way of life.[119] The American historian Lois Banner comments: 'It did not occur to [Sanger] that they might have come from a world in which sexuality was open and prostitution just another kind of work.'[120] There is much to Banner's thought, but more needs to be said. Jane Addams, writing in 1912, stressed some of the psychic needs which prompted 'unemployed, friendless immigrant' girls towards prostitution; and our convict and free poor women were, after all, only too often 'unemployed, friendless' immigrants. 'Loneliness and detachment . . . is easily intensified in such a girl into isolation and a desolating feeling of belonging nowhere . . . At such a moment of black oppression, the instinctive fear of solitude will send a lonely girl restlessly to walk the streets even when she is "too tired to stand" and where her desire for companionship in itself constitutes a grave danger'[121] (Caroline Chisholm's Highland girl Flora!). Robert Riegel also points to an influence relevant to our own founding mothers. A high proportion of Sanger's interviewees came from broken homes, while many blamed 'ill treatment by family', and, Riegel comments, 'Certain other explanations, such as the desire for an easier, more pleasant, more exciting life, while possibly classifiable as economic, might just as plausibly be interpreted as suggesting psychological troubles . . .' 'Certainly', he concludes, 'emotional maladjustments were important, even though they cannot be measured precisely.'[122]

And I think Lois Banner's 'just another kind of work' verdict, while not without its point, side-steps a question central to women's self-esteem and, through the generalized contempt men adopt to women *via* widespread prostitution, women's *overall* role-definition and standing. To demean in any way, especially to commercialize, one's sexuality places at great risk one's total self-esteem. No defence mechanisms can succeed in hiding from ourselves what we do to and with our bodies.* And neither can one fail to internalize male contempt and society's contempt. It suits many males – in fact it underlies *Playboy*-type trendiness – to pretend women can operate schizoid mechanisms with long-term success and psychic impunity. Many women adopt the stance of the ruling group, identify with their ideology, as is common with 'victims', and believe they can operate such mechanisms with impunity. But I submit there are no hiding places from the self.

If there is a sense in which convict women were outcast, is there anything about the way they were punished, or experienced punishment, which fits this ? For myself, the more I reconstruct in imagination bits of the universe I think our convict women inhabited, the more I find myself recalling De Tocqueville's 'civilized shock' in 1840: 'the English seem disposed carefully to retain the bloody traces of the dark ages in their penal legislation'; for, while there certainly are cases of women convicts being punished moderately, or with consideration, the evidence often suggests a savouring of vulnerability only too obvious. For example, in 1820, evidently precipitated by Commissioner Bigge's inquiries,[123] the case of Alice Blackstone came up for investigation, with Surgeon R. W. Owen answering questions. While pregnant, Alice Blackstone had been beaten by her husband 'about the face and head with a Stick $2\frac{1}{2}$ Inches Circumference, on which the Scar now remained, and from her head downwards as far as the legs; from the violence of the blows on her head, she fell, and Blackstone [her husband], not content with the Brutal manner in which he had treated her, Kicked and jumped on her . . .'[124] When Alice Blackstone had her baby, she was soon sent on a long trip with Surgeon Owen's approval. 'Fatigued', suckling her child, she walked thirty-five

* On my shelves as I write I can see a work published by the Boston Women's Health Collective called *Our Bodies Ourselves*. That title encapsulates volumes!

miles from 'George Town to Launceston with an Iron Collar weighing 5¼ pounds' around her neck.[125]

The following is an examination of Mr Matthew John Gibbons, Storekeeper to the Engineer in the Lumber Yard, Sydney, on 6 May 1829:

Do you recollect any collar irons being made during your former residence in the Colony? . . . I recollect such having been made by order of Lieutenant Governor Grose about the year 1793 or 1794; they were made for women convicts, who at that time were behaving so ill that it was found the only means of keeping them in order. What was the construction of these collar [sic]? – It was a round bolt of iron formed with a collar for the neck, and rivetted through two projections extending from a foot to eighteen inches from the collar. What was their weight? – . . . about fourteen or fifteen pounds each. [126]

In Van Diemen's Land, in 1836, women convicts 'were punished by solitary confinement, . . . an iron collar was sometimes used for the worst characters and . . . stocks had been erected at Launceston for detaining them for a short time.'[127] They could also have their heads shaved.[128] In Hobart, the *Colonial Times* reported in 1842 that the Governor's wife, Lady Jane Franklin, formed a Ladies' Committee to manage the Female Convict Establishment. In many ways Lady Jane had a punitive approach to the poor, certainly towards women convicts,[129] and her Committee intended to see that in the 'lowest crime yard', women convicts spent their time in 'breaking stones for the finishing course on the roads'; 'a certain task [had] to be fixed and finished daily, under the penalty of an extension of sentence.' In other 'crime yards', women convicts washed, sewed, spun and made clothes.[130] In 1836 the Tolpuddle Martyr George Loveless wrote this about women convicts:

. . . if they offend their masters by being insolent, neglectful of their duty, etc. etc., they are taken and charged before the magistrates, who sentence them, not to be flogged, but to have their heads shorn, and to be sent to the factory from one month to three years, to work at the wash tub, according to the nature of the offence. I have been told that a practice once prevailed, if the woman committed a misdemeanour after they were in the factory, to put iron collars round their necks, with spikes in them, to increase their punishment. This horrid practice, I believe, is not in existence now, but they have lately built a treadmill for them.[131]

Michael Cannon describes this treadmill:

The treadmill, one of the cruellest yet most overlooked methods of convict punishment inflicted in recent centuries, consisted of a large revolving cylinder to which was fastened a circular iron frame. This was fitted with steps around the circumference, rather like the paddle wheel of an early steamship. The drum could either be filled with stones or connected to a flour mill or pump. When the convict put his foot on to a step, the drum revolved, and to avoid falling off he had to keep on mounting continuously to the next step above. This process continued for whatever number of hours each day were thought appropriate by the authorities.[132]

The treadmill was devised with the physique of males in mind. But it was also in fact used for female convicts. Their suffering was consequently more acute, and, in cases like the following, more humiliating:

Dr. Good found that the chief effect of the treadmill on female convicts was 'a very horrible pain in the loins', the forerunner of greatly intensified menstruation . . . The bleeding took place 'even in the presence of the male keepers', until a sympathetic local magistrate substituted female keepers and had a linen screen erected a few feet above the platform. Dr. Good told of one woman, pregnant for two months, who was put on the wheel and 'thrown into a miscarriage' . . . In reply to Dr. Good's allegations, the chairman of Surrey Sessions, Thomas Harrison, informed the public that the treadmill was a marvellous specific against rheumatism and particularly good for women because it prevented them from getting varicose veins.[133]

In 1836, James Backhouse found the 'forty females . . . employed in field labour' at Eagle Farm near Brisbane were 'kept in close confinement during the night, and strictly watched in the day time . . . Some of them wear chains, to prevent their absconding.'[134] We know solitary confinement placed male convicts under extreme stress, but female convicts, Marjoribanks wrote, might have 'actually become mad altogether'[135] as a result. The same treatment given to men, then, could be experienced far more severely by women, as we saw happened with the tread-mill, where women could haemorrhage and miscarry when they were pregnant or menstruating.

In order to fulfil the condition that they should stand lower than convict men, and perhaps than all groups apart from Aborigines, then, perhaps convict women were treated some-what like an outcast group. If, as repeated use of the term by historians suggests, there is such a thing as a 'formative' period for a culture's folkways, we have to ask whether the caste-like situation of convict women has contributed to shaping our sociosexual patterns. We will never know. But if out of distaste for the thought, we reject the possibility, then we ought also to reject the very notion of a 'formative' period. Or is it only admirable, or at any rate less horrifying, qualities that can be handed down from formative times?

At any rate, from the first, one finds observers who believed the influence of convict women on that small community was far-reaching. Shaw, we noted at the beginning of this chapter, describes a letter from Mrs Elizabeth Leake to Mrs Taylor: it was 'almost impossible for those families who study the quiet and morality of their children to endure Female Convicts'.[136] Harriet Beecher Stowe believed the entire fabric of family and sexuality in the American slave South was permeated and moulded by the institution of slavery. We've had indications that nineteenth century observers sensed something of the psychic spin-offs from convictism. Keeping in mind Mrs Leake's statement, here is Charles Darwin's comment in 1836:

There are many serious drawbacks to the comforts of families; the chief of which, perhaps, is being surrounded by convict servants. How thoroughly odious to every feeling to be waited on by a man, who the day before, perhaps, was flogged, from your representation, for some trifling misdemeanour. *The female servants are of course much worse; hence children learn the vilest expressions, and it is fortunate if not equally vile ideas.* [My emphasis][137]

The report of the Molesworth Committee in 1838 says: 'It can easily be imagined, what a pernicious effect must be produced upon the character of the children of settlers being, too frequently, in their tenderest years, under the charge of such persons.' The Committee was also told that a female convict servant had 'corrupted' the 'daughters of a respectable individual'. She 'was made a kind of companion for them'. The daughters thereby evolved into 'almost the same condition as prostitutes, not to one servant, but to all the servants of the establishment', and were alleged to be 'in the habit of having intercourse with a road party of men'.[138] In 1840 a writer in the Hobart *Colonial Times* was of much the same opinion:

Good God. When we consider that these wretches in human form are scattered through the Colony, and admitted into the houses of respectable families, coming into hourly association with their sons and *daughters* [emphasis in original], we shudder at the consequences . . .[139]

A more recent researcher draws a similar conclusion on Tasmanian women convicts: 'Those who left the Factory and went into service became degrading influences in the families where they worked.'[140] And in 1844 Mrs Charles Meredith pointed to a similar process when she wrote that the 'largest portion' of female convict servants were 'totally unfit for a respectable place . . . from their inherent propensities to do evil, every shape of vice and depravity seeming as familiar to them as the air they breathe'.[141]

In 1886 a former Van Diemen's Land convict chaplain who served in the late 1830s, wrote a novel which touched on the domestic impact of convict women:

The settlers, many of them married men, were in many cases improperly intimate with their female servants, many of whom had been on the streets of the great cities at home . . . Young men, who, however wild they may have been when at college or away from their parents, found themselves when staying at the houses of the settlers in veritable brothels, each house containing in the shape of domestic servants its quota of unblushing prostitutes . . . the most disgraceful scenes were enacted under the roof where the mothers and grown daughters dwelt, and who to their shame be it said were well aware of what was being done.[142]

This diary of an American slave owner's wife might perhaps suggest what those 'well aware' respectable Van Diemen's Land mothers and daughters felt: 'God forgive us, but ours is a monstrous system . . . Like the patriarchs of old, our men live all in one house with their wives and their concubines . . .'[143]

If women wrote history, or if women – and children – were deemed subjects worthy of serious concern by Australian historians, could A. G. L. Shaw, one of our major authorities on convictism, still have come to the conclusion that 'socially [it] . . . did no great harm'?

At some level of their being, people in all social strata in the penal colonies must have been aware that theirs was an outcast society. Manning Clark's portraits of many of our early leaders are often portraits of deeply dissatisfied and driven men, soured, sometimes a little poisoned, by a sense of lack, of unfulfilment.* Underlying my thinking about our founding mothers, then, was this question: since there weren't enough Aboriginal women, did convict women fulfil an essential function as a visible, stigmatized outcast group, and thus lessen the pain of an entire outcast society? With that question in mind, I looked at the 'victim'-like self-image of convict women, their treatment, the language which that self-image and treatment elicited in the master (not forgetting that the master's language, as Fanon shows in *The Wretched of the Earth*, was also influenced by the need to diminish guilt by vilifying those he had crippled). Prostitution, too, commanded our attention partly in the context of thinking about outcasts. As we try to assess the 'imprinting' effect on Australian folkways of our founding mothers in formative decades, these then are some of the issues which demand attention.

* I'm not sure this applies to the penal colonies alone, and suggest why in the concluding chapter when I discuss one of Philip Slater's points.

Notes

1. Henry Reynolds, ' "That Hated Stain": The Aftermath of Transportation in Tasmania', *Historical Studies, Australia and New Zealand*, vol. 14, no. 53, October 1969, p. 19.

2. Cited in Henry Reynolds, loc. cit.

3. A. G. L. Shaw, *Convicts and the Colonies*, Faber and Faber, London, 1966, p. 240.

4. ibid., p. 358.

5. *Report from the Select Committee on Transportation*, 1837, vol. 1, Minutes of Evidence, Colonel G. Arthur, 27 June 1837, question 4281, p. 286.

6. W. Ullathorne, *The Horrors of Transportation*, Richard Coyne, Dublin, 1838, pp. 7, 15 and 26.

7. W. Ullathorne, *The Catholic Mission in Australasia*, Reckliff and Dickworth, Liverpool, 1837, p. 2.

8. *Sir William Molesworth's Speech in the House of Commons, March 6, 1838 on the State of the Colonies*, London, 1838, p. 5.

9. Henry Parkes, *An Emigrant's Home Letters*, Angus and Robertson, Sydney, 1896.

10. C. M. H. Clark, 'The Case of John and Jane Franklin', Tasmanian Historical Research Association, *Papers and Proceedings*, vol. 20, no. 2, June 1973, pp. 67–81, 71–2.

11. The petition is to be found at the Royal Commonwealth Society Library, London. The problem of dating it is discussed in: *Royal Commonwealth Society Library Notes with List of Accessions*, New Series, no. 59. November 1961.

12. Quoted in R. Conway, op. cit., p. 27.

13. Francis Adams, *The Australians. A Social Sketch*, T. Fisher Unwin, London, 1893, pp. 26–7.

14. C. M. H. Clark, *A History of Australia*, vol. 1, Melbourne University Press, Melbourne, 1962, p. 95.

15. Patrick O'Farrell, *The Catholic Church in Australia: A Short History 1788-1967*, Nelson, Melbourne, 1968, p. 10.

16. Douglas Pike, *The Quiet Continent*, Cambridge University Press, 1970, p. 47.

17. B. Argyle, op. cit., p. 5, citing A. C. De Tocqueville, *Democracy in America* (abridged), London, 1961, p. 434.

18. M. Cannon, op. cit.; Cannon gives dramatic evidence for his thesis in 'Violence: The Australian Heritage', *National Times*, 5–12 March 1973.

19. Xavier Herbert, in the *Australian*, 29 July 1974.

20. K. M. Dallas, 'Slavery in Australia – Convicts, Emigrants, Aborigines', Tasmanian Historical Research Association, *Papers and Proceedings*, vol. 16, no. 2, September 1968, pp. 61–77.

21. ibid., p. 63.

22. L. L. Robson, *The Convict Settlers* . . ., p. 4.

23. ibid., p. 74.

24. 'Report of the Select Committee on Transportation, 1812', *Parliamentary Papers*, House of Commons, 1812, vol. 2, pp. 581–2.

25. A. J. Gray, 'Anne Smith of the "Lady Penrhyn" ', Royal Australian Historical Society, *Journal and Proceedings*, vol. 43, 1957, p. 253.

26. R. Ward, *The Australian Legend*, 2nd edition, p. 22; L. L. Robson, *The Convict Settlers* . . ., p. 181; C. M. H. Clark, 'The Origins of the Convicts Transported to Eastern Australia 1787–1852', *Historical Studies, Australia and New Zealand*, vol. 7, nos. 26–7, 1956, p. 130.

27. L. L. Robson, 'The Origin of the Women Convicts Sent to Australia, 1787–1852', *Historical Studies, Australia and New Zealand*, vol. 11, November 1963, p. 45; *The Convict Settlers* . . ., especially pp. 176–88.

28. L. L. Robson, *The Convict Settlers* . . ., p. 130.

29. Barbara M. Richmond, 'Some Aspects of Transportation and Immigration in Van Diemen's Land, 1824–1855', M. A. thesis, University of Tasmania, 1956, p. 90.

30. Peter F. McDonald, *Marriage in Australia*, Australian Family Formation Project, Monograph no. 2, Department of Demography, Institute of Advanced Studies, A.N.U., Canberra, 1974, p. 40.

31. Max Harris, op. cit., p. 39.

32. Robert Connell and T. H. Irving, 'Class Structure in Australian History', chapter 3, p. 5 and p. 11. My thanks to the authors for generously letting me read their work in manuscript form.

33. *Australian Dictionary of Biography*, vols. 1 and 2, Melbourne University Press, 1966 and 1967; Gwynneth M. Dow, *Samuel Terry: The Botany Bay Rothschild*, Sydney University Press, 1974.

34. Connell and Irving, op. cit., chapter 3, p. 25.

35. Sibella Macarthur Onslow, *Some Early Records of the Macarthurs of Camden*, Angus and Robertson, Sydney, 1914; *Australian Dictionary of Biography*, vols. 1 and 2.

36. Connell and Irving, op. cit., chapter 3, p. 23.

37. ibid., chapter 3, p. 53.

38. Gordon Allport, *The Nature of Prejudice*, Doubleday Anchor Books, New York, 1958.

39. Alexander Harris, 'An Emigrant Mechanic', *Settlers and Convicts*, London, 1847, reprinted by Melbourne University Press, 1964, pp. 230–1.

40. A. J. Hammerton, 'A Study of Middle Class Female Emigration from Great Britain, 1830–1914', Ph.D. thesis, University of British Columbia, 1969, pp. 33–4, citing *Hansard*, 3rd series, 2, 22 February 1831, c. 875–906; 5, 8 August 1831, c. 927–9.

41. R. and F. Hill, op. cit., p. 39.

42. One modern scholar concludes, however, that while in general Bowes was 'a thoughtful commentator . . . on occasions he couched his opinions in rather intemperate language . . . However much they may have annoyed him at the time, the women on the *Lady Penrhyn* were not an "abandon'd set of wretches". A study of their lives at Sydney Cove and Norfolk Island makes this quite clear.' (A. J. Gray, op. cit., p. 254.)

43. Hunter to Portland, 18 November 1796, *Historical Records of New South Wales*, vol. 3, p. 182.

44. Hunter to Portland, 1 May 1799, *H.R.A.*, series 1, vol. 4, p. 360.

45. Hunter to Portland, 3 July 1799, ibid., p. 586.

46. General Orders 1799, 29 November 1798, *H.R.A.*, series 1, vol. 2.

47. King to Portland, 1 March 1802, *H.R.A.*, series 1, vol. 3, p. 434.

48. Examinations taken before John Thomas Bigge, 15 April 1820, *H.R.A.*, series 3, vol. 3, p. 407.

49. J. T. Bigge, 'Report of the Commissioner of Inquiry into the Colony of New South Wales', *Parliamentary Papers*, House of Commons, 1822, vol. 20, p. 584 (hereafter Bigge, *Report*).

50. P. Cunningham, op. cit., pp. 271–2.

51. A. Osborne, *Notes on the Present State and Prospects of Society in New South Wales*, J. Cross, London, 1833, p. 20.

52. W. Ullathorne, *The Catholic Mission in Australasia*, p. 26.

53. Cited in M. Cannon, op. cit., p. 58.

54. M. Cannon, op. cit., citing T. Potter Macqueen, *Australia As she is and As she May Be*, London, 1840.

55. 'Report of Select Committee on Transportation, 1837–38', *Parliamentary Papers*, House of Commons, 1837–38, vol. 22. Hereafter the House of Commons Select Committee on Transportation, 1837–38.

56.   B. P. Andrews, 'The Life, Position and Influence of Women in the early Settlement of Van Diemen's Land 1803–1850', M.A. thesis, 1942, University of Tasmania, p. 8.

57.   R. C. Hutchinson, 'Mrs Hutchinson and the Female Factories of Early Australia', Tasmanian Historical Research Association, *Papers and Proceedings*, vol. 2, no. 2, December 1963, p. 56.

58.   E. P. Thompson, 'The Moral Economy of the English Crowd in the Eighteenth Century', *Past and Present*, no. 50, February 1971, pp. 76–136.

59.   H. S. Payne, 'A Statistical Study of Female Convicts in Tasmania, 1843–53', Tasmanian Historical Research Association, *Papers and Proceedings*, vol. 9, no. 2, June 1961, pp. 56–66.

60.   Roger Therry, *Reminiscences of Thirty Years Residence in New South Wales and Victoria*, Sampson Low, London, 1863.

61.   Alexander Marjoribanks, *Travels in New South Wales*, London, 1847, pp. 226–7.

62.   M. De M. Laplace, *Voyage Autour du Monde*, 3, Paris, 1835, pp. 328–30, cited in Joan Cobb, 'The History of the Female Convict Factory at Parramatta', History Honours thesis, University of New England, 1958, p. 32.

63.   G. C. Munday, *Our Antipodes*, Bentley, London, 1855, p. 499.

64.   R. C. Hutchinson, op. cit., p. 57.

65.   James Jervis, *Story of Parramatta*, Shakespeare Head Press, 1933, pp. 13–14, 36–7, cited in J. Cobb, 'Female Convict Factory', p. 5.

66.   Hunter to Portland, 20 June 1797, *H.R.A.*, series 1, vol. 2, p. 24.

67.   Hunter to Portland, 20 August 1796, *H.R.A.*, series 1, vol. 1, pp. 594–5, cited in J. Cobb, 'Female Convict Factory', p. 5.

68.   King to Hobart, 14 August, 1804, *H.R.A.*, series 1, vol. 5, p. 12.

69.   Bigge, *Report*, p. 611.

70.   Marion Phillips, *A Colonial Autocracy: New South Wales under Governor Macquarie*, London, 1908 (Reprint 1971), p. 177.

71.   Michael Saclier, 'Sam Marsden's Colony: Notes on a Manuscript in the Mitchell Library Sydney'. *Journal of the Royal Australian Historical Society*, vol. 52, pt 6, August 1967, p. 103.

72.   ibid, p. 104.

73.   Marsden tried to salvage a cow and some clothes belonging to twenty-year-old Jane Smith. Jane Smith was locked up in Windsor fourteen days after having her baby, and couldn't sleep for fear rats would eat it. She was soon force-marched to Parramatta, where she died. Marsden hoped her sole property might be given to the baby: 'I felt much for her' (cited in John

Barrett, *That Better Country. The Religious Aspect of Life in Eastern Australia 1835–1850*, Melbourne University Press, 1966, p. 179).

74. Macquarie to Bathurst, 4 December 1817, *H.R.A.*, 1817, series 1, vol. 9, p. 541.

75. See Bathurst to Brisbane, 1 April 1823, *H.R.A.*, series 1, vol. 11, p. 74; Stephen to Horton, 2 September 1824, *H.R.A.*, series 4, vol. 1, pp. 556–7.

76. Samuel Marsden, *An Answer to Certain Calumnies in the Late Governor Macquarie's Pamphlet and the Third Edition of Mr Wentworth's Account of Australasia*, London, 1826, p. 23.

77. Michael Saclier, op. cit., p. 110.

78. Sorell to Macquarie, 26 March 1818, *H.R.A.*, series 3, vol. 2, p. 309.

79. B. P. Andrews, op. cit., p. 4.

80. ibid, p. 4.

81. Bigge, *Report*, p. 613.

82. A. G. L. Shaw, op. cit., pp. 100–1.

83. ibid., p. 242.

84. Kathleen Fitzpatrick, *Sir John Franklin in Tasmania 1837–1843*, Melbourne University Press, 1949, p. 332.

85. Bigge, *Report*, p. 611.

86. Hunter to Portland, 18 November 1796, *Historical Records of New South Wales*, vol. 3, p. 182.

87. James Backhouse, op. cit., p. 360.

88. *Report from the Select Committee on Transportation*, vol. 2, p. xiii, 3 August 1838, and vol. 1, 1837, Appendix No. 6, p. 197. An extract from the *New South Wales Government Gazette*, Wednesday 7 September 1836, *State of the Female Factory, Parramatta*, 3 September 1836.

89. Mary Douglas, Introduction to L. Dumont, op. cit., pp. 16–17.

90. Cited in R. C. Hutchinson, op. cit., p. 62.

91. Scandinavian mythology assigns the bondsmen ('trälar') clear bodily or stigmatic characteristics. The first baby called Träl is described in the Rigstula thus: 'dark of hue ... wrinkled the skin was upon his hands, crooked knuckles, malformed nails, and ugly face, bowed back and long heels' (Vilhelm Moberg, *A History of the Swedish People*, P. A. Norstedt, Stockholm, 1970, pp. 8–10).

92. R. C. Hutchinson, op. cit., p. 59.

93. *True Colonist*, 25 May 1838, cited in R. C. Hutchinson, op. cit., p. 60.

94. R. C. Hutchinson, loc. cit.

95.   King to Johnson and others, 17 August 1800, *H.R.A.*, series 1, vol. 2, pp. 534-5.

96.   Betty and Theodore Roszak, eds., *Masculine/Feminine. Readings in Sexual Mythology and the Liberation of Women*, Harper, Colophon Books, New York, 1969. Roszak means the so-called female parts of the male's personality.

97.   R. Thompson, op. cit., p. 51.

98.   Phyllis Chesler, op. cit., p. 100.

99.   Robert E. Riegel, 'Changing American Attitudes Towards Prostitution 1800-1920', *Journal of the History of Ideas*, vol. 29, no. 3, July-September 1968, p. 438.

100.   R. Thompson, op. cit., p. 65.

101.   Rev. William Henry to London Missionary Society, 29 August 1799, *Historical Records of New South Wales*, vol. 3, p. 715.

102.   Peter F. McDonald, op. cit., p. 30 and H. S. Payne, op. cit., pp. 56-69.

103.   'Report of the Select Committee on Transportation, 1812', *Parliamentary Papers*, House of Commons, 1812, vol. 2, pp. 584-5.

104.   Enclosure in Bathurst to Macquarie, 24 January 1817, *H.R.A.*, series 1, vol. 9, p. 198.

105.   See Egal Feldman, 'Prostitution, the Alien Woman and the Progressive Imagination, 1910-1915', *American Quarterly*, vol. 19, no. 2, part 1, Summer 1967, pp. 199-200.

106.   Macquarie to Bathurst, 3 March 1818, *H.R.A.*, series 1, vol. 9, pp. 750-1.

107.   Vale to Bathurst, 16 April 1818, *H.R.A.*, series 4, vol. 1, p. 287.

108.   We have seen, however, that this was not wholly true.

109.   T. H. Braim, *History of New South Wales, from its Settlement to the Close of the Year 1844*, 2 vols, Bentley, London, 1846, vol. 1, p. 240.

110.   Frank Fowler, op. cit., p. 44.

111.   N.S.W. Select Committee on the Working Classes, 1859-60, p. 1290.

112.   Anon., *Girl Life in Australia*, Rowland A. Elliot, Liverpool, 1876, p. 50, 61.

113.   The Diary of Sophia Phillips 1853-71, Battye Library, Perth.

114.   R. and F. Hill, op. cit., p. 276.

115.   R. E. N. Twopeny, *Town Life in Australia*, Elliott Stock, London, 1883, p. 124.

116.   *Sydney Morning Herald*, 10 June 1891.

117.   ibid., 15 November 1891.

118. G. Meudell, *The Pleasant Career of a Spendthrift*, Routledge, London, 1924, p. 269.

119. Robert Riegel, op. cit., p. 446.

120. Lois Banner, op. cit., p. 78.

121. Jane Addams, *A New Conscience and an Ancient Evil*, Macmillan, New York, 1912, p. 89.

122. Robert Riegel, op. cit., pp. 446–7.

123. *H.R.A.*, series 3, vol. 3, pp. 848–53.

124. ibid., p. 854.

125. ibid., p. 408.

126. Darling to Murray, 28 May 1829, *H.R.A.*, series 1, vol. 14, pp. 885–6. Enclosure G. to the Proceedings of the Executive Council.

127. B. P. Andrews, op. cit., p. 5, citing J. B. Boothman to Bigge, Despatch no. 10, 3 December 1836, Government Records Office.

128. R. C. Hutchinson, op. cit., p. 57. At the Hobart Female Factory, head shaving, along with wearing iron collars, stopped after Mrs Mary Hutchinson became Matron (1832–1851).

129. P. W. Boyer, 'Souls and Minds. Jane Franklin's dichotomous approach to human improvement: the theory and reality in Van Diemen's Land 1837–1843', M.A. thesis, University of Tasmania, 1972; 'Leaders and Helpers: Jane Franklin's Plan for Van Diemen's Land', Tasmanian Historical Research Association, *Papers and Proceedings*, vol. 21, no. 2, June 1974, pp. 47–65.

130. *Colonial Times*, 1 February 1842, p. 2.

131. George Loveless, *The Victims of Whiggery*, London, 1837, p. 24.

132. Michael Cannon, op. cit., p. 64.

133. ibid., pp. 65–6.

134. J. Backhouse, op. cit., p. 364.

135. A. Marjoribanks, op. cit., p. 226.

136. E. Leake, cited in A. G. L. Shaw, op. cit., p. 240.

137. Charles Darwin, *Narrative of the Surveying Voyages of His Majesty's Ships Adventure and Beagle between the Years 1826 and 1836 . . .* in 3 volumes, vol. 3, H. Colburn, London, 1839, p. 530. Cf. James Backhouse, op. cit., p. 464.

138. Cited in Kathleen Fitzpatrick, op. cit., p. 67.

139. *Colonial Times*, 10 March 1840.

140.   B. P. Andrews, op. cit., p. 4.

141.   Mrs Charles Meredith, *Notes and Sketches of New South Wales During a Residence in that Colony from 1839 to 1844*, John Murray, London, 1844, pp. 162–3. Cf. Robert E. Riegel, on prostitution in nineteenth century America: 'Parents everywhere were worried about the effects on their children of seeing women soliciting in the streets; of hearing boisterous mirth, cursing and obscenities . . .' op. cit., p. 438.

142.   Robert Crooke, 'The Convict', unpublished MS of a novel, p. 400, written 1886 by a former Van Diemen's Land convict chaplain. In the possession of Miss K. Crooke, Melbourne. Cited in Kathleen Fitzpatrick, op. cit., pp. 74–6.

143.   Cited in Gerda Lerner, *The Woman in American History*, op. cit., p. 62.

Chapter 5

The Irish

'Purity, Purity, was the everlasting cry . . .'

(HERBERT M. MORAN)

In the nineteenth century between one-third and one-quarter
of Australia's population was Irish, the percentage of single
female immigrants sometimes running far higher. The Irish
clustered most markedly on the lowest rungs of the status
hierarchy. Russel Ward has argued that the Irish influence on
early Australian working-class attitudes was disproportionately
strong[1] and consequently 'Irish working-class attitudes formed
another important ingredient in the distinctive Australian ethos
which was developing.'[2] Although I agree with his appraisal of
the strength of Irish influence, I suggest we substitute 'lower-
class' for 'working-class' and more important, adopt a view of
the Irish as not-quite-Western, and as primitive in the sense
of pre-modern. This was a view commonly held by the English
at the time: 'The men of the establishment in Sydney thought
the Irish Catholics so benighted . . . that, in their eyes, there
was nothing but the shade of a Catholic's skin to distinguish
him from an aborigine.'[3] In this way the Irish male, like the
black, became a 'victim' of English colonial arrogance and he
passed on to his woman the humiliation and blighted self-image
which imperialism enforced on the colonized Irish male. The
humble, quasi-Western status of Irish women, Irish rigid sex-
role stereotyping and Irish fear of sexuality have done a good
deal to shape the curiously low standing and impoverished
self-identity of Australian women.

Irish males were the victims of long centuries of English

colonial cruelty, despoliation, contempt and arrogance.* By coming to Australia, the Irish did not shake off their past heritage, neither its treasures, its dreams nor its nightmares. The Irish were classed as 'victims', and as masters are prone to do, the English defined their victims as wretchedly unworthy beings. Even if and as a victim passionately rejects his master's definition, a deep and treacherous corner of the heart accepts it and turns in inward in self-hate and self-denigration. Survival demands he turns it *back, outwards*, as much as he can. Usually, a victim achieves only limited success in this; changing early versions of the self is hard going. But nothing stops him trying. Part of their self-hate, thus, Irish males turned outwards on to the Anglo-Saxon Protestant master; part, alas, on to Irish women. Irish women are thus the 'victim of victims' (Lenin's phrase, the 'slave of slaves', rises to haunt us again).

Premodern-ness and primitivity in themselves certainly cannot explain Irish woman's low standing. The Finns are the most traditional, the last to modernize, and in that sense the most 'primitive' of the Scandinavians, but there is a good case for arguing that the standing of Finnish women is highest. What, then, are the specific features of *Irish* primitivity which can help explain our problem? First, Irish primitivity produced a curiously *ambivalent reaction among English masters*. The English simultaneously envied and despised Irish primitivity, but they chose to hide their envy from themselves by emphasizing their contempt, and thus added to Irish self-contempt.† Second, Irish primitivity was related to a persisting *clan-structure*, which in turn was associated with a pre-modern 'collectivism'.** Irish residual clan-collectivism in Australia preserved within

---

* Sweden seems to have entered on an imperialist path at roughly the same time, and the contrast between Sweden's effect on her Finnish colony, for example, and England's on Ireland, is striking.

† A similar dialectic between envy and contempt helps explain the low self-esteem of the most universal 'victim' in patriarchal society: woman.

** Not, be it noted, the 'instrumental' collectivism of the modern industrial proletariat.

the communal bond the traditional low standing of woman in Irish society. It acted to reinforce this low standing in several ways. First, residual clan-collectivism tended to isolate Irish women from the diversifying effects of other cultures here. Second, it helped give the Irish a sharply defined group identity in a general climate marked with bewildering *anomie*, and so it bestowed on Irish folkways a greater potential for imprinting the entire culture with, among other things, its vision of woman.

The Australian mateship ethos, world-renowned for its misogyny, encompasses amongst its several layers this element of collectivism. Thus Irish clan-based collectivism, itself a factor in the impoverishment of Irish women's self-image, also demands our attention as a formidable early substratum of Australian mateship, an institution grossly antipathetic to women.

To trace the implications of these notions, it is necessary to touch briefly on the nature of English imperialism in Ireland, its relation to Irish primitivity and poverty; and the way in which the imperial situation contributed to Irish social forms and self-image. Pre-sixteenth century Ireland was a most 'fruitful and prosperous land',[4] with a fairly nutritious diet.[5] However, 'Ireland was the first substantial object in the Western world of those forces which have been described as "imperialist".'[6] Ireland, Marx wrote:

has been stunted in its development by the English invasion and thrown centuries back . . . By consistent oppression [the Irish] have been artificially converted into an utterly impoverished nation.

De Tocqueville put it in his own way:

If you want to know what can be done by the spirit of conquest and religious hatred combined with the abuses of aristocracy, but without any of its advantages, go to Ireland.[7]

De Beaumont said: 'In all countries, more or less, paupers may be discovered, but an entire nation of paupers is what never was seen until it was shown in Ireland.'[8] Centuries of poverty left deep marks, which the sea voyages of Irish migrants were slow to change. E. J. Hobsbawn points out that the Irish took to nineteenth century England the 'habits of a peasantry on the verge of starvation',[9] and of course they took those same habits to nineteenth century Australia.

Collectively bolstered in their habituation to the ways of a poverty-culture, for most of Australian history the Irish occupied a disproportionately large place amongst Australia's poorest citizens. In 1902, for example, it was alleged in the *Australasian Catholic Record*:

It will be readily admitted that the only satisfactory reason which can be assigned for the fewness of Catholic marriages is the poverty of Catholics. The same reason, the only adequate one, may be assigned as the cause why we have more than our share of Criminals . . . Why should Catholics constitute the poorest section of the community?[10]

However, Father Ullathorne writes that one of New South Wales' early priests, Father J. J. Therry, had 'landed property . . . bequeathed to him in several places by Catholics',[11] and it is clear from Waldersee's recent research that the Irish ranged more widely over the status ladder than we've usually thought.[12] For example, while Oliver MacDonagh notes that Victorian Catholics between 1851 and 1890 were 'on the average . . . poorer than the other major elements in the population', he adds that 'the social differences between groups in the colonial community were comparatively small.'[13] But while a much overdue reshading on status and the early Irish is now under way, the substance of K. S. Inglis's point (noted earlier) stands firm: at least to about 1870, if not longer, 'the vast majority of Irish emigrants and emancipists were Catholic and poor . . . the highest praise for [eminent Catholics like Plunkett, Roger Therry and Terence Murray] on the lips of their countrymen was that they had not forgotten the mass of their humbler brothers.'[14] And whatever the degree of upward mobility, no one has yet begun to consider the issues central to *our* problem: whether, to what extent and over what cycle of generations, upward mobility alters 'the habits of a peasantry on the verge of starvation'. Our quarry concerns the attitudes to sexuality, women, child-raising, drinking, violence, work and authority embedded in that word 'habits': an elusive quarry, true. But modern research leaves no doubt that such 'habits' and attitudes help to shape the grand issues of politics, economics and international relations to such an extent that historians may be forced to come to terms with them.

The English were the first people in the world to modernize, to undergo metamorphosis into 'scrubbed protagonists of the . . . individualistic straining-striving' achievement ethos.[15] The English achievers were extreme in their behaviour and language towards the Irish. While guilt over ill-treatment helps explain this, one senses also that perhaps the English achievers were still grappling with vestiges of primitivism within themselves. They were more aware than they cared to admit that modernization was in many ways stunting their own humanity. They were also more susceptible than was safe, to a rich primitivity in the Irish

sense of wonder, . . . awareness of magic in the world . . . [belief that] the race was not to the swift, nor the battle to the strong.[16]

Nor were Englishmen oblivious to other aspects of Irish primitivity, the 'intensity and other-worldliness of Irish faith, its charm, nobility, humanity and astonishing perseverance'.[17]

Colonialism kept the Irish 'primitive', and that primitivity provoked ambiguous and ambivalent responses in the modernizing English – responses which ultimately had their consequences for Irish (and hence for Australian) women. Well before New South Wales was established, the English had perfected the art of diminishing the moral worth of the Irish, and we suggested that Irish males tried to counter this partly by diminishing Irish women. Sheridan pinned down some of the psychodynamics at work nicely, when he described how Irish peasants were calumniated 'by those men who would degrade them below the level of human creation in order to palliate their own inhumanity towards them'.[18]

In early New South Wales we can see in the Reverend Samuel Marsden a good example of an English high-achiever who hated the Irish, partly in an unconscious effort to subdue echoes of a richer, humbler, and sexually less impoverished version of . . . Samuel Marsden. The Reverend Marsden, whose mission was initiated by Wilberforce himself,[19] can indeed stand as a paradigm of the upwardly mobile, pious, individualist achiever. Of poorish Yorkshire farmer stock, he was sent first to Hull Grammar School, then to Magdalene College, Cambridge ('a nest of Methodists', according to Manning Clark)[20] by the Elland Society, a group of Anglican Ministers. Marsden had a 'tendency to see vice everywhere',[21] detested 'sin', and was stern in sexual morality. His inner restlessness points to a deep inner struggle.[22] Marsden's vocabulary in reference to the Irish is so vehement as to alert us to the fact that, amongst other things, he is fighting demons *within himself*, for he surely protests too much: the Irish, he wrote, were 'the most wild, ignorant and savage Race . . . governed entirely by the impulse of Passion, . . . fond of Riot Drunkeness [sic] and Cabals . . . '[23] Marsden, like many of the harshly puritanical élite in early Australian history, excelled at pious cruelty. Indeed the Bigge Report described his magistracy as stamped with severity, his very name 'almost a byword for harshness as an early clerical magistrate'.[24] Marsden was responsible for ordering the inhuman flogging of the Irishman Paddy Galvin,[25] and sentenced to death the leaders of the 1804 convict rebellion, many of whom were Irish but none of them killers.[26]

The vocabulary the British used when they talked about the Irish carried an emotional charge extravagant for an élite noted for its rigid 'character-armour' and consequent cult of understatement. Language gives many games away, and the language applied to the Irish, we suggest, spelled out the ironies of the colonial game, encapsulating the ambiguities of British feeling towards their Irish victims: contempt, guilt and envy at the primitivity colonialism enforced. Thus, according to one writer, every governor before Macquarie regarded the Irish as a 'separate class or type',[27] Governor Hunter spoke of 'those turbulent and worthless characters called Irish defenders', while Governor King described some Irish as 'ruthless, violent and turbulent characters with diabolical schemes for the destruction of all industry, public and private property, order and regularity'.[28] Governor Darling wrote to Earl Bathurst in 1826:

. . . a large proportion of the Convicts [is] of the lowest class of Irish Catholics, ignorant in the extreme, and in proportion bigotted and under the domination of their priest . . .[29]

Archdeacon McEnroe told the N.S.W. 1858 Select Committee on Irish Female Immigration that Irish people were still being called 'dirty Irish', 'ignorant Irish Papists' and 'low Papists'. J. V. Gorman also claimed that Irish girls were 'taunted':

Well, it is a very common term, 'Oh! they are Irish'; and there is nothing more taunting to an Irish girl than that.[30]

Wilhelm Moberg's portrait of Swedish peasant migrants to the United States in *The Emigrants* forms a comparison with that given by Gorman:

When those girls arrive in this country they have heavy shoes and thick woollen stockings, and all that sort of thing . . . in this Colony, where parties' means are so limited as only to allow of their having one servant, in such service the servant is more of a drudge, and the Irish girl much more likely to suit.[31]

Archdeacon McEnroe also claimed Irish girls were capable of very hard work. One thinks of Henry Mayhew, who said in 1851 of the Irish women street sellers in London (the least skilled and lowest paid): '. . . as regards mere toil, such as the carrying of a heavy burthen, [they] are by far the most laborious.' An Irish woman, Mayhew added, more 'readily unites begging with selling than the English'.[32] Constantia Maxwell notes that in 1812 Wakefield wrote 'females . . . [were] treated more like beasts of burden than rational beings.' They were subjected to all the 'drudgery' generally performed by men, setting potatoes, digging turf, and carrying heavy loads, so that they acquired at 'a very early period every mark of old age'.[33]

White-Anglo-Saxon-Protestant (WASP) prejudice in Australia was not only extravagant, it was ubiquitous. When the *Roman Emperor* docked at Port Adelaide on 23 October 1848, the Adelaide *Register* greeted its cargo of Irish female immigrants with the gloomy certainty that the colony would become 'a receptacle for unfledged thieves, juvenile bastards and incipient prostitutes'.[34] Mayhew, however, was at pains to point out that the humble Irish street-seller women in mid-century London were infinitely more 'chaste' than their English counterparts. I tend to accept Archdeacon McEnroe's view on prostitution among poor Irish women:

The Government would better employ a sum of money in sending them [Irish girl immigrants in Sydney] up the country rather than throw them on the streets of Sydney, and send them to perdition, for that is the result of this neglect.[35]

Shall we recapitulate likely Irish *inner responses* to such arrogance and bigotry? Given the long centuries of English colonial rule, the Irish in Australia for the most part found themselves re-enacting the roles of colonized 'victims'. Even those who visibly 'rose' to become respected citizens cannot be assumed to have shaken off old ghosts. Man's personality is not moulded by status alone. 'Victims', even while protesting their spiritual triumph over 'masters', unconsciously accept that master's concept of their worth as human beings. The Irish certainly mounted brave defences, to some extent locking themselves into mind-fortresses or ghettos in the process. But I submit that it was too late, and had been too late for a long time; the enemy had penetrated their hearts before the fortresses were built. So a core part of an Irish man *was* a 'dirty Irish', 'an ignorant Papist', just as a core part of every woman is a second-rate 'crypto-servant' human. Yes, we are always more than the dominant strata say we are: but we are never quite *not* what they say we are. It all starts too early. And we can affirm their definitions as much by defying them as by accepting them: that's the cruellest blow of all.

Frantz Fanon, a psychiatrist working with the Algerian Liberation Forces, sketches psychodynamic mechanisms which also applied to the Irish. Even while the Algerians were engaged in deadly physical combat with their French masters, the Algerian tended to accept those masters' concept of him: lying, lazy, violent, drunken . . . An Algerian never robs but he murders . . . Can't you hear an echo of Governors Hunter,

King and Darling on the Irish: 'turbulent and worthless', 'ruthless and violent', 'ignorant and bigotted'? Fanon found his Algerian patients commonly 'passed on' their self-hate to their own families, in one form or another; often in the form of physical violence, but they also deployed psychic, frequently unconscious, mechanisms.[36] And then, if all other forms of compensation are denied us, do we not fall back on devices of keeping others at a *relational distance*: a sort of 'banishing' and sending away?

We argued that one crucial early source of mateship, which enshrines and perpetuates a minimum human fellowship between men and women, was Irish residual clan-collectivism. The effect of this clannishness was to help provoke and exacerbate English contempt, and to reinforce the traditionally 'Irish' standing of woman in the Australian national identity. But in the early nineteenth century the Irish desperately needed that clan-collectivism, and before we can hope to call it all off and start living in the present, we'll have to look with sympathy at the relentless inevitability of that past need.

Hunger and humiliation cemented and perpetuated early Irish clan-based collectivistic 'mateship'. Addressing the Select Committee on Emigration from the United Kingdom in 1826, the Rt Reverend Bishop of Limerick leaves one in little doubt of its living reality:

When tenantry . . . are dispossessed, after a season of patient suffering, they go into some other district, perhaps a peaceable one; where they fail not to find friends, clansmen and fellow factionaries, whom they bring back with them . . . to avenge their cause . . . in blood . . . This will be quite intelligible to those who know the system of mutual understanding that pervades the districts I may say, of each province.[37]

The English often sensed the menace of Irish collectivism without always being able to articulate what it was that frightened them. Thus the 1831 'Report of the Select Committee on the State of Ireland' spoke of a 'Whiteboy *system*' [my emphasis] reaching back at least about sixty years, while the Chief Judge of Ireland described a 'mysterious engine of secret combination, shifting from place to place . . . [and]

wielded by some invisible hand . . . now against one part of the island, and now against another'.[38] (Mao's guerillas swimming like fish in a peasant sea spring to mind, but were Mao's guerillas cousins, or clan-kin to the fish?) In the 1830s, one source of disquiet for the British in Ireland was the prevalence of 'factions' in the 'dark and more uncivilized parts of the country'. But 'factions', George Cornewall Lewis tells us in 1836, were 'numerous families who act together . . . families forming into bodies', while the faction system 'is a remnant of the old barbarous Irish system of clanship, which still continues in practice'. Indeed, in Lewis's view, at that time 'the clannish spirit was still prevalent among the peasantry.' He also records a sort of collectivism arising from the existence of the clan spirit. For example, poor Irishmen would join the Whiteboy 'system' at times to help others: 'though they may not be personally concerned, yet their kinsmen and friends and fellows are concerned. [Some people can't seem to grasp that] . . . it is possible for men to be swayed by a regard for the general advantage of their order, without reaping any individual and immediate benefit.'[39] This passage evokes some descriptions of antipodean 'mateship' in Alexander Harris's *Settlers and Convicts*. W. Steuart Trench, a land agent in Ireland for the Marquis of Bath and others, also may suggest a residual 'clannish spirit' in his *Realities of Irish Life*, published in 1868 but drawing on personal experiences from earlier decades. He describes, for example, 'the Ribbon Societies . . . those dark and mysterious confederacies'.[40] As late as 1957, Estyn Evans could write about the 'strength of blood-ties in extended family groups still maintained even in many urban families . . . [while] in remote rural areas the blood-tie is a dominant force governing economic as well as social relationships'.[41]

The very numbers of the early Irish help explain their central contribution to Australian folkways. But even more important, I think, was that relative sharpness in definition of their identity which owed a lot to vestigial clan-collectivism and their consequent cohesiveness. The Irish existed as a community in a way other nineteenth century new Australians, for all their loud protestations, tragically failed to do. Modern *anomie*, I think, found one of its first homes in our broken, cold and unnatural land . . . Irish cohesiveness thus provoked greater antagonism while it simultaneously made Irish folkways the more contagious.

But *did* the Irish bring their vestigial clan-collectivism to Australia? Writing in 1974 about Irish Australian Catholics in New South Wales before 1860, James Waldersee repeatedly points to 'clan'-like qualities:

> It must be borne in mind that, whatever the contributing factors that led to violence – factiousness, ignorance, patriotism, vengeance, clannishness – the tempers and temperaments that had been the downfall of these village Ishmaels in Ireland were the very same that they brought to New South Wales.[42]

We noted that George Cornewall Lewis insisted that 'factions' were themselves 'a remnant of the old barbarous Irish system of clanship, which still continues in practice'. Thus Waldersee's adjectives 'factiousness' and 'clannishness' are related to clan, hence to the quality of 'anthropological' or tribal 'collectivism', which I submit is one component of Australia's misogynistic institution of mateship. He makes it clear that the 'clannish' aspects of Irish 'temperaments' did indeed persist in New South Wales:

> On perusing the records even cursorily, it became quite apparent that there was a considerable degree of association between the convicts in the sample. In rural Ireland, to a far greater extent than in England or even Dublin, a crime, particularly of violence, was likely to be a family affair . . . [A malefactor] might well be supported in his actions by the hands of ubiquitous and clannish relatives. The proportion of Irish convicts transported with a relative or two, with relatives in transit, or already in the colony was surprisingly high – far greater than mere probability might indicate.[43]

Irish girl migrants to Australia displayed a cohesiveness which ought perhaps to be seen in the context of 'clannishness'. On 19 December 1848, for example, Mrs Maria Cooper, Matron on board the female orphan immigration ship *Earl Grey*, told the Orphan Immigration Committee that 'the girls from the various parts have invariably kept together. For instance, the

Banbridge girls would not think of associating with the Belfast girls,'[44] while Judge Therry, writing in 1863 but also drawing on earlier decades, bears her out:

In the Irish . . . ships the girls formed themselves into detachments, taking their names from the counties from which they respectively came . . . these girls were called on the ship's roll, 'Turn up, ye Kilkennys', 'Turn up, ye Limericks' . . . There was much rivalry amongst these ladies on the passage, in their speculations as to their future destiny, the ground of jealousy being whether the Kilkennys or the Limericks would get on best in the Colony.[45]

Waldersee further refers to the 'vague but none the less strong bonds of clannishness and more remote kinship . . .' which persisted in nineteenth century Australia. Here, finally, is a part of the conclusion of his study:

. . . if there is any cause for celebration, it lies in the survival of Catholicism as a quietly accepted tradition, to a great extent bound up with Hibernicism, but, very likely, equally bound up with clannishness.[46]

Other writers suggest that Irish Australians of later decades experienced an unusual sense of 'community' and 'cohesion',[47] and while the influence of religious oppression cannot be denied here, we should also take into account persisting 'clannishness'.

It's possible that certain late eighteenth century events intensified community feeling among the Irish during the formative decades, a time of peculiar sensitivity for Australian folkways. For example, to explain 'the conduct of the Irish prisoner in Australia', Eris O'Brien asks us to remember the far-reaching influence of the United Irishmen, under the leadership of Wolf Tone. That

. . . intimate sway . . . over the minds of the United Irishmen in Ireland and exercised by deputies of the supreme control stationed throughout the country, and the enthusiasm and loyalty felt by the members for their leaders, were phenomena far in advance of those that had characterized other rebellions. This devotion was more in evidence in the later period of the movement, when it became accentuated by the English practices of espionage and cruelty, and finally, after defeat, it persisted vividly in the minds of the victims, who refused to acknowledge that the cause for which they had suffered was irrevocably lost.[48]

Such a deeply-felt experience, so close to the 'moment of birth' of New South Wales, could well have burned itself deeply into both Irish and official attitudes, the one reinforcing the intensity of the other. O'Brien fails to point out, however, that any enhanced sense of community Irishmen felt as a result of this particular experience, must have meshed in with and reinforced older 'clan'-derived feelings of community. But he does us a signal service in pointing up the possibly traumatic associations of 1798 for rebel and ruler alike, translated into the antipodean universe:

. . . it must be recognized that the influence of this large body in a small incompetently controlled community of felons was disquieting to governors.[49]

Time softened it all, of course, as time can. But in the meantime, 1798 and its consequences probably intensified Irish feelings of desperation and hence, of collectivistic community.

Since in old Ireland, woman's standing in society at large was extremely low, any tendency for Irish Australians to maintain traditional communal bonds would tend to reproduce that standing in the new world. And if Australian mateship can partly be understood in terms of the Irish need to defend their sense of dignity against WASP élites through maintaining those bonds, that, too, boded ill for woman: for as we know, mateship embodies deep hostility to her. Woman's standing in old Ireland was strikingly low. Her notorious dominance in the Irish family was – and is – not *in spite of* her low standing in the wider society but *because of it* (we've already outlined the often-destructive compensation mechanisms victims must try to implement while structures pivoted about victimhood persist).

Politics provides one indication of the low standing of Irish women in the past (as it does of Australian women right at this moment). In general Irish women were drawn into political protest in the national cause to a fairly small degree.* There is a vivid contrast between the role they played and the role played by, say, Indian, Finnish or French women. This unusually overall low level of political participation[51] was re-enacted, *mutatis mutandis*, by Irish women in, say, early Van Diemen's Land. Many Irish women sent to Van Diemen's Land were convicted of arson which, for Irish men, was commonly a deliberate political offence. But contrary to 'the general historical opinion . . . that Irish female arsonists were taking part in rural revolt and agrarian agitations . . . [the] evidence suggests that arson for many women was a means of escape rather than a form of protest'.[52] There were many cases of women physically injuring people quite unknown to them, out of blind personalized anguish, and so it seems improbable that their violence arose directly out of political or social motives. Irish men are known to have been associated with 'well organized . . . groups . . . faction fighting' but women are not mentioned in such contexts. Perhaps custom forbade mention, but it is more likely that rigid Irish sex role stereotyping excluded most women from the strongly masculine domain of politics. Hence Van Diemen's Land Irish women could rarely aspire to the dignified title of 'political criminals'. One authority concludes: 'Most of the vagrants were an indifferent group of women although some [some!] were forced into that situation by the famine. Nearly two-fifths of the women transported for vagrancy were prostitutes . . .'[53] The protests expressed by Irish women, then, if we can accept male accounts of them, tended to be intensely personalized, unfocused and thus less politically effective than male protests. This is basically because Irish tradition saw women's standing as too lowly to allow her to meddle with politics. Thus in early twentieth century Australia, Cardinal Moran expressed impatience at the general reluctance of Irish-

---

* This is a point about scale, a comparative point. It does not deny the existence of, say, the Fenian Sisterhood, the Ladies' Land League – though here women stepped back into the 'ladies auxiliary role' famed throughout

Australian men to have 'their' women voting. The Catholic *Freeman's Journal* 'virtually ignored the [suffrage] question, even in its women's page, except to note the final passage of the 1902 Act',[54] though by contrast the *Catholic Press* 'was very much aware of antagonism among Catholics in general and went on to urge Catholic women to vote, exhorting conservative Irish men to encourage them . . .' But 'there was positive antagonism from Irish Labour Party members.'[55]

We conclude by exploring some overlaps between Irish and Australian folkways, relevant to sexuality and women. How much we owe to the Irish can never be known: the most we can do, finally, is think about it all.

We've suggested that in the Irish we can locate one major early source of Australian mateship, a form of male-bonding unusually intense and exclusive for a Western country. Australians are also regarded as fairly unusual in their dedication to drinking, and some authorities link mateship and drinking. A 1971 survey by the National Health and Medical Research Council commented that Australia had 'one of the highest alcoholism rates', 'about 6 per cent of Australians are estimated to be alcoholics', while 'more than half Australian men and a third of women were classified as heavy drinkers'. 'Roman Catholics are the heaviest drinking religious group.'[56] One expert on Australian drinking who links it with mateship writes that the 'cultural attitudes which seem to affect Australian drinking as a whole, and have particular reference to heavy drinking . . . [include] drinking as a symbol of mateship and social solidarity'.[57]

Somewhere during the nineteenth century, the unusual prevalence of male drinking seems to show up as a much-noted aspect of emerging national patterns – though in 1844 Mrs Charles Meredith emphasized the incidence of drink among

---

Australia today, when men were able to reclaim the lead; it does not deny the election of ten Irish women parliamentarians in 1921, or the example of Constance de Markievicz.[50]

poor women* in her indictment of our 'universal addiction to drink'.[58]

If there is a case for thinking our style of drinking owes something to the Irish through a link with mateship, we may also owe them a second characteristic. In a letter to me, the anthropologist Margaret Mead recalled that, during her visit to Australia in the 1950s, she'd been quite struck by the degree of discontinuity between eating and drinking (far less pronounced now, of course!). This is an Irish pattern. One authority on Irish drinking notes that the Irish 'have had a long . . . history with alcohol . . . in which the use of alcohol has . . . penetrated deeply into nearly every aspect of their social life . . . Alcohol addiction rates for Irish males in the United States during the period between 1900 and 1940 were relatively high in comparison to other groups.' Assuming a modal age of thirty-five to forty for these addicts, this writer estimated their birth and socialization fell into the last quarter of the nineteenth century, while that of their parents fell in the first part of the nineteenth. This places such parents alongside those of Irish-Australians. He also noted a somewhat 'careless', 'depreciatory' attitude to food, a willingness to fast, a certain shame connected with eating, and a tendency to neglect meals.[59] Irishmen, he said, drink fasting, while Englishmen are more prone to drink with and after food. In 1911, M. J. F. McCarthy wrote: 'Amongst the Irish Catholics, drink is the synonym for hospitality. It stands alone and is not associated with food . . . Drink is more idealized in Ireland than in England, through not being kept in the home and taken there with meals as it is in England.'[60]

As to relationships between men and women, the Irish have doubtless contributed a good deal to the well-known coolness between the sexes in Australia. V. S. Pritchett captures the Irish sexual ambience as well as any generalization can:

There is now a small increase in the number of early marriages. This

---

* As Victorian concepts of 'femininity' gradually filtered to the 'lower orders' from their earlier home among the middle classes, women tended to hide their drinking. So today we have more 'wardrobe' or 'cupboard' women drinkers.

must be due to some loosening of the severe restraints of Irish life, though it still strikes one that Dublin is a male-dominated society and that the object of the male is never to go home. And especially always to be late for dinner* . . . It is often said that the sexes *do not like each other* [my emphasis] and fear sexual life. . . . The reason given for this is that, since the father is always out at the street corner, or the bar, or the sports ground, with his friends, the power of the woman in the home increases. The mother dominates the son, and his feelings are directed first to her and then to his sisters: this tends to make him idealize and – eventually – to despise women. Guilt about the mother is a recurring subject in Irish literature: the peculiar relationship in James Joyce's family and described in *Ulysses* is an example. One has the impression of Irish love being militant flirtation, a meeting of enemies who unite for a moment and then return chastely to their own separate ways of living. . . Gogarty, in one of his outbursts about the censorship which up to a few years ago was the most repressive in the world, has this sentence: 'It is high time the people of this country found some other way of loving God than by hating women.'[62]

The Irish in Australia seem to have carried with them a kind of revulsion for the flesh; though qualities peculiar to the curiously ungiving body of this land of ours must have also entered their hearts. Thus, reminiscing about his boyhood in the New South Wales Catholic community between the 1890s and 1920s, Herbert M. Moran wrote:

All round us, at that age, there was much drunkenness . . . Ten Commandments there were, but only one sin really mattered – the sin of the flesh . . . Alcoholic over-indulgence was therefore deplored . . . But the person who sinned carnally was damned – damned irrevocably. Purity, Purity, was the everlasting cry . . .[63]

An unnamed author in an early twentieth century copy of the *Imperial Review* described the 'Austral-Irish Girl', whose

* 'A Daughter of the Soil' writes from Melbourne in 1862: 'One cause of dissension [between wife and husband] . . . which is a perfect epidemic here is a general way of being too late for everything, meals especially.'[64] Sheer coincidence? But too delightful to leave out.

... pattern is the Virgin Mother ... The Australian Daughters of Mary form an unsurpassable phalanx of future Mothers. As disciples of Father Hayes, and the League of the Cross, their resolve is: The lips that touch Liquor shall never touch mine. So they ban beer, and whiskey, and wine.

The notorious Australian tendency for the sexes to accept separateness as 'natural', to a far greater extent than is the case, say, in France, can also be noted in some areas of Ireland. During the late eighteenth and nineteenth centuries, from economic necessity, men used to leave their farms and their women, for six months or so of each year and work as labourers in England. In *Family and Community in Ireland*, a study begun in 1931, Arensberg and Kimbal wrote:

Men and women are much more often to be seen in the company of members of their own sex than otherwise, except in the house itself. Except upon ceremonial occasions in family life or in the considerable affluence of owning a gig or a motor car, in Clare at least they go to mass, to town, or to sportive gatherings with companions of their own sex.

Yet such apartheid was not a matter of 'separate but equal':

Till recently and even now in remote districts, a conventional peasant woman always kept several paces behind her man, *even if they were walking somewhere together*. [My emphasis][64]

The combination of superior status with relational and physical distance begins early. Of Irish children Michael McCarthy wrote in 1911:

The boys are taught to look upon themselves as superior to the girls at a very early age and soon cease to associate with them; the average boy of nine or ten being ashamed to be seen in the company of his sisters, lest he be called a Sheelah. The peasants' cottages, especially of the old mud-walled type, are so small, and the families usually so large, that the boys and girls are of necessity very much together indoors. But their modesty is exemplary; and, though sleeping perhaps, in the same apartment, the boys are as separate from the girls as if they were in the different bedrooms of a large mansion.[65]

In 1972 a demographer studying 'The Social Status of the Sexes and Their Relative Mortality in Ireland' wrote:

... the son in the Irish family system was generally given preferential treatment. Sons were subordinate to their father but above everyone else in the household in the way their mother treated them. In both rural and urban areas and among all social classes, daughters were expected to provide their brothers with special service and comforts. As a 26-year-old Dublin woman told an observer ... in the early 1950s, speaking in front of her mother and brothers (who agreed with her comments): 'If I am sitting in the easy chair there and Matt or Charlie come home, I am expected to get up and give them the chair. They just say "Pardon me" and up I get ... There is no use fighting against it. I used to, but I soon found out which way the wind blew – we have to wait on the boys from sole to crown ... Mammy is just a slave to them, a willing slave, and we are expected to be, too. And that is general. That's the common attitude.'

While the Irish husband was bound by custom to provide for his wife and family, this was 'only after looking after his own personal needs and those of the farm and livestock ... Under this system the wife and children were liable to suffer if the husband over-indulged in drink and gambling ... As in eating priorities, the wife and children would probably be supported by leftovers, with the sons getting the largest share.' And the writer concludes:

The Irish case illustrates well how male dominance is associated with relatively high female mortality, a linkage that before the 20th century may have been common in some European societies ... Ireland has been unusual in that social customs sustaining male dominance persisted into the mid-20th century.[66]

Australians widely acknowledge their debts to the Irish over attitudes and folkways. We conclude this chapter by asking: 'Do these debts include attitudes to heavy, perhaps sublimatory drinking, to sexuality, and do they also include a status for women which is unusually diminished, considering we are a Western democracy?' However we answer these questions, surely we must keep in mind Ireland's bitter centuries of colonial oppression?

Notes

1. Russel Ward, *The Australian Legend*, pp. 44–5.

2. ibid., p. 49.

3. C. M. H. Clark, *A Short History of Australia*, Mentor, New American Library, New York, 1963, pp. 70–71.

4. George O'Brien, *The Economic History of Ireland in the Seventeenth Century*, Maunsel, Dublin, 1919, p. 30.

5. R. N. Salaman, *The Influence of the Potato on the Course of Irish History*, Dublin, 1943, cited in K. H. Connell, *The Population of Ireland 1750-1845*, Clarendon Press, Oxford, 1950, p. 127.

6. Emil Strauss, *Irish Nationalism and British Democracy*, Methuen, London, 1951, pp. 2–3, 5.

7. A. C. De Tocqueville, *Journeys to England and Ireland*, ed. by J. P. Mayer, Faber and Faber, London, 1958, p. 122.

8. Cited in Russel Ward, *The Australian Legend*, pp. 46–7.

9. E. J. Hobsbawn, *Industry and Empire*, Penguin Books, 1968, p. 310.

10. M. MacNamara, 'The Catholic Church in N.S.W. and the Census', *Australian Catholic Record*, vol. 8, 1902, cited in Patrick O'Farrell, *Documents in Australian Catholic History*, vol. 2, 1884–1968, Chapman, London, 1969, p. 65.

11. Eris O'Brien, *The Foundation of Catholicism in Australia: Life and Letters of Archpriest John Joseph Therry*, in two vols., vol. 1, Angus and Robertson, Sydney, 1922, pp. 161–2.

12. James Waldersee, *Catholic Society in New South Wales 1788-1860*, Sydney University Press, Sydney, 1974.

13. Oliver MacDonagh, 'The Irish in Victoria 1851–91: A Demographic Essay', p. 81.

14. K. S. Inglis, *The Australian Colonists: An exploration of social history 1788-1870*, Melbourne University Press, Melbourne, 1974, p. 88.

15. Robert Endleman, *Personality and Social Life*, p. 205.

16. C. M. H. Clark, *A History of Australia*, vol. 1, New American Library, New York, 1963, pp. 103–107.

17. Patrick O'Farrell, *The Catholic Church in Australia: A Short History 1788–1967*, Nelson, Melbourne, 1968, pp. 9–10.

18. Sheridan, cited in K. H. Connell, op. cit., p. 60.

19. J. A. Ferguson, 'The Rev. Samuel Marsden: his life and work', Royal Australian Historical Society, *Journal and Proceedings*, vol. 12, part 5, 1926.

20. C. M. H. Clark, *A History of Australia*, vol. 1, p. 131.

21. M. H. Ellis, *John Macarthur*, Angus & Robertson, Sydney, 1955, p. 84.

22. A. T. Yarwood, *Samuel Marsden*, Oxford University Press, Melbourne, 1968, p. 5. See too 'Writing an Ecclesiastic Biography', Armidale and District Historical Society, *Journal and Proceedings*, no. 16, January 1973, pp. 30–36.

23. Samuel Marsden, 'A few observations on the Toleration of the Catholic Religion in N. South Wales', c. 1806-7. From the Marsden Manuscripts, Mitchell Library, Sydney, cited in Patrick O'Farrell, *Documents in Australian Catholic History*, vol. 1: 1788–1884, pp. 73–4.

24. John Barrett, *That Better Country*, p. 179. In an earlier chapter we saw a softer side to the man. In three essays attributed to Marsden, 'a few observations on the Situation of the Female Convicts in New South Wales', one catches awareness of the misery of the women even though his main concern is immorality. See Michael Saclier, op. cit., p. 100.

25. C. M. H. Clark, *A History of Australia*, vol. 1, p. 156.

26. ibid., pp. 171-3; R. W. Connell, 'The Convict Rebellion of 1804', *Melbourne Historical Journal*, vol. 5, 1965, p. 35.

27. T. J. Kiernan, *Transportation from Ireland to Sydney 1791–1816*, Australian National University, Canberra, 1954, p. 2.

28. C. M. H. Clark, *A History of Australia*, vol. 1, p. 169.

29. Darling to Bathurst, 6 September 1826, *H.R.A.*, series 1, vol. 12, p. 54.

30. Select Committee on Irish Female Immigration, *Report*, New South Wales Legislative Assembly, *Votes and Proceedings*, 1858-9, vol. 2, p. 13, 14.

31. ibid., p. 14.

32. Henry Mayhew, *London Labour and the London Poor* (Frank Cass edition), p. 457.

33. Constantia Maxwell, *Country and Town in Ireland Under the Georges*, W. Tempest, Dundalk, 1949, p. 150.

34. Cited in C. W. Parkin, 'Irish Female Immigration to South Australia . . .', p. 27.

35. Select Committee on Irish Female Immigration, *Report*, p. 4.

36. Frantz Fanon, *The Wretched of the Earth*, Penguin Books, 1967.

37. *Parliamentary Papers*, 1826, vol. 4, p. 404, cited in C. M. H. Clark, ed., *Select Documents in Australian History 1788–1850*, Angus & Robertson, Sydney, 1950, p. 172.

38. 'Report of the Select Committee on the State of Ireland', *Parliamentary Papers*, House of Commons, 1831-2, vol. 16, pp. 11–12, p. 568. See too Edmund Curtis, *A History of Ireland*, Methuen, London, 1936, pp. 305–6.

39. George Cornewall Lewis, *On local disturbances in Ireland: and on the Irish Church Question*, B. Fellowes, London, 1836, p. 279, 292, 296.

40. Steuart W. Trench, *Realities of Irish Life*, Longmans, Green, London, 1868, pp. 47–61.

41. Estyn Evans, *Irish Folk Ways*, Routledge & Kegan Paul, London, 1957, p. 10. Some other sources from which I have put together a picture of residual collectivist patterns amongst the Irish include: Conrad M. Arensberg, *The Irish Countryman*, Macmillan, London, 1937; Conrad M. Arensberg and Solon T. Kimbal, *Family and Community in Ireland*, 2nd ed., Harvard University Press, Cambridge, Massachusetts, 1968 (in a preface written in 1939 to the first ed., Lloyd Warner points out that the study was begun in 1931, so it catches generations going back into the nineteenth century); Robert F. Bales, 'Attitudes toward Drinking in the Irish Culture', in David J. Pittman and Charles R. Snyder, eds., *Society, Culture and Drinking Patterns*, Wiley, London, 1962; J. B. Bryan, *A Practical View of Ireland, from the Period of the Union*, W. F. Wakeman, Dublin, 1831; George O'Brien, *The Economic History of Ireland in the Seventeenth Century*, Dublin, 1919; *The Economic History of Ireland in the Eighteenth Century*, Maunsel, Dublin, 1918; *The Economic History of Ireland from the Union to the Famine*, Longmans, Green, London, 1921; K. H. Connell, *Irish Peasant Society*, Oxford, 1968; Lynn Lees, 'Patterns of Lower-Class Life: Irish Slum Communities in Nineteenth Century London', in Richard Sennett and Stephen Thernstrom, eds, *Nineteenth Century Cities: Essays in the New Urban History*, Yale Univerity Press, New Haven, 1969.

42. This is true, too, for Victoria. Oliver MacDonagh writes: 'The Catholic and Irish communities can be treated as substantially synonymous . . .' ('The Irish in Victoria 1851–91: A Demographic Essay', p. 72).

43. James Waldersee, op. cit., pp. 66–7.

44. Fitzroy to Grey, 19 December 1848, *H.R.A.*, series 1, vol. 26, p. 756.

45. Roger Therry, *Reminiscences of Thirty Years' Residence in New South Wales*, pp. 413–14.

46. James Waldersee, op. cit., p. 264.

47. Patrick J. O'Farrell and J. J. McGovern, 'Australia', vol. 6, pt 6 of P. J. Corish, ed., *A History of Irish Catholicism*, Gill & Macmillan, Dublin, 1971; and Patrick J. O'Farrell, *Ireland's English Question: Anglo-Irish Relations 1534–1970*, Batsford, London, 1971.

48. Eris O'Brien, *The Foundation of Australia (1786–1800). A Study in English Criminal Practice and Penal Colonization in the Eighteenth Century*, Greenwood Press, Westport, Conn., 1970 (1937), pp. 203–4.

49. loc. cit.

50. See Jacqueline Van Voris, *Constance de Markievicz: In the Cause of Ireland*, University of Massachusetts Press, 1967.

51. John Williams, 'Irish convicts and Van Diemen's Land', Master of Arts thesis, History Department, University of Tasmania, 1972; and 'Irish Convicts and Van Diemen's Land', Tasmanian Historical Research Association, *Papers and Proceedings*, vol. 19, no. 3, September 1972, pp. 100–120. For Irish women in the United States, see W. G. Broehl, *The Molly Maguires*, Harvard University Press, Cambridge, Mass., 1965, p. 25.

52. John Williams, 'Irish Convicts and Van Diemen's Land', *Papers and Proceedings*, p. 117.

53. John Williams, 'Irish Convicts and Van Diemen's Land', *Papers and Proceedings*, p. 118.

54. Joan Cobb, 'The Women's Movement in New South Wales 1880–1914', M.A. thesis, History Department, University of New England, 1966, p. 197.

55. ibid., p. 198, 200.

56. *National Times*, 29 November – 4 December 1971, p. 4.

57. Margaret J. Sargent, 'Heavy Drinking and its Relation to Alcoholism – with special reference to Australia', *Australian and New Zealand Journal of Sociology*, vol. 4, no. 2, October 1968, pp. 148–50.

58. Mrs Charles Meredith, op. cit., pp. 76–7, 125, 58.

59. Robert F. Bales, op. cit., pp. 158–9.

60. M. J. F. McCarthy, *Irish Land and Liberty*, R. Scott, London, 1911, p. 293.

61. 'A Daughter of the Soil' [Mrs Nugent Wood], *Woman's Work in Australia*, S. Mullen, Melbourne, 1862, p. 11.

62. V. S. Pritchett, *Dublin: A Portrait*, Bodley Head, London, 1967, pp. 90–1.

63.   H. M. Moran, *Viewless Winds*, London, 1939, cited in **Patrick O'Farrell**, ed., *Documents in Australian Catholic History*, vol. 2, 1884–1968, pp. 23–4. Marvin Opler's study of Irish and Italian schizophrenic patients in *Scientific American* offers food for thought: 'All of our Irish schizophrenic patients were either pallidly asexual or latently homosexual. Most of them avoided females. Their homosexuality was repressed because sexuality in general is inhibited in the Irish culture . . . Nearly all the Irish schizophrenics tormented themselves with preoccupations of guilt about sex, whereas most of the Italians had no trace of such Puritanism.' ('Schizophrenia and Culture', in *Frontiers of Psychological Research, Readings from Scientific American*, selected and introduced by Stanley Coopersmith, W. H. Freeman, San Francisco, 1957, p. 120.)

64.   Conrad M. Arensberg and Solon T. Kimbal, op. cit., p. 196.

65.   M. J. F. McCarthy, op. cit., p. 110.

66.   Robert E. Kennedy, Jr., 'The Social Status of the Sexes and Their Relative Mortality in Ireland', in William Petersen, ed., *Readings in Population*, Macmillan, New York, 1972, pp. 123, 134.

Chapter 6

Models for Female Identity Formation in a Frontier Land

The Frontier: 'all right for men and dogs, but it's hell on women and horses.' (ANON.)

We begin this chapter by looking at role models for female identity in relation to the frontier, pioneering and to demography. Then we consider the paucity of *robust* female role models, an historical fact which sprang from the class structure of a land that was not only a frontier country but a colony. Colonies often lack solid upper social strata – an aristocracy, *haute bourgeoisie* and an 'aristocracy of the mind'. I suspect most Australian colonies also lacked a really solid middle bourgeoisie, and this might suggest an important reason for the failure of Protestantism to attain the level of moral hegemony reached in analogous countries. That failure is itself relevant to the situation of Australian women: religion has often played an important (if always ambivalent) part in nurturing confident role models for women. Such models have also tended to emerge from the higher social strata enumerated above. Perhaps like the frontier, democracy is good for men and dogs . . . ? Hence this chapter on role models and identity begins by exploring the relevance of the frontier to our subject, and ends by exploring that of class and colony.

The Australian frontier experience was a formative period in the development of attitudes towards 'minority groups' such as Aborigines and women. In the United States, the implications of the frontier for men have been explored by Frederick Jackson Turner and his many critics, and its implications for women by David Potter. But among Australian male historians, the latter set of implications has so far remained virtually a non-question, though historians have come to recognize the importance of frontier social interaction for the

development of attitudes towards Aborigines. In this chapter I
ask a question for which answers will be hard to come by, if
only because historians have never seriously asked the questions.
What values arose out of the Australian frontier experience that
might be relevant to the standing and self-image of Australian
women? Perhaps there is no such thing as 'the Australian
frontier experience': the anti-generalizers will surely have a
field day here. And in any case at this stage the answer, or
answers, to the question can turn out to be, at best, *fruitfully
wrong*. And doubtless (and hopefully) wrong-*headed* enough
to coax others to put the whole thing straight.

Many pioneer women responded with exuberance to the
challenge of a harsh environment. Take, for example, Jane
Henty of Victoria's western district, and Charlotte May
McKenzie, Judith Wright's grandmother. One thinks of the
delight some of the early Bussell women expressed at exchang-
ing what they evidently felt as stifling English gentility, for the
tasks of mastering a pioneering situation in Western Australia.[1]
In 1857, Emma Lucille Frances Thomson described fragments
of a life she enjoyed at Brookhampton, Western Australia:
1 January 1857 – 'Danced the New Year in at Govt House . . .';
28 Wednesday – 'Beautiful day'; 20 July 1857 – 'Lovely day.
Jim, Dr Arden and Mr Travers went to Guildford to shoot
pigeons'; 21 Tuesday – 'Spent the day at Mrs Lefroys . . .';
23 Thursday – 'Went to a large cristening [sic] dance to the
Travers enjoyed it very much.'[2] Describing visits as a child
to 'Western Australia in 1854 and 1856', Amy Hale told of her
delight on one occasion:

Well all pleasant things come too soon to an end, and so to us did this
happy visit to the Vasse, and all the simple joys, the riding parties, the
strolls in the bush to gather wild flowers and fresh gum, the house-
warmings, the birthday parties, and above all the parties at Mrs John's
and last but not least the walks and talks on the banks of the river
when Emily repeated poetry, and Capel told us romantic tales. Of
all these joys I tasted during this memorable visit, it seemed to me
as if I had gone through the experiences of a lifetime and as if another
would hardly suffice for their recital to the little sister left at home.[3]

Letters to Maria S. Rye from poor 'gentlewomen' in Australia often express pleasure at being accepted into unpretentious and welcoming families as governesses, and zest at having to tackle farming chores.[4]

Working hard at shared tasks has proved a rich source of fellowship between woman and man through the ages. Thus in 1863, Mrs J. S. Maley of Greenough, Western Australia, told her diary about work shared with her husband. And in the midst of details about limestone for the mill floor, sacks of flour and meal, we read: 'I am sorely . . . distressed not seeing my dear husband. I feel very miserable. Never looked so much as I have today for him and cannot see his dear face.'[5] In other pioneer lands, comradeship and joy sprang from work shared in situations often more gruelling than ours. Sarah Roberts, for example, left a family farm sixty-five miles east of the railhead at Stettler, Alberta, Canada, after five years (1906–1911) because she could no longer bear the winter cold. But she looked back on the time as 'an exhilarating challenge', a time of 'sweet companionship of working together in daily tasks and of sharing with each other hardship and heart-break and trial and triumph and sorrow and joy'. In 'Homesteading and Homemaking on the Plains . . .',[6] Mary Hargreaves tells us of more than one such experience. All her informants, however, she describes as 'well-educated', and we may suspect the Australian women we named had, if not formal education, then a greater ease with things of the mind than most early *small* settlers' women. There were many Australian counterparts of these Canadian women, working alongside their husbands in friendship and dignity, sharing triumphs and defeats, though, through child-bearing, knowing degrees of exhaustion and danger denied to men.

Though Australian countrywomen have been more devoted to local-level association than their city counterparts, they fell and fall far short of North American women. About the Canadians, for example, Mary Hargreaves writes: 'Loneliness was a general complaint, but women's insistence upon the organisation of schools and churches generated the institutional basis for a wide range of social activities – reading and singing groups, community dances, programs of seasonal celebration.' Vigorous local-level association enriches women's experience of pioneering and the frontier and ultimately, through encouraging a kind of female sub-culture, their visibility and confidence in settled community life. In America, for example, in the seventeenth and early eighteenth centuries there were wide scale local self-help bodies for childbirth and illness and for setting up and funding churches. As training grounds for female activism, these can be seen as forerunners of the early-nineteenth century revivalist groups where women were trained in public speaking and political campaigning. That training carried over into the Abolitionist movement in the 1830s, thence into the feminist movement of the 1850s.

Now let us consider the greyer implications of 'the frontier' for women in Australia. Shipboard experiences seem to have lodged firmly in the memories of many pioneer women. Analysis of contemporary migrant experience is teaching us how deeply first approaches to a new land can colour subsequent experiences. 'John Gardiner Pioneer and Overlander', in Australia in the 1830s, clearly rose to the challenge of pioneering. However, his biographer makes no mention of how John's wife Mary felt, an omission which makes sense when one in fact finds out. Her version is tucked into John Gardiner's biography at the Royal Commonwealth Society Library on separate sheets of paper. Here is what she thought of a boat trip from Sydney to Port Phillip on 14 March 1837:

Oh the nausea and weariness attending [sic] board ship even when actual sea-sickness does not confine one to their [sic] berth . . . Oh how heart sickening are those words 'the wind has changed' . . . The whistling of the wind, the raging of the waves and pitching of a vessel have no charms for me . . .

As the ship pulled in to harbour Mary 'felt less terrified, though my teeth continued to chatter and my knees to shake'.[7] Like Mary Gardiner, Sarah Brunskill hated the sea voyage essential to pioneering and its glories. On her way to South Australia in 1837, she wrote to her parents back in England: 'no tongue can express with truth, the pain and agony of the heart . . .'[8]

Sarah Brunskill lost two children on the voyage. Rosina Ferguson sailed to South Australia in 1836. On board she 'was delivered of a little Australian girl', and 'had a very trying time of it all the voyage'. Her life prospered thereafter, but fifteen years later in 1852, she refers to even those years of prosperity in a way suggesting she experienced them as transient. How fully did she *live*, then, since to live is to accept the present: 'we did not expect to have been here till now, but it seems we must stay a little longer.'[9] Anna Ey, wife of the Lutheran pastor of Lobethal, sailed to South Australia on the *Gellert*, 28 August 1847. During the voyage, she tells us, 'a sailor got hold of me and dangled me over the side of the ship. I screamed dreadfully, and in my fright I struggled with arms and legs. My hat and sewing basket fell into the sea and we never saw them again. How easily I could have fallen in too!'[10]

What was early Australia like for poor *women*? Ward's argument bearing on the question focuses very strongly on poor *men*. As earlier chapters showed, our national identity was and is unusually deeply imprinted with the values of the so-called 'lower orders'; in Erikson's terms, their values formed one of its major early configurations. Ward submits that the 'lower orders' experienced an earlier and stronger local, Australia-oriented, sense of belonging than more prosperous people did. He gives a reason for this:

From that day to this the standard of living for ordinary people, whatever it may have lacked in culture and refinement, was very much better in a material sense than it was for the same people in Britain at the same period. It seems implausible but it is true that even convicts serving their sentences in Australia usually ate more and better food than did unskilled labourers in Britain . . .[11]

In 1851, from Melbourne, Lucy Hart wrote in similar vein to her mother, brothers and sisters in Winchester:

Should I have been so well off in England NO [sic] work hard and be half starved Australia is the place to live . . . [we saved our money] so that my husband should not allways work under a Master and happy am I to inform you that we have gained that point he is now his own Master . . . [sic][12]

This would have been important in determining how poor women, as well as poor men, felt about their new land. Indeed, Ward quotes Ellen W. writing from Sydney in 1846:

We pay eight shillings a week rent but it is well we get on. Oh, what a difference there is between this country and Home for poor folks. I know I would not go back again – I know what England is. Old England is a fine place for the rich, but the Lord help the poor.[13]

However, neither women nor men live by bread alone, and for those who 'believe' in words, we should first of all note that Ellen W. used the word 'home' in reference to England, and a sense of community, whose absence hurts women most consciously and acutely, was and is far more real in England than in Australia. Next, I question whether poor women in New South Wales felt anything like the same sense of 'belonging' to their new country, anything like the same sense of 'local patriotism', as poor men felt. When nineteenth century travellers said Australia is 'the poor man's country', their choice of gender was accurate.

But what was early *frontier* Australia like for women? David Potter challenges the idea that Turner's frontier thesis was valid for American women. 'Our social generalization', he points out in 'American Women and the American Character':

is mostly in masculine terms . . . This masculine orientation is to be expected, of course, in a society which is traditionally and culturally male-dominated – in what we call a patriarchal rather than a matriarchal society . . . When Turner states that [the frontier] furnishes 'a new field of opportunity, a gate of escape from the bondage of the past', one must ask, exactly what was the nature of women's participation in this opportunity?

Potter is not denying that there *was* opportunity, just as I wouldn't deny poor women were economically better-off in early New South Wales than in the slums of early industrializing England. But Potter continues: 'In fact, the frontier was brutally harsh for females, and it furnished its own verdict on its differential impact upon the sexes. "This country" said the frontier aphorism, "is all right for men and dogs, but it's hell on women and horses".'[14]

The general view of the frontier and the outback in Australia, as in the United States, tends to be strongly male-oriented. Here, for example, is a grim celebration of the outback by a non-family-oriented male. His name is Henry Lawson.

And I've carried swag for months out-back in Australia – and it was life, in spite of its 'squalidness' and meanness and wretchedness and hardship . . . the land of self-reliance, and never-give-in, and help-your-mate . . . Australia! My country! Her very name is music to me.[15]

To a woman, experiencing child-bearing and rearing in loneliness, such a life would be more likely to call for endurance rather than celebration. It is a measure of how crippled the female sub-culture has been in Australia that so few writers have challenged the spiritual aridities of the mateship universe, or even explored them from the vantage point of women. In 1893 Francis Adams said of the females in the families of small farmers (whom he likened to 'mean whites' of the American south): 'The life of their women is pitiable.'[16]

'We were drinking mates together.' Thus did Henry Lawson describe one of the closest forms of human friendship he knew. But what might mateship have meant for the *wives* of 'mean white' farmers? We repeat Judith Wright:

The 'mateship' ingredient in Australian tradition was always and is is necessarily one-sided; it left out of account the whole relationship with woman.[17]

Next, thinking specifically of poor women in the outback, we could examine the picture painted by Barbara Baynton, in *Bush Studies*, 1903. In her, one reviewer writes, 'we have an artist who instinctively chooses to draw an Australia which is not of Rolf Boldrewood or . . . Mrs Campbell Praed, It is grey and drouthy [sic] and blasphemous. It is lonely and it offers cavernous leisure for the doing of foul things . . .'[18] Baynton said:

Women of the bush have little to share, and nursing the belief that how they live is quite unknown to one another they have no inclination to entertain a caller.

Here is Mrs E. M. Everton, thinking about her life after 1851 in Tea Tree Gully, a village close to Adelaide. She, unlike Barbara Baynton, points to a sisterhood unsung by male historians but richer than 'drinking' mateship.

Does anyone remember when typhoid fever, that dread disease, struck the little village ? . . . There were no trained nurses in those days. Any sickness was coped with by the women of the little community, those who could taking it in turns for day and night duty. But typhoid fever was a dread scourge . . .[19]

Next, a fragment from the life of a South Australian poor farmer's wife, Mrs John Gilbert, in 1848:

Come to a Crick to Camp verry Dirty Rainin narly all day . . . Confind son Thursday 25 of May at the Crick
Monday 29 May
Lave the Crick Arfter my Confinment [sic] to go [?] scrub 15 mills to Leak Bony . . . Chasin the Bulluck up all night this is my first Days travel arfter my Confinment no Warter here . . .[20]

In *The Timber Getters*, a novel written in Perth, 1899, Mrs Baldwin Hodge gives us a picture of life for poor women among very poor men. Her picture is far darker than the one Katharine Susannah Prichard paints of a similar *milieu* in *Working Bullocks*, for, like Henry Lawson, Prichard is ideologically dedicated to celebrating the noble poor *man*, so she cannot confront his brutality towards 'his' woman. In *The Timber Getters*, John Boyce, a timber getter, lost his wife because her baby came on prematurely while she was helping him clear timber. His wife dead, John is then helped by his son Jem and daughter Bella. Bella 'worked like a man without a man's pay or relaxation'.* During periods of discontent,

* A few years later Barbara Baynton noted acidly that 'manhood suffrage in Australia most certainly limited the working man's labours to eight hours.' When would this blessing be extended to women workers, she wondered ?[22]

Bella 'had misty thoughts of rebellion that never got beyond the thick fog of her comprehension'. Her resentment smouldered and grew, fed on loneliness and hard labour utterly beyond her strength. She became, finally, cruel and bitter, and killed her brother Jem. Outside the courtroom where sentence was passed on her:

she threw her weather-beaten, toil-hardened hands above her head and fell in an unconscious heap on the floor. They picked her up, a creature harmless and helpless – a woman without a mind.[21]

Depending then on social status, physical health, personal aspirations of the woman concerned, and her relations with her husband or father, a woman could experience the 'frontier', pioneering, as a kind of outrage. Writing of Darling Downs wheat farmers in the 1890s, where 'pride of ownership was sometimes marred by virtual slave labour, as whole families struggled to increase the area under crop to 70,000 acres', Duncan Waterson comments: 'Racking tensions between patriarch and his sons were not uncommon and remorseless routine often made drudges of the women.'[23] My own grandmother, Margaret Bertha Shann, was a deeply intellectual woman. But because she married a farmer in north-east Victoria, the life of the mind was often denied her, for example, by the need to cook for farm labour during harvest, by tasks such as carrying water to the kitchen (Grandfather was reluctant to 'waste' money needed for capital improvement by piping water to the kitchen)[24] and hand sewing clothes for Dad and my aunts. Though Grandma died when I was nine, she had a crucial influence on my life – Freud has a curious passage about the affinity between grandparent and grandchild which I've come to accept. Reading her diaries now, I often think of her as I day-dream about the lives of other farmers' wives. The *Perth Gazette*, 3 October 1851: 'Money-making engrosses the men – everlasting stitching the women! books are at a discount . . .'[25] On Sunday mornings, outside a one-roomed wooden church at Yarroweah in north-east Victoria, Grandpa Dixson used to join the other farmers in discussing money-making, weather and crops. In Victoria's prosperous western district between 1834 and 1890 one settler's wife lamented: 'The chief topics of conversation in the bush . . . are dips, the strength of tobacco, the best way of growing and drying it, whether it is hot or cold, and so on and so on . . .'[26] Grandma was devoted to her diary so for me the words of the novelist, Mrs Campbell Praed, struck home:

. . . alas!, it is difficult to find anything poetic in the mean hardships which fall upon gracious women, who in their springtime had reasonably expected something better from life. For them it is a bad business when the country happens on evil days. No servant and seven children! and the boys obliged to go to a state school . . .! Oh, I call it just slavery, working all day and never feeling tidy – washing pots and pans and cleaning knives, which is what I hate most – and the brick-dust gets so under one's nails! This is the kind of woman-like plaint which tells the squalid tragedy of bad times.[27]

I would feel different about my grandmother had women's contribution to the building of our present been authentically explored and affirmed. Historians, as we've noted earlier, are as much Australians as wharfies, farmers, scientists and business-men, and share the profound unconscious contempt for women that pervades the Australian ethos. Thus, with some exceptions, their treatment of women can too often be shallow and awk-ward: like Xavier Herbert, they usually lack a feel for that women's side of *themselves* imprisoned only too securely in the dungeons of their psyche. So they need to 'research' women, as Herbert told us he did to write *Soldiers' Women* (soldiers' food, soldiers' boots, soldiers' *women* . . .). Historians have not usually granted women the respect careful consideration and spontaneous fellow-feeling brings, and listing women's richer attributes out of the context of their imperfections is thus a kind of insult: 'Once upon a pedestal' . . . Fleeing from women, domesticity, ordinariness, into loneliness, the bush, into achievement up to breaking-point and beyond, American men, it has been contended,[28] manifest a deep fear of women. Erikson bears this out, tracing causes back far into a pioneering land's history.[29] Thus Leslie Fiedler argues that in the American novel women are commonly portrayed not as ordinary, many-sided, flawed fellow-humans, but as 'monsters of virtue or bitchery'.[30] Australian historians also tend to treat women as monsters of virtue and perhaps occasionally (as the novelists tend to do) 'monsters of mateyness', but for the most part they cope with them by ignoring them. For example, in the burgeoning literature on national character, as we noted before, women are scarcely mentioned. Books written after the women's movement began to make some impression, have more entries in their indexes under the word 'women'.[31] But even now, the value system by which our pattern-setting historians decide whom to include and whom to exclude from a supposedly-communal history, is hidden, airless and élite-oriented. Far more than American and more than English, Australian history still unknowingly tends to take its bearings from nineteenth century historiography.[32] In its time this was invaluable as vocational training for an élite destined to rule England and her Empire. Careful questioning of my own students, however, has so far uncovered very few who intend to rule Burma or even staff the higher reaches of the British civil service and Church, and this might throw some light on the alarming pace at which history is vanishing from Australian schools. In those schools and universities, history teachers persist in naming their discipline 'history'. The word carries the implication of an overall approach to societal process and change, of a framework capable of attempting integration between disparate areas and broad stretches of population. But in reality what we tend to teach concerns highly compartmentalized or fragmented slices of history, never even aiming at integration. So therefore we are duty-bound to call our courses what they really are: parliamentary-political history, political history, constitutional history, military history; there is 'great man' history, diplomatic history, religious history, intellectual history (not much of this in Australia). And, impartially devoting about as much attention to women as allegedly élitist types of history, there is also labour history (quite big in Australia). Finally, we should not leave out Humphrey McQueen's history, for, while he is just as androcentric as the erring souls he is devoted to 'revising', he is *militantly* androcentric.

Common, then, to all these fragmentary histories – and indeed to those purporting to analyse 'national' character, etc.– is the exclusion of women and children: the majority. In naming fragmentary slices of history 'history', we perpetuate a semantic outrage for which, quite rightly, we would fail the humble student (fortunately in order to pass exams students have the sense to do what we *say* and not what we *do*). The only semantic justification we can plead is that what we teach is literally HISTORY. At present, Australian historiography is so backward that women and children are not even accorded the token place they are finding in other countries. But they will assume an integral and central place only when historians come clean as to what they are really at, spell out in simple language the now-hidden value system they use in defining who is a worthy historical actor (ACTOR) and what is a valid historical area of inquiry. In the meantime, the trickle of references to women in Australian history books comes across, for the most part, as a token gesture to assuage a new-born guilt, a dim sense of professional inadequacy, of the need to 'keep up', to stay with it, to be trendy. Still, we've made a start, and if as yet there are no William L. O'Neills among Australian historians, that is, after all, because our historians are at heart true-blue Australians: in all honesty they cannot 'see' women as authentic historical subjects.

Historians in Australia tend, on the whole, to pay very little attention to pioneer women, and probably for that reason, when women *are* discussed, historians tend to bend over backwards, making women larger than life (again, 'once upon a pedestal'), thus replacing an insult of omission by an insult of commission. So, for example, Stephen Roberts, *The Squatting Age in Australia 1835–1847*, and N. Bartley, *Australian Pioneers and Reminiscences*,[33] tend to portray pioneer women as 'monsters of virtue'. The coming of European women often exacerbated white-black relations here, as in Brazil, Fiji and Madagascar, but that is scarcely recognized[34] (more on this later). If it were, Australian historians would have had to think carefully about women in their ordinariness, their humanity, 'warts and all', and they'd have to confront the sexual jealousy of white women for native women.

How have small farmers felt about women, and how have their women felt about themselves? Small farmers have placed a mark on Australian *mores* that is hard to isolate but clearly strong. In the national identity debate, writers now stress the overlap in folkways between small farmers and rural proletarians: 'Countless shearers, teamsters, fencers and other bush workers shared a smallholder's background', one writer points out.[35]

Geoffrey Blainey implies that any half-way canny farmer of means from the 'Old Country' would have kept well clear of Australia:

While dear land financed the coming of migrants, it probably deterred those British emigrants who hoped to be farmers. An Englishman who possessed a little capital and the hope of ploughing his own soil was foolish to migrate to Australia in preference to North America. Dear land cursed farmers. One of Australia's tragedies in the second half of the nineteenth century was the failure of the tens of thousands of farmers and their families to make a living from small farms after slaving for years.[36]

So what manner of men did we come by, then? In *The Chosen Vessel* (part of *Bush Studies*), Barbara Baynton sketches some of the texture of life for a mean white farmer's wife. The woman in this incident is frightened of a cow. June Lee takes up the story:

The husband also exhibits the same disregard for the woman, and in so doing, allies himself with the world of the animal. . . . 'but the woman's husband was angry and called her – the noun was cur' . . . He demands the subjection of the emotions of warmth and tenderness and forces the woman to overlay her basic aversion [to the cow] with indifference: '[He] forced her to run and meet the advancing cow, brandishing a stick, and uttering threatening words till the enemy turned and ran. "That's the way!" the man said, laughing at her white face. In many things he was worse than the cow . . .' The woman's husband is shown to have degenerated into a mere brute-like acceptance of a world motivated by basically inhuman instincts . . .

'more than once she thought of taking her baby and going to her husband. But in the past, when she had dared to speak of the dangers to which her loneliness exposed her, he had taunted her and sneered at her.'

June Lee believes Baynton's general feeling is that a mean white farmer's woman, as a symbol of warmth, love, sympathy and tenderness, must necessarily be destroyed by the oppression of dullness, insensitivity, brutality and cruelty.[37] In *Australian Life, Black and White* (1885), Mrs Campbell Praed captured some of the grossness of the small grazier-farmer feeling for women, recounting an incident concerning one Jackson, a widower, who was much attracted to a Miss Grant. He did not press his suit with much energy and, Mrs Praed's father having teased him on the question, Jackson admitted he was sorry he hadn't visited Eurogan, the property on which Miss Grant lived, so as to have courted her effectively:

The fact is, my dear Murray, ... the cattle hereabouts are too scattered, you can't inspect them properly. Next year I shall look over a heifer-paddock in Sydney and take my pick.

'N.B. – Heifer-paddock in Australian slang means a ladies' school', adds Mrs Praed.[38] She later tells the story of an acquaintance of her brother, a young man called Van Helmont, who described his plan to gain a wife. This is the sort of woman he wanted:

Any age from twenty to twenty-six would do. She must be used to the bush, and able to wash and cook for herself if necessary; all the better if she has no relations, and one with a little money preferred. And she must be of the same religion as myself, though that would not be of great consequence, as I mean to settle on the Ubi, and from all I hear, you are not much troubled with parsons there.

Van Helmont, Mrs Praed then adds, was 'small and ugly, with ferret-like eyes and a skin covered with pimples, and a wonderful mop of red hair which always stood on end. He was rough, uncouth, and ill-educated, but believed himself irresistible.'[39]

But perhaps so far our exploration of the impact on women

of the frontier and pioneering has missed the main point? The low standing of women in Australia, many observers have always insisted, stems above all from the sheer numerical shortage of women and the consequent imbalance of the sexes. As early as 1820, for example, the Hon. H. Grey Bennet, M.P., wrote to Lord Bathurst: nor, 'as long as such a disproportion exists between the two sexes, is it possible to prevent the system of general prostitution'.[40] In 1821 the Reverend Mr Cowper told Commissioner Bigge 'there was considerable concubinage, illegitimacy and crime in Sydney, but he attributed this to the disproportionate number of males'.[41] In 1837 Mr Hutt asked Lieutenant Colonel Breton, witness before the Molesworth Select Committee on Transportation: 'Does it appear to you that the paucity of women has a tendency to produce prostitution?' Breton answered: 'It might have: in the interior it certainly would.'[42] Witness James Macarthur accepted the numbers theory only up to a point. Mr Hutt:

May not the irregularities you have described as being common, in which women are concerned, arise from the paucity of women in the colony?

Macarthur:

In some degree it may, but not altogether . . .[43]

But in the same year in England Sir John Barrow, reviewing recent books on New South Wales, concluded: 'The women, with a few exceptions, are so ill-conducted, that the more respectable settlers are unwilling to receive them at all. Their numbers being small in comparison to the male convicts they are assailed by so many temptations, that reform seems hopeless. Their conduct is marked not only by idleness, drunkenness and unchastity, but too often by untameable ferocity.'[44] In 1870 James Bonwick gave a certain implicit support to the numbers theory[45] while in 1937 R. B. Madgwick awarded numbers a fairly important part: 'The amount of prostitution and illegitimacy in the twenties and thirties of last century was due as much to the marked disproportion of the sexes as to the moral decadence of sections of the population.'[46] Recent writers tend to follow suit. Rosemary Goddard, for example, notes that 'generally, the currency lasses were believed to be less virtuous than their male counterparts. This is not surprising in view of their background and the fact that they were among the most eligible women in a society where women were very much in the minority.'[47] Joan Cobb writes of a proposal in 1828 to place convict women on farms in the interior: 'At this stage women were so outnumbered in the country that their situation was often reported as little less than desperate.'[48] Later she adds: 'Assignment in the bush (or assignment at all) was a menace to the women because they were outnumbered by the men.'

But while this has been the general consensus, not all Australian historians have been happy with the numbers theory. Manning Clark, for example, calls our attention to 'that teaser for the social historian of why women accepted male domination in a society in which their scanty numbers seemed to present an opportunity of challenging such domination'.[49] The teaser becomes more intriguing if one widens the comparative canvas and looks at some seventeenth and eighteenth century American colonies. 'Women had always been a valuable commodity in colonial America', says Barbara Welter.[50] Roger Thompson notes the 'relative emancipation of women in the American colonies'.[51] Gerda Lerner writes: 'the American environment had a liberating influence on women . . .'[52] American colonial (early frontier, pioneering) women, then, enjoyed a relatively *high* standing. But this is widely explained by the numerical shortage of women; the same factor is invoked to help explain woman's relatively *low* standing in most Australian colonies. For example, of the American experience A. W. Calhoun writes:

In the pioneer regions women were usually scarce and hence were highly esteemed . . . The deficit of women on the frontier, accounts for their superior standing in some of the newest states.[53]

William L. O'Neill, a leading modern historian of the American women's movement, takes the same approach:

It has always been supposed that the frontier circumstances with which many women lived in the early nineteenth century, and which were part of the ancestral experience of most Americans, improved the status of women. Women were scarce on the frontier, and consequently more valuable.[54]

Roger Thompson develops the problem when he writes of the seventeenth century:

. . . there is little doubt that prostitution was rife and rising in London, and probably was considerable throughout the country as a whole. In the colonies, on the other hand, despite a shortage of women and thus a considerable class of unmarried men of marriageable age, I have been able to find hardly any evidence of the existence of the oldest profession.[55]

The 'sex ratio' is 'the number of males per hundred females'.[56] In the seventeenth century American colonies Thompson discusses, he describes the sex ratio as on the whole 'abnormally high'.[57] That is, there were far more men than women. In seventeenth century Virginia there were four males to one female. Arrivals counted in Massachusetts were three to two, though, and by the end of the century there was a surplus of women in larger towns, especially, for example, in Boston.[58] For Massachusetts as a whole, by the 1690s, 'the overall sex ratio [was] around the 100 mark'[59] (about even numbers of each sex).

Thus while numbers have their place in shaping attitudes to, and the overall standing of, women in a given community, there's a good deal more to be said. Where Geoffrey Gorer finds the nineteenth century one in which the standing of women is at an all-time low throughout western Europe,[60] there are stretches in seventeenth century England where the climate was in certain respects more encouraging (a medievalist might interpret this as the tail-end of medieval folkways; a seventeenth century expert might argue his century is in some ways *sui generis*). Thompson writes: 'The middle years of the [seventeenth] century saw profound social as well as political change. In this upheaval women took the stage in religious, political, legal and business affairs.'[61] So while numbers must always be taken seriously, in the seventeenth century other historical currents were also at work. Colonial American women were, in general, not only more firmly committed to religion than our founding mothers but also stood higher on the status ladder. De Tocqueville, for example, wrote that, though often possessed of 'a masculine strength of understanding and a manly energy', the women of America generally 'preserve great delicacy of personal appearance, and always retain the manners of women'.[62] Thompson describes a Virginian frontier woman in 1710: 'She is a very civil woman and shews nothing of ruggedness, or Immodesty in her carriage, yett she will carry a gunn . . . and perform the most manful exercises . . .[sic]'[63] We could say such women manifested behaviour patterns associated with 'gentlewomen', or 'bourgeois' strata, while lacking the a-sexual quality of genteel, pallid insipidness which would finally distinguish the 'feminine' human being from the 'female' human being. But those colonial American frontier women also came from social strata where legal marriage was the norm, and where religion prescribed firm guidelines for sexual relations and self-esteem. By contrast, among the nineteenth century casual poor, from which many of our own founding mothers sprang, 'pairing' was probably much more widespread than legal marriage. And one does not know how long-term the 'pairing' was, this after all, being crucial to the well-being and security of women and children. But with women held in such low regard as they were among the casual poor, it's hard to be too optimistic about the chances of constancy.

As for the higher standing of American women on the frontier, we should also note that Americans more typically settled with and through the family than did Australians. Norman MacKenzie indeed writes '. . . family life, in the strict sense, is a comparatively recent phenomenon in Australia . . . it was only in the middle of the 19th century that normal married life became possible for a majority of adults.'[64] Russel Ward gives him some support:

Assuming women to be distributed more or less evenly through the different economic groups of the outback population, it is obvious at a glance that, even at the end of the decade [1851], four out of

196

every seven men must still have been doomed to bachelorhood. Actually, of course, the proportion of single men among the nomad tribe of pastoral labourers was very much higher than this. . . . In the older and more fertile areas of the 'nineteen counties' there were some small agricultural holdings worked by family groups. But . . . beyond the boundaries of location individual small holdings, worked by family groups, were almost unknown.[65]

What can we say of Aboriginal women in the context of formative, frontier experiences? In *Childhood and Society*, Erikson attributes aspects of American racism partly to reaction-formations developed to hold at bay what he calls the 'sensual and oral temptations'[66] black women held for Southern white men – black mammies had often suckled them. It's worth asking whether early and repeated encounters between our lonely men and Aboriginal women have left traces, less powerful, different in many ways, but still quite real. After all, the term 'black velvet' encapsulates a world of 'sensual and oral temptations', luxury Anglo-Saxon women perhaps could not provide even when they were present. But sexual gratification is often fused with feelings of murkiness, dirt and blackness in capitalist cultures.* Since European men were often brutal to Aboriginal women, this increased the burden of guilt. Guilt, almost unbearable if experienced passively, can be managed better – so we imagine – if we actively turn it against our victims. The jack-booted stormtrooper kicking a frail old Jewish grandfather is not guilty of brutality: quite the contrary. The grandfather is actually guilty, and the Nazi is the victim. The grandfather is part of an international Jewish-Marxist plot, sucking the rich red blood of the German *Volk*. Guilt is thus a common component and cause of racism. So those formative, frontier encounters between Australian men and Aboriginal women have possibly made Australian racism rather more ugly and, at the same time, strengthened negative feelings about the body – '*black* velvet' – and sexuality. Since there is some final sense in which all women are one, though each man is an

* Freud's phrase 'the anal-obsessive' character is, as Norman O. Brown points out in *Life Against Death*, the capitalist character.

individual, negative feelings about sexuality and black women, especially in formative times, meant negative feelings about sexuality and women. A bonus, surely? There were plenty of negative feelings around in any case . . .

Sexual jealousy goes some way towards explaining the cold indifference most of our own respectable women displayed towards the manifest and desperate situation of convict women,[67] and a long way towards explaining the positive hostility they often showed towards Aboriginal women.[68] (Early respectable ladies of the American south often displayed cruel indifference to the anguish of Negro slave women and sexual jealousy is an important reason for that, too:[69] there's a closer parallel here with early New South Wales than generally recognized.) The relatively poor sense of commitment to community, especially to less fortunate women, displayed by our own early élite women is thus not only to be understood in terms of the fact that our male élite evinced a similar attitude. Early élite women had their own reasons, and these helped impoverish the entire feeling of community.

White women tended to arrive here later than men, and Australian historians – when they look at the question at all – give an overall impression that white women acted as a civilizing influence on relations between Aborigines and Europeans. However, the same historians give specific items of evidence contradicting this, showing, for example, white women using guns against Aborigines, while still leaving the reader with an overall impression of heroines bringing a mythic gentling. To repeat Leslie Fiedler's[70] phrase, bush women have usually been depicted as 'monsters of virtue'. Historians have thus not usually granted them the flawed humanity that goes with real respect.[71] Yet recent research[72] throws decisive doubt on the gentling-heroine picture, making it clear that early Australian women were as brave and able to defend hearth and home as colonial American pioneer women,[73] and as prone to jealousy over the 'sensual and oral temptations' of black women.

We've now looked at the possible female role models associated with the frontier and women on the land. We turn finally to look at role models associated with higher social strata –

wealthy women, bourgeois women, intellectual and professional women. Taking liberties with language for the sake of getting across an overall picture, I've called these 'élite women'. How might élite women have contributed to overall female role-definition in Australia? How might they have contributed to that range or pool of role-models that history decrees is relevant for female identity formation in a given community? We have to start by going back, very quickly, over some old ground.

Colonies, we said, often lack solid upper strata – an aristocracy, *haute bourgeoisie*, an aristocracy of the mind. Most West-European-style communities took their main range of models for identity formation from the top of the status ladder. But because of freak influences associated with our birth and formative times, Australians have taken theirs from, broadly speaking, two areas: the middle and the bottom rungs (there was no 'top'). Two main clusters of values have thus coexisted within our national identity (not as uneasily as one might expect, because, to a major extent, the bottom layers have accepted basic values deriving from hierarchy and have often also tried to be 'top at the bottom'). But in most states, we have not had an especially robust bourgeois or middle strata. Indeed as early as 1843 an English observer, John Hood, could sense a weakness in the bourgeois strata, a thinness which Marxists rightly see as a common feature of colonial social structures:* 'There does not seem to be any middle class in the colony to take a leading part . . .'[74] We have argued through this book that, if one is to get at the sources of identity formation for women in a given group, one must begin by looking at those sources for men. Uncertainty and a feeling of something missing, of inadequacy in relation to an English matrix or reference group, is a key feature of identity in relation to Australian male élites, and an important source of their uncertainty about issues of authority. Manning Clark uses as one of his conceptual categories 'the age of the bourgeoisie'. Compared with West-European, especially

---

* Though bourgeois strata were to prove weaker in New South Wales and Queensland than in South Australia and Victoria, the latter states still fall into the 'colonial' category in this matter.

English, bourgeois strata, our bourgeoisie is a *bourgeoisie man-qué*: and our bourgeois males relentlessly, often consciously, compared themselves with English élites. Thus they suffered acutely from a sense of being less than whole, from a sense of something missing. The uncertainty characterizing the middle layers, combined with the militant philistinism of the bottom, produced a 'notably derivative and dependent society in its culture and institutions',[75] and a 'strongly imitative, conventional . . . people who have never quite ceased to feel insecure'.[76]

This sense of inadequacy in relation to England contoured the outlook of the Australian élite in endless ways: it gave rise to what A. A. Phillips has called the 'cultural cringe',[77] to much of what Roe describes as 'the derivative element'[78] in our culture, which we can probably run to earth in an undefined desire to be more English than the English, more genteel than the genteel. Governor Gipps suggests one early source of that desire:

The ordinary proprieties of Society are observed amongst the better portion of New South Wales, in as great and perhaps in a greater degree than amongst persons of the same class elsewhere. The fear indeed of being suspected of the taint of Convictism operates in a wholesome manner as a restraint upon those who are free from it.[79]

If we are to take seriously the idea of 'imprinting' and 'formative experiences', we can scarcely ignore the importance, within our early élite, of military men. High and low alike, their souls were pervaded and poisoned by the logic of their vocation, 'war, the most absurd and vicious of all the games that men play'.[80] Military men are probably finer specimens of male-bonders than mateship men – though as the celebrants of Anzac have reverently demonstrated – the categories are hardly exclusive. Military institutions are best understood as western analogues to Melanesian men's houses, whose atmosphere, Kate Millett tells us, 'is not very remote from that of military institutions in the modern world: they reek of physical exertion, violence, the aura of the kill, and the throb of homosexual sentiment . . . Citadels of virility, they reinforce the most saliently power-oriented characteristics of patriarchy.'[81] An early value-structure imprinted with military *mores* could therefore contain few notable feelings of fellowship towards women, who were largely irrelevant institutionally, economically and, to a curious extent, sexually.

The significance of formative experiences compels us, alas, to ponder Governor Hunter's 1797 comment on a crucial group of early authority figures and male élite identity models, the New South Wales Corps, from whom Hunter had every right to expect help in building some sense of community:

> . . . the manner in which this corps has . . . been recruited does in a great measure weaken the effect or service which we would expect to derive from the assistance of the military. Soldiers from the Savoy* and other characters who have been considered as disgraceful to every other regiment in his Majesty's service, have been thought fit and proper recruits for the New South Wales Corps . . . a set of the worst, the most atrocious characters that ever disgraced human nature.[82]

The élite fattened out, of course, but the picture Lady Forbes drew in 1831 showed it to be still pretty meagre:

> Society in Sydney at this time was composed almost entirely of the families of the Government officials, the Military and Naval Officers and their wives, and some few of the leading colonists.

Elsewhere she refers to her 'limited social circle'.[83]

Our male élite never experienced a cathartic separation from the English ruling class, often admirably achieved by a good blood-letting: the American War of Independence springs to mind. If our élite lacked solid upper strata with a sense of independence, it also lacked a robust sense of autonomy. But ease about issues of authority is impossible without a reasonably secure feeling of autonomy, and both are crucial to a robust sense of identity. Michael Roe is one of the few Australian explorers of the tiger-country concerned with 'authority', and he notes 'the absence of a strong middle class'.[84] Sometimes nothing can act more powerfully as a 'presence' than an 'absence'. For example, a sense of 'absence', of something missing that

* Savoy – a prison in London where military officers were confined.

'should' be present, explains the quality of protesting too much in the following (it is the N.S.W. Legislative Council speaking in 1838):

. . . in the opinion of this Council, the numerous Free Emigrants of character and capital, including many officers of the Army and Navy, and East India Company's Service, who have settled in the Colony with their families, together with a rising generation of Nativeborn Subjects [constitute as worthy a group as in any colony and have been able to] impress a character of respectability upon the Colony at large.[85]

Whatever they finally came to be, for long years, many of our early male élite were not sure whether they were travellers on the make, or migrants. Either way, they were commonly rapers of nature, whether on sea or land, robbing but not restoring and nurturing. Small wonder that, compared with older élites in settled lands, our élite failed to develop a pattern of abiding commitment to community (a *pattern*: individuals always did and do). Roe, paraphrasing James Macarthur in 1837, puts it only too well: 'In New South Wales the possession of property too often was unaccompanied by that sense of honour and obligation which ought to distinguish an élite.'[86] The irony of it was that while the community starved spiritually, so, too, did members of the élite, and they bequeathed a shallow cheated soul to the Australian ruling classes of today. Think how often they have handed over Australian earth to foreigners, and in foreign policy have gone all the way with the L.B.J.s . . .

What are some of the implications of this for women? First, as with élite men, from early days élite women seem to have lacked a sense of commitment to community of an intensity and scale displayed by their opposite numbers in England, America, Canada, Sweden and, I think, New Zealand. Another factor is relevant. Pattern-setting men tended to quieten their own feelings of inadequacy and illegitimacy by trying to be more bourgeois than the bourgeois (or perhaps more petit-bourgeois than the petit-bourgeois). Similarly, upper layers of the working class here, urgently aspiring to better themselves, tended to an exaggerated version of being bourgeois. They thus required an exaggerated version of the 'Victorian' ideal for 'their' women: childlike, pale and indeterminate, passive, submissive, mindless, genteel and 'nice' to a greater extent than that required of their more self-assured equivalents in England. Michael Roe draws our attention to one aspect of this:

In Australia more than in most countries propriety of behaviour has always won both respectability and respect. The wowser has scored many statutory victories . . .[87]

It's therefore not surprising that one student of the late-nineteenth century New South Wales' women's movement finds in it little that was original and finds it constricted in its aims.[88] The National Council of Women in New South Wales, unlike that, for example, of Canada,[89] remained neutral on the question of women's suffrage: too controversial![90] The Windeyer family canvassed every charitable organization in New South Wales to gain delegates for the state branch National Council of Women, and met with an astonishing initial lack of interest. Women working for charities were committed elsewhere, or could not attend during the day, or had too many domestic commitments. Small wonder the state National Council of Women was narrowly issue-oriented. At its first meeting, it skirted the issue of equal pay and adopted Lady Windeyer's suggestion that 'Home Literature' was a suitable item for discussion. The same meeting also supported Louisa McDonald's resolution 'that a knowledge of the domestic arts be included in the curriculum for girls in public schools'.[91] By 1901 many groups within the New South Wales' women's movement, Joan Cobb notes, seemed *obsessed with observing, and being seen to observe, absolute correctness*, when for decades at least some English aristocratic and upper class women had ventured beyond crippling stereotypes of femininity – sometimes ambivalently, like Caroline Norton, sometimes with superb contempt. Australian élite women, by contrast, were still pre-occupied and part-stifled with being more British than the British. In that year, for example, Lady Beaumont addressed the Women's Club, of which she was President:

. . . it was most important that at this period of the country's history
its women should stand clearly for the highest standards in everything.
The responsibility of keeping up such standards lies always very
largely with the women of any land . . . woe the land whose women
are less high minded than the men . . . [sic][92]

In 1904, here is Lady Rawson, president of the National Council
of Women, reminding women of their proper place in society:
'servicing' 'real' people:

. . . they should never forget that women's first duties were her home
duties. Her chief sphere of action was there and her first care should
be to secure the well-being of her husband and children, her servants
and those over whom she had influence.[93]

Lacking an aristocracy, an *haute bourgeoisie*, or established
middle bourgeois strata of any solidity, and being a pioneer
land, it is not surprising that, for the most part, Australia
lacked a strong and confident intelligentsia. J. A. Froude
wrote: 'The deficiency of the Sydney colonists is . . . that they
have no severe intellectual interests. They aim at little except
what money will buy.'[94] There are some outstanding exceptions,
of course, but in general Geoffrey Serle seems to have the right
of it: 'The cultural achievement of the first century was meagre
indeed . . . the tone of colonial society was set by *nouveau riche*
boors . . . There is little doubt that writers and artists felt
themselves to be confronted by a viciously hostile society.'[95]
English intellectual women were far more confident and visible
than Australian, and so could constitute more robust role models
for English girls as they grew up. But in some ways English
intellectual women themselves reflected the Victorian cult of
'true womanhood', a terminal stage of that social disease whereby
over the centuries female human beings withered into 'feminine'
human beings. Hippolyte Taine, for example, was much
surprised to find George Eliot and Elizabeth Barrett Browning
militantly affirming their domesticity and 'womanliness' and
denying their intellectuality in the presence of men: 'A great
French painter who spent several days with two women pos-
sessing genius, never even discovered they were women of

talent.' The contrast with proudly-learned French women seems embarrassing, and Taine was struck by the English combination of domesticity and learning in which domesticity predominated.[96]

It's not surprising that in a milieu positively hostile to the mind, the Australian novelist Ada Cambridge tells us that 'housework has all along been the business of life, novels have been squeezed into odd times . . .'[97] Ada Cambridge was an exception to the rule that 'colonial women seem to have been notably inarticulate'. But for Ada Cambridge, too, in the last instance, 'housework' did prove to be 'the business of life' and, in the words of A. G. Stephens, she finally 'did her duty . . . strangled her dreams, silenced her mind and conformed'.[98] In many ways Mary Gilmore too reflected the colonial tendency towards ultra-domesticity. In 1899 she wrote to her husband:

People here say that I mean to be a writer and that is why we resigned. They know nothing about it. I wouldn't be a writer in case I should let the love of it grow into my life and perhaps owe to it what I only want to owe to you – or that it might set up another aim or tie in which you would not be the centre.[99]

It is true that more women might have used their intellects had their energies not been absorbed in housework.* Ada Cambridge reports Bishop Perry's words on the burden of housework for clergymen's wives like herself: 'It was not the hardships of the clergy that troubled him, he said, but the killing strain upon their wives – literally killing, for he quoted figures to show the disproportionately high rate of sickness and ultimately death amongst them.'[100]

One historical consequence of the relative scarcity, lack of visibility and confidence of intellectual women was to impoverish

---

* Contemporary sources repeatedly stressed that girls preferred factory work to domestic service. Here is W. M. Alderson, a leather manufacturer, being asked by the N.S.W. 1875 Select Committee on the Employment of Children, whether girls could earn more with his company than in domestic service. 'No', but they chose to work in his factory because as domestics 'they would be more tied'.[101]

the stock of role models available for female identity formation. But that scarcity also had an institutional spin-off: it helped make the nineteenth century women's movement in Australia relatively small-scale and timid.[102] At that time, educated and intellectual women were few in any country, yet in England, Canada, the United States of America, France and Sweden, for example, educated and intellectual women played a far more important part in promoting causes relevant to women's well-being than they did in Australia. Where Australian university women graduates tended to stay 'aloof' from the developing women's movement,[103] by contrast in England, a valuable part was played by 'a steady stream of highly gifted women who virtually formed a feminine intelligentsia'.[104] Studies have shown the American and Canadian experience to have been somewhat similar.[105] Of French feminism in 1897, Virginia Crawford said, 'from the first it has been an intellectual and literary rather than a democratic movement: it has sprung from the imaginative brain of the writer and thinker rather than from the painful experience of the sufferer, and it is spreading today from the cultured few to the uneducated many.'[106] The importance for French feminism of robust and unfettered intellectuality is also brought out by Léopold Lacour in his study 'Les Origines du Féminisme Contemporaine',[107] but since this quality was missing from Australian intellectual life as a whole, we can hardly expect it to have flourished, though it certainly existed, in the Australian women's movement. The only Australian woman who can be compared with the brilliant, irreverent, outrageously witty French feminist Maria Déraismes, is Vida Goldstein, yet the comparison reveals the latter, admirable though she is, as lacking in originality and daring, and Victorian in personality-pattern. This is less true of the South Australian Catherine Spence, but then she was Scottish-born, and by no means wholly identified with the 'women's movement'.[108] In Sweden, where universities were opened to women between 1853 and 1859, university women, organized from 1904 in the Akademiskt Bildade Kvinnors Förening, played a central part in the suffrage movement, and during the twentieth century concerned themselves in a central way with the general problems of women, not merely those of academic women.[109] Ellen Key, a leader of the Swedish women's movement, was internationally renowned, both as ideologue and writer.[110]

But in most countries in the Western tradition, privileged women who were *not* intellectuals played a much more prominent part than they did here, both in the 'first wave' of the women's movement, and in general community problems. Most of us implicitly tend to think of the New South Wales élite in terms of West European élites, and so we should therefore surely ask why privileged women set up so few philanthropic organizations? Aside from domestic service, there was little demand for the labour of our founding mothers, where America's were the sturdy helpmates of the founding fathers. Thus, for example, in early Parramatta (then a settlement vying with Sydney in importance) women unable or unwilling to stay at the abysmal government Female Factory were often forced to prostitute themselves for lodging and food, hence joining 'what must have been a considerable band roaming the Parramatta streets'. But for a long time there were 'no organisations . . . to which destitute women could turn for help'.[111] The twenty-five poor girls boarded, clothed and educated in Elizabeth Macquarie's School of Industry[112] were fortunate, but the problem was scarcely solved by this, and Macquarie's own attitude, we noted before, was one of either indifference, impatience or misogyny. In 1825 Lady Darling set up a Female School of Industry to train poor girls belonging to the Church of England in cooking and general housework;[113] and, prompted by Lady Darling, for a while upper class women did give some help to the Parramatta Female Convict Factory.

Lady Darling conjured up the only lay-body of workers for the factory which ever came into existence, though it seems that many of its members were only flirting with reform movements and that it was only the presence and position of the Governor's wife which held it together . . . The Committee collapsed with Lady Darling's departure and no Governor tried to revivify it or re-introduce it.

But the sudden:

collapse of the Ladies' Committee on the departure of the Darlings indicates that it had not captured any general approbation and the results of its work were likely to be ignored. Bourke found on his arrival that the group had already disintegrated and in spite of suggestions from the Home Office in 1834 that a new group be formed, neither he nor Governor Gipps seriously considered doing so.[114]

Yet had responsible women seriously pressed Bourke or Gipps, would these governors really have failed to take up the chance to respond to Home Office suggestions? Married women and mothers within good family situations seem not to have done very much to help convict women, though their plight was well-known to them because they *saw* them, often within their own families. In 1837 the Reverend John Dunmore Lang told the Molesworth Select Committee on Transportation:

... the Government have not the means of employing women in the colony ... the defect of the system in regard to the assignment of women, arises from insufficient superintendence to which they are subjected in most of the families of the colony, and in fact, from the character of these families themselves.[115]

Joan Cobb again:

There were checks on assignment, but evidence is overwhelming that women were too often sent to families which exploited instead of protecting their servants. Nor was there any organised system of introducing women into families of good moral standing (which was constantly asserted to be the only means of effecting reformation); indeed the fact emerges that *better class families, not willing to take the risk of employing them at all, played little part in any campaign to help these women.* [My emphasis][116]

Could the relative lack of commitment of élite women to their less fortunate sisters be linked with the fact that élite women grew up with, and became hardened to, the plight of convict and free casual poor women? This is suggested in the words R. C. Hutchinson intended as rebuttal of contemporary charges that Mrs Mary Hutchinson, matron of several early female convict establishments, was indifferent and harsh towards women convicts:

It was in . . . this atmosphere of female degradation and licentiousness that Mary Oakes [later Hutchinson] grew up. There is little doubt that, from early childhood, she would have been familiar with the sight of hungry, ill-clad convict women, and their children, wandering the streets of Parramatta . . . It seems reasonable to assume that Mary Oakes *learnt to accept the wretchedness and debased behaviour of female convicts* as part of their way of life, *and an evil that the free people of the community was obliged to tolerate.* [My emphasis][117]

In general a woman's self-concept cannot be too different from her concept of other women in her culture. It seems likely that Australian women had a tendency to form low expectations of women from 'formative' times: this implies they held low expectations of and for themselves. Thus it is significant that foreign-born women often seem to have played a leading part in helping underprivileged women here. Charlotte Anley, an English Quaker disciple of Elizabeth Fry, behaved in a warm and accepting way towards the most violent convict women at the Parramatta Factory. Their response is a most moving affirmation of the power of love.[118] Caroline Chisholm behaved with tireless compassion towards poor women, but like Charlotte Anley, and unlike Mary Hutchinson, she was born in England and so did not grow up in a small community to be hardened against accepting shared humanity with poor women. Convictism thus helped lower the standing of Australian women by encouraging women to despise women: hence, also, themselves.

In 1875, the English reformers Rosamond and Florence Hill noted that New South Wales had no Discharged Prisoners' Aid Society, though certainly the community was familiar with their problems. However, the Hill sisters added '. . . a few ladies visit the women, and help in finding places for them when liberated.'[119] Noting the narrow range and timid nature of the women's movement taking shape after c.1880, Joan Cobb offers a part-explanation, referring to the Sydney élite as 'closely knit . . . composed of small factions'.[120] How much had its ethos changed, then, since 1831 when Lady Forbes, as we recall, described it as 'composed almost entirely of the families of the Government officials, the Military and Naval officers and their wives, and some few of the leading colonists'. In 1883 Frances Gillan Holden, Lady Superintendent of the Children's Hospital, wrote about 'the tremendous frivolity, whose fatal incubus is smothering and choking the womanhood of our days'.[121] In his *John Bull and Co.*, Max O'Rell records that he found among Australian 'society' women 'some of the most frivolous women to be found anywhere. Balls, dinners, soirées . . . appear to fill the life of hundreds of them.' Mrs Alexander Hirst, who quotes O'Rell, protests that his words apply only to 'a certain would-be fashionable, dwarf-minded minority, and a small minority at that',[122] but there is much to suggest that privileged women in New South Wales were not notable for their commitment to community, when viewed in international perspective.[123]

In Victoria, the bourgeoisie, apparently because of the differential impact there of the gold rushes during the 1850s,[124] was somewhat more robust than in New South Wales. Liberalism, liberal-radicalism, and the women's movement were all consequently more powerful. Even so, Vida Goldstein, outstanding leader of the Victorian women's movement in the late nineteenth and early twentieth centuries, found her work seriously hampered by a lack of 'wealthy members' willing and able to help her,[125] and by 1900 a report she gave on the achievements of American women clearly shows she felt they took on greater social responsibilities than her own countrywomen: 'When shall we have a Mother's Club in Melbourne?', she finishes.[126] During the twentieth century women from more privileged strata showed increasing interest in issues relevant to women, such as child welfare, equal pay, midwifery, excessive drinking, venereal diseases, film censorship, and the appearance of pornographic definitions of woman in a fast-developing mass culture. Yet in 1945 the much-travelled Ivy Brooks, like Vida Goldstein years earlier, recorded surprise at the extent of organization among American women, and observed how hard it had been to compile a history of the National Council of Women in Victoria 'since over the years the records have been kept at times very briefly and even erratically, and in other cases they have disappeared altogether and been lost'.[127]

In the late nineteenth century women's movement, some élite women certainly played a fine role. There is Lady Windeyer in New South Wales, for one, and Rose Scott, whose interests spread far beyond the vote. We find her organizing and writing a petition to the New South Wales Legislative Council showing 'that the age of Protection for young girls is lower [here] than in any other Australian State . . .'[128] In 1902 she addressed a monthly meeting of the Women's Political and Economic League on 'The Economic Dependence of Married Women';[129] in March 1904 on 'Peace and Arbitration'; and in April, she proposed to take as her text some aspects of John Stuart Mill's *The Subjection of Women.*[130] She was scarcely lacking in passion, commitment or intellect; though one could not claim she was an outstanding or original thinker. There were many other committed and capable women – Louisa Lawson, Annette Bear-Crawford, the Golding sisters, Vida Goldstein. Yet there is much to be said for the opinion of most historians that men played a relatively larger part in helping women gain the vote in Australia than elsewhere.* Women themselves were less roused to activity here than in New Zealand and most comparable countries at the time. Certainly there was nothing, for example, approaching the scale of activity of women in Finland, a country with a population much the same size as ours. We noted earlier that from 1907 the percentage of women in the Finnish national parliament ranged between seven and twenty-one†. The intensity with which the Finnish women campaigned before 1906 may be gauged from the fact that, as the Finnish National Council of Women explains, 'a general strike among women . . . was planned in case the demand for suffrage should not be accorded.'[131] Since women's

* It seems to be taking men longer to *visibly and publicly* associate themselves with the women's movement in Australia today, though there are a lot of deep but quiet sympathizers. However in 1975 the growth of men's consciousness-raising (or men-against-sexism) groups signalled the start of a breakthrough I believe absolutely crucial to women and to human liberation.

† See above, p. 45.

marches from all areas of Finland on Helsinki were also part of the campaign, it is not surprising that women's suffrage was 'accorded'. But in Australia by contrast, the Women's Christian Temperance Union's international organizer, Jessie Ackermann, said in 1913: 'I have talked to thousands of leading women and none could say how the franchise had been won . . .'[132] Referring to a talk she gave that same year to Sydney Women Graduates, Dora Montefiore, who worked in the women's movement in Australia and England, wondered whether Australian women had not 'obtained the vote before . . . prepared for it'; they had not experienced 'the long and hard fight which had been the lot of English women'; and she continued: 'I considered from my observations that in many respects Australian women were backward in organizing themselves, either politically or industrially.'[133] My reading of the New Zealand story confirms Dora Montefiore's impression.[134] Norman MacKenzie notes the comparatively slight part Australian women played in promoting the causes of Australian women from the late 1880s on, suggesting that men bulked larger in the women's cause here than in similar countries.[135] Peter Biskup endorses MacKenzie's view in relation to Western Australia, and, like Dora Montefiore, notes that Australian women made surprisingly little use of the vote once it was achieved.[136] Finally, Joan Cobb, echoing the same point, points to a derivative and imitative quality about leading Australian women, a quality historians and others have repeatedly attributed to leading circles in the community at large. New South Wales women

were, in fact, so inclined to take the lead from overseas that when they found instead that they were in possession of it, they were unable to strike out in a fresh direction.[137]

Sue Margaret Eade has recently challenged the Biskup-MacKenzie view that Australian women were somewhat passive over the suffrage campaign.[138] However, her main focus is South Australia, where foundation middle class and protestant dissenters played an important part in evolving cultural patterns. Here there might be more truth in her challenge, but far less for New South Wales; and on the wider international canvas in which MacKenzie viewed the suffrage process, he carries the day.

The reasons go deep into Australian traditions and the standing of women. By the 1880s, when the women's movement began to emerge in Australia, Australian women had settled into a standing uniquely low in Western-type communities, and from this flowed a curiously impoverished self-concept. Inevitably, that self-concept found reflection in the weakness, by international standards, of the women's movement. So that movement itself reveals unusual features about the situation of women in Australia, indeed, something distinctively Australian, which can be understood only in terms of the short history of our small tribe.

Notes

1 See, for example, 'Letters from Charlotte Bussell to her husband John G. Bussell, written from "Cattle Chosen" while he was at Bishop Hale's school in Perth, 1864.' Battye Library, Perth.

2. 'Diary of Emma Lucille Frances Thomson, wife of James Guy Thomson and Daughter of John Septimus Roe.' 1851, Battye Library, Perth.

3. Amy Hale, 'Reminiscences of Miss Amy Hale, Later Mrs Wilkinson, of Visits to Western Australia in 1854 and 1856', Battye Library, Perth.

4. Details given by Dr A. J. Hammerton in 'Feminism and Female Emigration, 1860–1914', a paper delivered to section 26, 46th ANZAAS congress, Canberra, January 1975.

5. Diaries of Mrs J. S. Maley, 1863 etc., 24 October 1863, Battye Library, Perth.

6. Mary Hargreaves, 'Homesteading and Homemaking on the Plains: A Review', *Agricultural History*, vol. 47, no. 2, April 1973, pp. 156–63.

7. Mary Gardiner's Diary, 'Sydney to Port Phillip by Sea', 14 March 1837. Royal Commonwealth Society Library, London.

8. 'Letter Written on Voyage to S. Australia of George and Sarah Norman Brunskill, to her parents in Ely, 1838/9.' State Archives of South Australia.

9. Geo. C. Morphett, ed., *William and Rosina Ferguson*. Published by the Pioneers' Association of South Australia, Adelaide, n.d., State Archives of South Australia.

10. 'Memoirs of Anna Ey', n.d. (early 1900s). Typescript, State Archives of South Australia.

11. Russel Ward, 'Two Kinds of Australian Patriotism', p. 3.

12. 'Letter written by Lucy Hart, Melbourne, to her mother, brothers and sisters in Winchester, England, 3 May 1851.' State Archives of South Australia.

13. Russel Ward, 'Two Kinds of Australian Patriotism', p. 3, citing Margaret Kiddle, *Caroline Chisholm*, Melbourne, 1957, (second edition), Appendix B, p. 251.

14. David Potter, op. cit., pp. 1, 2, and 5.

15. Henry Lawson, *Prose Works*, 2 vols, vol. 2, Angus & Robertson, Sydney, 1937, pp. 189–90.

16. Francis Adams, op. cit., p. 168.

17. Judith Wright, *Preoccupations in Australian Poetry*, pp. 138-9.

18. In A. A. D. Bayldon, newspaper cuttings, 1899–1911, Mitchell Library, p. 29. Exact source indecipherable.

19. Mrs E. M. Everton, *Reminiscences*. State Archives of South Australia.

20. 'Extracts from a Diary of Mrs John Gilbert 21 May – 7 June 1848.' State Archives of South Australia.

21. Cited in Beverley Smith, 'Early Western Australian Literature', Master of Arts thesis, University of Western Australia, 1961, p. 204.

22. A. A. D. Bayldon, newspaper cuttings, Mitchell Library, n.d., p. 34.

23. G. L. Buxton, in Frank Crowley, ed., *A New History of Australia*, Heinemann, Melbourne, 1974, Ch. 5 '1870–90', p. 179. Buxton is citing Duncan Waterson's *Squatter, Selector and Storekeeper: The Darling Downs 1859–1893*, Sydney, 1968.

24. My aunt, Dorothy Dixson, told me this in 1974.

25. Cited in Beverley Smith, op. cit., p. 33.

26. Margaret Kiddle, *Men of Yesterday. A Social History of the Western District of Victoria 1834–1890*, Melbourne University Press, 1961, pp. 91-2.

27. Mrs Campbell Praed, *My Australian Girlhood*, T. Fisher Unwin, London, 1902, p. 131.

28. Leslie Fiedler, *Love and Death in the American Novel*, Paladin, St. Albans, 1970 (1960).

29. E. H. Erikson, *Childhood and Society*, Ch. 8, 'Reflections on the American Identity'.

30. Leslie Fiedler, op. cit., p. 24.

31.   Some of my students seeking the face of women in history books have found a new avenue, and I therefore urge readers not to be discouraged by the mere absence in indexes of words such as 'woman', 'female', 'convict, female', etc. Subtlety yields unexpected rewards. 'Balance', for example, is often worth a try. It can mean sex-balance or sex-ratio.

32.   Professor Ron Neale of the University of New England first put the idea to me in this form, and for this among many other thoughts I thank him.

33.   S. H. Roberts, *The Squatting Age in Australia, 1835–1847*, Melbourne University Press, Melbourne, 1964; N. Bartley, *Australian Pioneers and Reminiscences*, Gordon & Gotch, Brisbane, 1896.

34.   Judith Murray-Prior, 'Women Settlers and Aborigines', B.A. Honours thesis, University of New England, November 1973.

35.   Douglas Pike, 'The Smallholders' Place . . .', p. 32.

36.   Geoffrey Blainey, op. cit., p. 166.

37.   June Lee, op. cit., p. 53, citing *Bush Studies*, p. 134, p. 58.

38.   Mrs R. Campbell Praed, *Australian Life, Black and White*, Chapman and Hall, London, 1885, pp. 44–50.

39.   ibid., pp. 122–3.

40.   H. Grey Bennet, *A Letter to Earl Bathurst, Secretary of State for the Colonial Department, on the Condition of the Colonies in New South Wales and Vandieman's* [sic] *Land, as set forth in the Evidence taken before the Prison Committee in 1819*, London, 1820, p. 72.

41.   Evidence of Cowper, 23 January 1821, B.T. Box 8, pp. 3343–72; Cowper to Bigge, 8 January 1821, B.T. Box 25, pp. 5626–7, cited in John Ritchie, *Punishment and Profit*, Heinemann, Melbourne, 1970, p. 198.

42.   House of Commons Select Committee on Transportation, 1837–38, p. 154.

43.   ibid., p. 197.

44.   Sir John Barrow, *New South Wales 1838. A Review of Five Pieces of Writing on New South Wales*, Royal Commonwealth Society, London, p. 484.

45.   James Bonwick, *Curious Facts of Old Colonial Days*, Sampson Low, London, 1870, p. 140.

46.   R. B. Madgwick, *Immigration into Eastern Australia, 1788–1851*, 1937, Sydney University Press reprint, 1969, p. 229.

47.   Rosemary Goddard, 'The Structure of New South Wales Society in 1828', M.A. thesis, History Department, University of Melbourne, 1967, p. 157.

48. Joan Cobb, 'The History of the Female Convict Factory at Parramatta', p. 17.

49. C. M. H. Clark, *Select Documents in Australian History, 1851–1900*, Angus and Robertson, Melbourne, 1968, p. 663.

50. Barbara Welter, 'The Cult of True Womanhood: 1820–1860' in Thomas E. Frazier, ed., *The Underside of American History*, vol. 1, to 1877, Harcourt Brace Jovanovich, New York, 1971.

51. Roger Thompson, op. cit., p. 11.

52. Gerda Lerner, op. cit., p. 9.

53. A. W. Calhoun, *A Social History of the American Family from Colonial Times to the Present*, 2 vols, vol. 2, A. Clark, Cleveland, 1918, p. 109.

54. William O'Neill, op. cit., p. 18.

55. Roger Thompson, op. cit., p. 65.

56. ibid., p. 21.

57. ibid., p. 31.

58. ibid., p. 29.

59. ibid., p. 30.

60. 'Fifty Years After', *Observer*, 13 August 1961.

61. Roger Thompson, op. cit., pp. 4–5.

62. Cited in A. W. Calhoun, op. cit., vol. 2, pp. 110–111.

63. Roger Thompson, op. cit., p. 105.

64. Norman MacKenzie, op. cit., p. 83.

65. Russel Ward, *The Australian Legend*, pp. 88–9.

66. E. Erikson, *Childhood and Society*, p. 234.

67. Joan Cobb, 'The History of the Female Convict Factory at Parramatta'; and 'The Women's Movement in New South Wales 1880–1914', M.A. thesis, History Department, University of New England, 1966 (hereafter, 'The Women's Movement').

68. Judith Murray-Prior, op. cit.

69. For an exploration of this element, see Calvin Hernton, *Sex and Racism*, Paladin, London, 1970.

70. Leslie Fiedler, op. cit., p. 24.

71. As examples of this approach one can instance N. Bartley, op. cit., S. H. Roberts, op. cit., and Eve Pownall, *Mary of Maranoa*, F. H. Johnston, Sydney, 1959.

72. Judith Murray-Prior, op. cit.

73. See, for example, Roger Thompson, op. cit., pp. 104ff., for Mrs Preston, 1622, in Virginia; Mary Rowlandson, 1670s, Massachusetts; and Mrs Drummer, 1639, York.

74. John Hood, *Australia and the East* . . ., Murray, London, 1843, p. 309.

75. John A. La Nauze, cited in Craig McGregor, op. cit., p. 54.

76. Rosalie Stephenson, *Women in Australian Society*, Heinemann Educational Australia, South Yarra, Vic., 1970, pp. 3-4.

77. A. A. Phillips, *The Australian Tradition*, F. W. Cheshire, Melbourne, 1958, p. 88.

78. Michael Roe, *Quest for Authority in Eastern Australia 1835-1851*, Melbourne University Press and A.N.U. Press, 1965, p. 201.

79. ibid., p. 195.

80. Philip Slater, op. cit., p. 73.

81. Kate Millett, *Sexual Politics*, Rupert Hart-Davis, London, 1969, p. 49.

82. Hunter to Portland, 10 August 1796, Despatch No. 13, *H.R.A.*, series 1, vol. 1, p. 574.

83. Lady Forbes, *Sydney Society in Crown Colony Days (being the Personal Reminiscences of the late Lady Forbes)*, edited for publication by George Forbes, Mitchell Library, pp. 46, 132.

84. Michael Roe, op. cit., p. 205.

85. New South Wales Legislative Council, *Votes and Proceedings*, 17 July 1838, cited in Michael Roe, op. cit., p. 36.

86. Michael Roe, op. cit., p. 43.

87. ibid., p. 204.

88. Joan Cobb, 'The Women's Movement'.

89. See Catherine Cleverdon, *The Woman Suffrage Movement in Canada*, University of Toronto Press, 1950.

90. State Councils affiliated to the National Council of Women between 1899 and 1911. Not all refused to support women's franchise. See for example *The First Fifty Years: History of the National Council of Women of Queensland*, The Council, Brisbane, 1959.

91. Manuscript Minutes, 1896, National Council of Women, cited in Joan Cobb, 'The Women's Movement', pp. 115-16.

92. Manuscript minutes of the Women's Club. In the possession of the Club, Elizabeth Street, Sydney. Cited in Joan Cobb, 'The Women's Movement', p. 101.

93. Manuscript minutes of the National Council of Women. At the Council's offices in Philip Street, Sydney. Cited in Joan Cobb, ibid., p. 102.

94. J. A. Froude, *Oceania or England and Her Colonies*, Longmans, Green, London, 1886, p. 191.

95. Geoffrey Serle, *From Deserts the Prophets Come*, pp. 52-5.

96. Marilyn Seaton, 'The Mid Victorian Ideal of Womanhood: its Pertinence and Veracity', History Honours thesis, University of Western Australia, 1971, pp. 43-4.

97. Ada Cambridge, *Thirty Years in Australia*, Methuen, London, 1903, p. 87.

98. Jill Roe, 'The Case of Ada Cambridge', op. cit., pp. 389, 400.

99. Mary Gilmore to her husband, 15 December 1899, cited in W. H. Wilde, 'Mary Gilmore – The Hidden Years', *Meanjin*, no. 4, 1973, p. 426.

100. Ada Cambridge, op. cit., p. 87.

101. Select Committee on the Employment of Children, Progress Report, New South Wales Legislative Assembly, *Votes and Proceedings*, 1875-6, vol. 6, p. 895. See too Beverley Kingston, 'Domestic Service as a Career for Girls in Australia in the late Nineteenth Century', *Refractory Girl*, Summer 1974-1975, pp. 4-9.

102. The movement made very little impact on our working class women. I came across a fascinating item of misreporting on this in Paris, in La Bibliothèque Marguérite Durande. On 9 January 1910, *La Française* said the Australian feminist cause claimed 'l'adhésion des masses ouvrières féminines . . . de l'Australie'.

103. Joan Cobb, 'The Women's Movement', pp. 3, 55-6, 86.

104. Roger Fulford, *Votes for Women*, Faber and Faber, London, 1957, p. 100.

105. For America: Eleanor Flexner, *Century of Struggle. The Woman's Rights Movement in the United States*, Belknap Press, Cambridge, Mass., 1959; Aileen S. Kraditor, *The Ideas of the Woman Suffrage Movement, 1890–1920*, Columbia University Press, New York, 1965; W. L. O'Neill, op. cit.; Andrew Sinclair, *The Better Half, The Emancipation of the American Woman*, Harper and Row, New York, 1965. For Canada: Catherine Cleverdon, op. cit., passim.

106. Virginia Crawford, 'Feminism in France', *Fortnightly Review*, vol. 67, 1897, p. 525.

107. Léopold Lacour, *Trois Femmes de la Révolution*, Plon-Nourrit, Paris, 1900.

108. Susan Margaret Eade, 'A Study of Catherine Helen Spence 1825–1910', M.A. thesis, History Department, School of General Studies, Australian National University, Canberra, 1971.

109. Gulli Högbom, 'Historique de l'Association des Femmes Universitaires en Suède, (Kvinnliga Akademikers Förening) to c. 1950'. Kindly sent to the author by Dr Karin Tarschys, Stockholm.

110. See Louise Nystrom-Hamilton, *Ellen Key. Her Life and Her Work*, Putnam's, New York, 1913. Louise Nystrom-Hamilton shows that Ellen Key's family took the life of the mind very seriously. Her father was a minor nobleman and founder of the Agrarian Party. For the quality of Ellen Key's thought, see, for example, her books *The Century of the Child* (Putnam's, New York, 1909), and *War, Peace and the Future* (Putnam, New York, 1916).

111. Joan Cobb, 'The History of the Female Convict Factory at Parramatta', p. 7.

112. J. Backhouse, op. cit., pp. 466-7.

113. S. W. Brooks, op. cit., p. 14.

114. Joan Cobb, 'The History of the Female Convict Factory at Parramatta', pp. 28–30.

115. House of Commons Select Committee on Transportation, 1837–38, p. 231.

116. Joan Cobb, 'The History of the Female Convict Factory at Parramatta', p. 20.

117. R. C. Hutchinson, op. cit., pp. 52–3.

118. Charlotte Anley, *The Prisoners of Australia*, J. Hatchard, London, 1841, pp. 18–29.

119. R. and F. Hill, op. cit., p. 277.

120. Joan Cobb, 'The Women's Movement', pp. 77–8.

121. Frances Gillan Holden, *Woman's Ignorance and the World's Need. A Plea for Physiology*, George Robertson, Melbourne, 1883 (signed 1878), p. 14.

122. Mrs Alexander Hirst, *Australasia*, Kegan Paul, Trench, Trübner, London, 1900, pp. 287–8, pp. 8–24.

123. See, for example, *Women in Social Life. The Transactions of The Social Section of the International Congress of Women*, London, July 1899, T. Fisher Unwin, London, 1900.

124. Geoffrey Serle, *The Golden Age*, Melbourne University Press, 1968.

125.   Rachel Cookson, 'The Role of Certain Women and Women's Organisations in Politics in New South Wales and Victoria between 1900 and 1920', B.A. Hons. thesis, Department of Government, University of Sydney, 1959, p. 51.

126.   Vida Goldstein in *Woman's Sphere*, October 1900, p. 16.

127.   Ivy Brooks in the introduction to Helen E. Gillan, *A Brief History of the National Council of Women of Victoria 1902–1945*, Spectator, Melbourne, 1959, [1945].

128.   Rose Scott Papers, Mitchell Library, uncat. ms. 38, 1, n.d.

129.   ibid., p. 8.

130.   ibid., p. 70.

131.   Marjatte Jannes for the National Council of Women of Finland, *40 Years of Woman Suffrage in Finland*, Helsinki, 1947, p. 3.

132.   Jessie Ackermann, *Australia from a Woman's Point of View*, Cassell, London, 1913, p. 210.

133.   Dora Montefiore, *From a Victorian to a Modern*, E. Archer, London, 1927, p. 138.

134.   Patricia Grimshaw, *Women's Suffrage in New Zealand*, Auckland University Press, 1971.

135.   Norman MacKenzie, op. cit., p. 52.

136.   Peter Biskup, 'The Westralian Feminist Movement', *University Studies in Western Australian History*, October 1959, vol. 3, no. 3, pp. 71–84.

137.   Joan Cobb, 'The Women's Movement', p. 183.

138.   Susan Margaret Eade, op. cit.

Chapter 7

Into the 1980s!

'Women need solidarity . . . to work on broad human projects that turn out to be mainly in their hands . . .'
> (DOROTHY DINNERSTEIN, *The Mermaid and the Minotaur*)

By the 1980s, in a society rent by massive contradiction and uncertainty, a question central to western feminism had made its appearance on the agenda of Australian women: greater autonomy. As they sought the higher public status essential to that greater autonomy, a minority of women won gains outlined by the women's movement for a century or more.

The present chapter sketches these gains and some of the obstacles which now block their fuller achievement. That in turn leads to the unspoken agendas and psychic costs of what has happened so far. We uncover a central conflict within and between women – the conflict between the demands of autonomy and nurturance.[1] The conflict is central to the divisions in the women's movement and to the silence with which most women have greeted what may well prove the key to future social development: greater female autonomy, the movement's core demand.

For the majority of women in the 1980s, issues of autonomy entered their world largely in subliminal fashion, or as a potential rather than a reality: only a minority of female pattern-setters had won the reality of fuller autonomy. In a limited but significant way, this minority achieved higher status in the public sphere, and in the process generated ripple effects throughout the Australian community. The project of fuller female autonomy ranks among the significant historical dramas of the late twentieth century. Despite still formidable external barriers, many of the major remaining obstacles to fuller autonomy for women are to be found within and between women. As Australian women in the 1980s confront an existential dilemma, this paradox provides the hidden script of our seventh chapter on women and identity. But what precipitated the process?

To answer the question and begin to grasp its meaning for women today, we must first turn to history, to the nineteenth century when western middle-class women achieved astonishing gains in status. (As we see later, these were shot through with ambivalent implications.) Gains largely in terms of the roles of mother and wife, they brought an increase in domestic or private power. However constricted or defective that power appears when we compare it with today's possibilities for fuller autonomy, at the time it was unmatched in quality and unparalleled in scale. The real and imagined dividends arising from this change of course took on very different meanings according to class and national context – for example, the dividends did not operate for Australian women as they operated for American women. But in contemporary dress and with massive power those dividends persist today, and the majority of women are doubtful about or flatly unwilling to exchange them for fuller autonomy. For such autonomy appears to threaten the progress made in domestic power, and that progress brought greater fulfilment of women's need for nurturance. Thus most women experience today's challenge of fuller autonomy in terms of profound inner conflict: as a dubious trade-off against precious nurturance needs and domestic power, but also as a star which beckons irresistibly even while it terrifies. And our paradox is compounded: for this ambivalence about autonomy applies to feminists quite as much as to anti-feminists; and beyond both, to the majority who answer each group with silence.

Examining Australia in the context of comparable societies, this book has proposed a significant and consistent lag in the status of women throughout a brief history. During the 1970s the lag did not close but it became less marked, and a real advance occurred for women. Those who gained most were part of a highly visible and articulate minority which operates as general pattern-setter for women, and so Australia has only begun to experience ripple effects from the advance. In colonial Australia, a minority of white middle-class women served as the significant pattern-setters. Their contemporary successors can be found among today's visible and articulate minority, and within it, especially among aspiring, junior or middle-echelon members of a new corporate élite which acts as vanguard. Nineteenth century middle-class pattern-setters sometimes adopted forms of nineteenth century feminism, generally 'domestic feminism', the public counterpart of the new private or domestic power exercised by urban middle-class women.[2] Where they are feminists, today's aspiring or successful members of the new corporate élite tend to embrace diluted forms of contemporary American reform feminism, though other kinds of feminism play an important part (for example, the role of radical feminism has been critical). And once alerted by feminists, certain socialists (mostly centralist-socialist) embraced feminism, rapidly setting their stamp to an unusual degree upon its thinking in this country.

Whether in the bureaucracy, media, the teaching and helping professions or management, the new élite women are usually genuine, and sometimes passionate, about their feminism. They embrace it as sincerely as the sixteenth century western bourgeoisie embraced the protestant religion, or its late eighteenth century counterpart the ideals of liberty and equality. And however central the role of new élite women, in one form or another feminism has taken stubborn root among women well outside their ranks. Indeed it now operates beyond gender as an independent historical dynamic in Australian society and has already altered community awareness in both tangible and unconscious ways. If feminism can develop so as to meet the fateful new challenges of the late twentieth century, it may go far toward changing the way Australians construct their social reality. It could alter the entire institutional fabric, for our gender script – which radical feminism threw into central focus – lies close to the core of that fabric. Whether this happens depends largely on whether feminism can progress beyond the 1970s forms which claim it at present: for as we show later, despite their new (largely government- and bureaucracy-inspired) visibility, such forms now threaten to condemn feminists to marginality if not a dead end in terms of deeper community imperatives.

Charting the recent advance in status of Australian women, the emergence of feminism in the 1970s, and the prospects for a new feminism relevant to the tasks of the late twentieth century, we begin with a broad-brush sketch of the corporate system which assumed clearer shape after the end of the second world war.

After 1945, the Australian economy became more capital intensive. Bureaucrats, managers, professionals and experts, assisted by
an invasive mass media, functioned as the muscle of big government, big business and big unions. Together they formed the nerve
centre of the corporate system and its agencies. The 'individual' who
typified an earlier stage of the industrial revolution is being sup-
planted by a new ideal type: over-administered, mass man and mass
woman, who are most visible in urban areas. Mass man and mass
woman are perfect consumers in the making, ideally passive and
compliant. But their triumph is far from universal. Even today they
represent at best a powerful tendency – though exceptions are
shrinking in number and confidence. For its part, the Australian
family now labours under unparalleled stress. The family certainly
continues to function as a partly separate, protective space in which
'authentic human alternatives to market relations and values [still
hold], however shakily and imperfectly,' and contributes vitally to
preserving 'the human face and the human scale even through bleak
and awesome times'.[3] But as a separate psychic space the family is
increasingly invaded by the combined and controlling influences of
the media, the expert and the professional, which, to a growing
extent, cross the boundaries of ethnic, regional and class difference.
From infancy the child is now more directly raised ('socialized') not
by her imperfect parents, but by extra-familial agencies of the corporate system: by the media, and by educational, welfare and health
experts. Crucial to the shaping of the ideal consumer, these agencies
(whatever the avowed ideologies of individuals within them), have
helped diminish the child's potential for autonomy as an adult, as
over decades they have significantly eroded parental confidence and
authority within the family. Thus in asserting women's need for
fuller autonomy, women face more formidable barriers than first
meets the eye. Overall, the agencies of corporatism have played an
indispensable part in altering the mode of authority informing the
social fabric. We now see the emergence of a new form of male
domination or code of authority. For personal authority, this substitutes an impersonal, bureaucratic, 'rational' form of male domination, one excellently suited to the corporate system.[4] Feminists who
see this substitution as a gain for female power against male power
are tragically misled: the confidence of the individual mother, hence

daughter and woman, is threatened just as much as that of the individual father, hence man. *Citizen* autonomy stands at serious risk in the face of impersonal, machine-like forces of male domination in its corporate shape.

Economic change in the decades since 1945 sheds light on both the drive to fuller autonomy among women and the resistance it evokes from them. A long-term increase in female and a long-term decrease in male paid employment[5] underpins a good deal of the thrust to autonomy, while the accelerated suburbanization made possible by such change, helps explain the fear, hostility and silence with which so many women respond to that thrust.* After 1945, migrant labour and overseas capital led a long boom, but by the 1970s, recession and structural economic change began to bite deep, signalled by a decline in the proportion of workers in both primary and secondary industry. However the proportion engaged in the service or tertiary sector, a major area for women, expanded. Although responding late to change, by the second half of the 1960s or early 1970s, the economy had begun to apply new technologies to certain long-established industries and to deploy resources away from older low-skilled to newer high-skilled industries.

After the war, with women in administrative, clerical, executive, professional and technical employment leading the way, a sharp drop in family size took place, and with it a drop in the age of completed fertility. By 1976 annual marital fertility rates were lower than they had ever been.[6] Along with late-arriving new Anglo-American attitudes towards women's autonomy, these demographic changes helped ensure that women, especially married women, would continue their steady move into the paid workforce, and by 1980 married women made up 39.6 per cent of the employed civil population.[7] Yet Australian gender-role perceptions continued to be solidly traditional, so that women and men alike continued to see women chiefly in the roles of wife and mother.[8]

Within manufacturing, the light consumer goods – textiles, footwear and electrical appliances for example – absorbed large

---

*Post-war suburbanization intensified an extremely powerful tendency towards domesticity which predated but gained impetus from the 1880s onset of suburbanization. That domesticity constitutes one of feminism's strongest obstacles in the 1980s.

numbers of women in repetitive and low-paid work.[9] No matter how these opportunities are rated, rural women, black and white, missed out on them, as they fell to migrant[10] and other unskilled women based in the city. Here, in the mushrooming service sector, women also constituted a big proportion of salespersons, clerks, typists, telephonists, and tellers in wholesale, retail, banking and insurance industries. But from the start women also gained modestly at middle and sometimes senior level in the tertiary sector. Before the 1970s, lobbying by women lessened the gap between male and female average weekly earnings (lobbies included the National Council of Women, the Women's Electoral Lobby and the Union of Australian Women). Success was registered in notable decisions handed down by arbitration authorities in 1958, 1969, 1972 and 1974, but despite these and other gains at later dates, recent statistics continue to reveal a 'remarkable difference', 'a continuing wide disparity' between male and female average weekly earnings.[11]

After 1974 the long boom collapsed. Australia's tariff-sheltered industries wilted under many combined blows: our own long-standing structural maladjustments, rural droughts of cruel stubbornness and intensity, moves offshore by capital in search of more competitive labour costs. And to them we must add the rise of new and economically more efficient international rivals and the onset of global recession. To date our response to this batch of challenges has been dismayingly ineffective in economic terms while in social terms our response has resulted in a steady increase of centralization and bureaucratization, and has thus intensified existing tendencies to deskill the labour and diminish the autonomy of the citizen. Seeking fuller autonomy for women, feminism has therefore encountered many barriers.

In the major transformation of economic base which confronts us, automation and microelectronics will continue to be important in rationalizing and restructuring it, causing further shedding of the less skilled in favour of smaller numbers of technicians and professionals in female-labour salient productive and service sectors alike. We can instance banking, with new-generation technology such as electronic telling machines; insurance, where the number of female workers falls with the advent of ever more sophisticated computers, microfiche and word processors; commerce, where self-service and computerized point-of-sale terminals threaten to convert supermarkets into ghost emporiums. Libraries emerged from the 1970s with males increasingly prominent in senior and administrative positions, and apparently set to control the new library technology. Also significant for women is the expanded use of word processors and cutbacks in public-sector funding[12], heavily affecting officers of the fourth division where women are over-represented. An econometric model developed by the Industries Assistance Commission (the 'IMPACT' model) predicted a displacement of 1.6 million jobs by the 1990s, and in 1980, the Committee of Inquiry into Technological Change in Australia nominated women as a group likely to bear 'the larger burden of adjustment to technological change'.[13]

Both main political parties agreed. Opening the National Conference on Women and Technological Change in July 1982, the then-Federal Minister for Employment and Industrial Relations in the Liberal-National Party administration said that 'current microprocessor technologies' might have 'the greatest direct employment impact in the clerical, sales, and service areas, where women tend to be concentrated'.[14] Similarly, Labor leader Hawke's 1983 election policy speech identified women as 'most susceptible' to rapid technological change.[15] In 1976 Dame Margaret Guilfoyle, Federal Minister for Social Security, reported that 80 per cent or 3.2 million of her department's clients were women, and during the 1980s government instrumentalities reported that the 'feminization of poverty' was intesifying.[16] In 1982 the National Women's Advisory Council called for assurances that women were 'not asked to bear the brunt of economic downturn'.[17] If feminism has done nothing else (and it has), it can claim that discourse on economic futures in the late twentieth century might well marginalize but will find it hard to ignore the specifics of women's situation.

The current employment situation of women suggests paradox. Given the contraction of traditional male industries such as iron and steel, coal and building, recession has accelerated the post-1945 shift in overall employment toward female labour, with the number of women growing about twice as fast as men[18] (an increasing percentage of women work part time).[19] On the other hand the gross incidence of female unemployment after 1974 was greater than male, [20] and among young women for example, at about 23 per cent, it was a good deal greater. Why, among women, do we see growing employment on the one hand, and growing unemployment on the other? Briefly, while a majority of women have been hit hard by recession, a minority have done well, and sex segregation of the labour market is the prime culprit. Within a sex-segmented labour market, about half of all women workers cluster into five, generally low-skilled occupational groups which are extremely vulnerable to technological change. Moreover particular groups of women were unusually disadvantaged, with estimates of female migrant unemployment at about 22 per cent [21] and in July 1979, of Aboriginal women at about 25 per cent.[22] Some two-thirds of unemployed teenage women continued to seek work in the industries of greatest female unemployment, such as the clerical and sales areas which our main socializing agencies (family, media and school) continue to emphasize. Hence within Australia's total unemployment figure (10.7 per cent in March 1983) unskilled, inexperienced, young, migrant and black women were greatly over-represented. Yet a minority of women was outstripping not only less skilled women but significant groups of men.*

Where private industry is upgrading through automation and microelectronics, more highly educated and/or experienced Australian women are fast replacing younger, migrant and less-educated women. Thus for example, between 1974 and 1979 women's employment improved in finance, insurance and business services by 2.8 per cent (though technology threatened retrenchment here too) and in entertainment and recreational services by 2.5 per cent. However the big advance for women occurred in the government sector, where the annual rate of increase was 3.2 per cent between June 1974 and June 1977. Community services, for example, increased its female workforce over that period by 20.2 per cent, public administration and communications by 20.3 per cent[23], while in April 1983 the number of women in senior positions in the public sector reached the highest level ever recorded.[24]

In its submission to the 1980 O.E.C.D. conference on women's

---

*These include men socially considered as the classic breadwinners of the late twenties to forties age bracket. The urban members of this bracket are beginning at last to join their rural counterparts long familiar with displacement.

employment, Australia proposed an hypothesis to explain the paradox of a simultaneous contraction and growth in female paid work over the years 1974–78: '… the labour market for females is split into two distinct segments, one of which was buoyant over the four years because of growth in the "non-market" sector of the economy while the other was even more depressed than the corresponding market for male labour'.[25] The women who have conspicuously improved their position are a small but significant minority, and the case for an advance in Australian women's status applies in the first instance to them. But partly because they are visible and highly articulate, they are major pattern-setters for all women, so their gains have begun to generate pressures with a profound influence throughout the community. They are also central to our current questioning of gender role and this contribution, though indirect, can hardly be underestimated. For male-dominated society has repeatedly accommodated shifts in its patterns of hierarchy and domination (whether non-class or class in form). But it cannot survive a fundamental change in gender role.[26]

We turn now to issues of women, identity and status in selected areas of politics, the unions, the professions and the church. In politics, first the Labor Party.

Nineteenth century feminism found its way into the Labor Party from the start, but was then and remained until recently greatly limited by the party's 'mateship' ambience and the overall weakness of Australian feminism. Because it was a middle-class movement, Australian feminism was constricted in its ideological and social impact, and the main reasons for these limitations overlap with historical influences accounting for the constricted nature of the Australian middle class itself. Those influences can be schematically outlined in terms of interaction between two forces: on the one hand, as compared to similar societies, the relative material poverty, cultural thinness and lack of self-confidence of all elements of the Australian élite, including the pattern-setting middle class; and on the other hand, the relative, indeed internationally unique, confidence of the 'lower orders', though not of its women. We have also noted the lack of overall confidence of urban pre-working-class English and peasant Irish women; convictism intensified but did not originate this long-standing condition. In Australia female bonding was unusually weak among such women, partly because of the unusual strength of male bonding (mateship). That strength helps account for the unique input of such males into the Australian national identity along with the unusual power of the unions and the Labor Party.

Late twentieth century Australian women carry with them the heritage of their brief history, the more powerful because it remains largely unacknowledged. Throughout the west during the industrial and post-industrial eras, middle-class men have had no easy time with issues of male identity. But the experience of working-class men has been especially difficult. Hence in Australia, the Labor Party with its trade union base, has proved more wary of women than the Liberal Party, and thus more wary about allowing Labor women to share in decision making. And so while women registered important advances during the time of the Whitlam Federal Labor administration (1972 - 75), Labor women lagged well behind their Liberal counterparts in terms of power within party decision-making structures. In 1978 the A.L.P. established a National Committee of Inquiry into Labor's policies and structure. The Committee identified 'women' as a central concern. To women – 'the group most neglected by the A.L.P.' – the Party's appeal 'may not be all it could be'. The Committee 'recognized'

that the problem is not one peculiar to the A.L.P., but that the sources of this discrimination lie deep-rooted in Australian attitudes, perhaps particularly in the attitude of mateship, traditionally strong in the Australian Labor Party. And it is sustained by the role structures of women in Australian society ... and by the nature of other institutions ... including some unions ...

In the 10 per cent of Australian unions affiliated with the A.L.P. and representing 'the great majority of the Australian workforce', women were 'not commonly' found in positions of influence, and here again, the Committee pointed to mateship: 'the tradition of mateship, reflecting the solidarity of individual unions, encourages the principle that a mate is first supported for elected positions ...' 'Some means of removing the oppression of women by the spirit of mateship must be found.'[27] The A.L.P. National Committee of Inquiry (N.C.I.) recommended measures to give women a significantly stronger presence in the party's organization, public image and policies. (The Committee had noted one submission that alleged women would have been 'better off being whales' during the 1977 Federal election campaign.) Labor women throughout Australia were quick to appraise and publicize the N.C.I. report. Operating through state branches, they often took pains to find out the views of rank-and-file Labor women, using mass meetings, day workshops and questionnaires. ('I am nobody's fraternally anything!', ran an exasperated aside on one questionnaire. As we also see later in the protests of Christian feminists, language conditions gender role at stubborn and subliminal sources.) In 1983, Senator Susan Ryan, then Minister Assisting the Prime Minister on the Status of Women and Minister for Education and Youth Affairs, could look back to 1981 and discern a 'real sense of dissatisfaction and frustration amongst Labor women'.[28] But in July that year the A.L.P. national conference endorsed a policy of positive discrimination and resolved that over a ten-year period, the party should guarantee women representation in State and Federal parliaments in numbers proportional to their party membership (about 30 per cent). With this and other advances, A.L.P. women could look forward to real change in the 1980s.

In the first seventy-five years after Federation, only sixteen women had ever been elected to Federal parliament. In the House of Representatives, until well into 1981 only four women had ever held seats, but by 1982 there were twelve women in all. The three women in the House were Labor, while in the Senate, four were Labor and four were Liberal-National Party. Although the gap between Labor and non-Labor votes had narrowed during the 1970s, women still tended to be more conservative in their voting than men (there are sharp age-based differences within them as a group).[29] Hence during (as distinct from after) the 1983 election campaign, politicians across the party spectrum perceived 'the family' as a bigger vote-catcher than 'women', hoping to appeal to women while not alienating men, and so, for one thing, the appeals of the Women's Electoral Lobby, dramatically effective a decade earlier, drew little overt response.[30] The Liberal-National Party Coalition subsumed the concerns of women under the heading of the family: 'We are the family party', said the coalition leader and then-Prime Minister Malcolm Fraser in announcing Liberal Party policy on 15

February.[31] Fraser pointed to earlier family-related achievements of his administration, specifying increased family allowances and child-care finance, and promising new child-care projects along with improved old age pension assistance. Women's issues were somewhat more prominent in the policy speech of Labor leader Hawke, but nevertheless 'women' fell among the four areas given least wordage ('women' ran two lines ahead of 'sport', eight lines ahead of 'rural policy' and three behind 'Aborigines'). 'Labor', said Mr Hawke, possessed 'a comprehensive women's affairs policy'. Labor recognized women's lack of full equality with men, named women as 'most susceptible' to rapid technological change, and promised immediate Commonwealth Sex Discrimination legislation over a wide range of issues including employment and education.[32]

According to the Liberal Party, the 'special concerns of women' must be considered within 'the framework of individual policy areas',[33] while the effective pursuit of women's concerns demanded a more robust economy. Such an economy would be characterized by 'vigorous and adaptive private enterprise in all areas of industry', and would demonstrate a positive respect for 'the stimulus of competition'.[34]

Issues the Party identified as specifically relating to women derived ultimately from principles of nineteenth century liberal individualism which the Party deeply respected. However their application to women was largely ignored until forced into party-political discourse by the Women's Electoral Lobby after 1972.[35] By 1982 the Liberal Party Federal Platform specified such matters as 'equality of opportunity and freedom of choice to engage in political, civil and community activities, employment and education', together with 'removal of remaining areas of discrimination against women', 'encouragement of training and re-training schemes for women wishing to re-enter the workforce', child-care facilities, 'the realignment of working hours to accord with family responsibilities, and the encouragement of arrangements for part-time work ...' The Platform placed central stress on an essentially nuclear family:

The family is the fundamental and most important social and cohesive force in society and should be encouraged to take the primary responsibility for the care and development of children and providing for its members a source of personal happiness, economic security and social and psychological support. Liberals acknowledge the vital contribution of the family in the development of the individual.

In its section headed 'Women', the Platform gave 'recognition [to] the vital role of women in the stability and development of the family', and upheld the 'opportunity and choice for mothers to fulfil their family role...' Despite an increasing divergence from it in hard fact, this ideal continues to command broad consensus in Australia.

Women possess considerable power in the Liberal Party, and if they want something strongly enough, they can probably get it. Where they are feminists, Liberal women tend to be domestic feminists[36], though again, increasingly, exceptions can be found. For example, after the 1983 elections, the founders of the Victorian Liberal Feminist Network were reported to say: 'despite the equal representation which the Liberal Party gives women in Victoria, its own influential women tend to be highly conservative and traditional...' Domestic feminism has exerted a formidable female power on behalf of gender-role stability, but maintains a low public profile. Most Liberal women were thus not as eager as Labor women for political visibility, and the Liberal Feminist reproach to Liberalism's 'influential' women concluded: 'with a few notable exceptions [they] have not stood for preselection or actively sought out potential women candidates to groom for office.'[37] Recent A.L.P. women's initiatives no doubt helped prompt Liberal feminist dissatisfaction, but Liberal and non-Labor women had nevertheless long been pacemakers in the Australian party system. The first woman elected to any Australian parliament was a Westralian Nationalist returned in 1921, and the first women elected in all other states also represented non-Labor parties (N.S.W. 1925, Queensland 1929, Victoria 1933, Tasmania 1955, S.A. 1955). The first woman member of the House of Representatives was the United Australia Party's Dame Enid Lyons in 1943. The constitution of the Federal Liberal Party, since its foundation in the 1940s, has directed that certain organizational positions be reserved expressly for women. The constitution also provided for a Federal Women's Committee, and a guarantee of high-level representation in all State Party branches: in N.S.W. in 1981 for example, two of the four vice-presidents were women, while in Victoria women were guaranteed equal representation at all levels. All State branches had some form of separate women's organization. In 1981 three State branches elected women presidents, while in the Young Liberal Movement, this was true of five of the State branches.[38]

The National Party is widely held to be the backbone of Australian conservatism. Like rural Australia itself, its philosophy and policies are distorted where not obliterated by an urban-oriented media, intelligentsia and power structure. Essentially urban and middle class, feminism is in general at best insensitive towards issues specific to the rural sector or to class divisions within it.[39] Indeed most feminists appear to have little time for rural women, though they list them in token fashion under headings such as 'disadvantaged', and praise them for nobleness (fortitude in the face of drought and rural depression, etc.). National Party women now participate confidently in its conferences and appear increasingly, though in modest numbers, on decision-making committees. Yet, measured in programme and structure, women's visible presence significantly trails that of Labor and Liberal women.[40] Country women are certainly not satisfied with their visible political role: one former National Party Senate candidate, for example, her background 'conservative in the extreme', and for years State president of the Country Women's Association, believed that country women were increasingly prone to 'resent patronising attitudes from men'. 'If men keep on refusing to take women seriously, they might even form a party of their own.'[41] Any list of reasons for the scarcity of feminist initiatives in the National Party could begin by recognizing women's solidarity with a rural community in basic ways at odds with and excluded from urban-dominated Australia. Though ready to concede that Black solidarity and working-class solidarity might be authentic for Aboriginal and working-class women, feminists generally appear unaware of rural parallels. The rural solidarity which helps undercut feminism is fed by rural fears about urban union bureaucrats and the centralist urban thrust of Labor government. Also important however is the fact that a remarkable number of country women now play indispensable and recognized roles in maintaining embattled family farms[42], while gender role itself tends to work better in the country where the family is more cohesive. Rural families still appear to provide rather more of a 'haven in a heartless world' than their urban counterparts.

The year 1983 was to see a new impetus in the drive to raise the status of women in Australia. To begin with, the total number of women in the new parliament rose from twelve to eighteen, thirteen of them A.L.P., an increase partly reflecting the efforts of Labor women. We noted that by the 1970s new élite women had gained more than other women (and many men) from the new forms of polarization characterizing corporate society. Thus the massive increase of welfare and education experts now found clear reflection in the expanded power of A.L.P. women, while Liberal women, traditionally in a stronger position within the party organization, were beginning to reappraise strategies and manoeuvre for greater impact. By 1983 feminist initiatives had lodged women's concerns more securely within Australian political parties, and during the following year, those initiatives would begin to bear fruit.

The Whitlam Labor administration had taken important initial steps towards implementing such reforms as equal pay, a minimum wage for women, and paid maternity leave. The administration ratified the International Labor Organization Convention on discrimination, and set up Federal and State committees to carry its work further. It also set up anti-discrimination legislation in some States[43], together with certain programmes and services for women covering employment[44], women's refuges and child-care centres. During the seventies, formal and verbal public acceptance of elementary ideas about women's rights became a little more widespread, while there were signs of increased understanding of sex role stereotyping. If progress in all these areas remained slim, one major reason was the economic recession which dated from the early 1970s and weighed heavily on the Hawke Labor Government in 1983. Nevertheless Labor, by then holding office in most States, attempted to press ahead with its women's rights programme. On 2 June 1983 Senator Susan Ryan introduced the Sex Discrimination Bill 1983 'to give effect to certain provisions of the U.N. Convention on the Elimination of All Forms of Discrimination against women'. This included discrimination on the ground of sex, marital status, or pregnancy in the areas of employment, education and accommodation.[45] With this Australia had begun to challenge the United States in the field of women's rights, for the United States signed but failed to ratify the U.N. Convention, while the Equal Rights' Amendment to the Constitution was stalemated. From the start Labor politicians were alert to community fear about gender issues, though it is not clear to what extent they appreciated their extraordinary sensitivity and thus respected such fear. Thus in July the Minister for Foreign Affairs and the Federal Attorney General joined Senator Ryan in insisting that Labor's ratification of the U.N. Convention 'would not force women into the workforce, children into creches, ... lead to a unisex society, [or] give power to anyone outside Australia to make laws for Australia'.[46] Labor also proposed educational reform for women. In August 1983 Senator Ryan, as Minister for Education and Youth Affairs, announced that her Government proposed a 'programme for the elimination of sexism in education.' Among other things, Labor would fund projects to improve education for girls (with equal access to computer education), encourage the development of non-sexist teaching materials, and require the Schools Commission to report on the impact of all its programmes on the education of girls.[47] Labor also planned an affirmative action programme in relation to women. In all Government instrumentalities, and in companies over a certain size, management would be required to reassess recruitment and other policies in relation to women. Companies would submit forward programmes to a new Government body, the Affirmative Action Commission. Where these were deemed unsatisfactory, Government would bring pressure to bear where companies had Commonwealth contracts. Where no such contracts existed, the Government might refer cases to the Human Rights Commission, and hence to parliament or a Federal court.

By the 1980s, Australian women could also report certain advances in the trade union movement. Australian unions enjoy an order of legitimacy in the national value structure[48] and a degree of power which is unmatched internationally, but they have not proved eager to accommodate women or women's issues. During the 1970s, while the level of membership in unions of male employees remained constant at about 60 per cent, the union membership of women rose from about 36 per cent of women employees in 1970 to 47 per cent in 1979.[49] Women's advance to positions of influence in our unions is very late, ironically in part because of the internationally unique standing working-class males occupy in the Australian national identity. Nevertheless women are gaining ground in unions, though mainly at minor official level. Indeed union women here played a possibly unique role in developing the second wave of feminism. In 1970, radical feminist thinking led left-wing union women in Victoria to protest angrily over their unions' stance on the 1969 equal pay decision, and socialist feminist Zelda d'Aprano founded a Women's Action Committee.[50] Set in the peculiarly fertile ideological soil of the Melbourne labour movement, this committee drew up a list of demands which would serve as a basis for action among women unionists for over a decade. These included demands for equal employment, maternity leave, part-time work, retraining, and education to edge women away from female ghetto areas in the labour market. After 1970 organizational initiatives came thick and fast. In 1971, dissatisfied with the male preoccupations of the Australian Council of Trade Unions (A.C.T.U.), union women set up an Alternative Trade Union Women's Conference, and in the same year the powerful 'peak' union council, the Council of Australian Government Employees' Organisations (C.A.G.E.O.) set up a women's committee. The Canberra branch of the Australian Clerical Officers' Association followed suit in 1972, while in 1974 the Australian Council of Salaried and Professional Officers' Associations established an Executive Advisory Committee on Women's Affairs.[51] This was instrumental in helping to establish the Working Women's Centre in Melbourne, in 1975.[52] Over these years trade union women had developed a Working Women's Charter, and in 1977, the first female advocate for the A.C.T.U., Jan Marsh, successfully sought its acceptance at the A.C.T.U. congress. Based essentially on the 1970 Melbourne Women's Action Committee programme, the 1977 Charter signalled a formal break with the union movement's single (male) breadwinner wage philosophy, and also insisted that women would have to participate more fully in union decision making if unions were to claim they represented their female as well as male members.

And there lay the rub. Though after 1973 a small number of

much-publicized women union officials was appointed, by 1976, to take Victoria (perhaps the most advanced state in this respect) as an example, only ten unions had a significant number of women in full-time executive or paid positions. These included nurses, insurance and bank employees, airline hostesses, fourth division Australian public servants, primary teachers, shop assistants and clerks – all areas in which women form more than half the employees. Over recent years there have been few women delegates to state Labor Councils and fewer than 5 per cent of delegates to A.C.T.U. congresses are women. Most women rank-and-file unionists interviewed before 1980 by Kaye Hargreaves, author of *Women at Work*, felt that union officials had little interest in them apart from dues' collection, and in any case management sometimes took care of dues.[53] To be sure, this is often true for male rank-and-file unionists, but women incurred extra official distrust when they formed ginger groups in order to bring women's issues to the attention of local officials (despite formal union support). Thus hostility often arose because bureaucratic hierarchy in the unions can rest easy only when the rank and file, male or female, is passive. However gender role certainly also enters the picture. Apart from the more obvious sources of stress built into working-class male gender role,[54] men honestly fear the breakdown of the family wage concept, fear job fragmentation by part-time and/or unskilled women, and fear (as they have since the 1880s) that employers will use women as 'coolie labour'. For their part, women unionists, including migrants, have been increasingly influenced by aspects of feminist thought.

Thus issues of sexism can now be raised as such in the union movement, though as yet mainly in professional areas. Some unions – for example, the New South Wales Teachers' Federation, the Queensland Teachers' Union, the South Australian Teachers' Union and the Victorian Teachers' Union[55] – have appointed coordinators to combat sexism.[56] As the decade moves forward, one glimpses more women in leading union positions: Beryl Ashe, the first Women's Advisory Officer of the N.S.W. Labor Council, member of the Federated Clerks' Union (New South Wales) State Council, and of its Federal Council; Ann Forward, National Vice President and Victorian Branch President of the Administrative and Clerical Officers' Association of the Commonwealth Public Service;

and, the first woman member of the executive of the Australian Council of Trade Unions, Jenny George (Australian Council of Salaried and Professional Officers' Association).[57] There was also a clear (if still small) tendency for women to be elected as union shop stewards, organizers, committee of management members, and participants in trade union training schemes. Despite this, the general forecast for rank-and-file union women in the 1980s is not encouraging[58], though there is ground for cautious optimism in a fact which historically has had ambivalent consequences for the status of Australian women: the unusual power of Australian unions. Thus if the main architects of advance tailor feminist ideas to suit the uncongenial (but not unresponsive) union milieu and if union women do not concede too much ground, Australian women as a whole stand to gain. For today's unions have inherited important nineteenth century traditions which continue to exert a subtle buried influence. And so (to take one example) since unions have helped shape broad Australian attitudes to gender role, and gender role deeply influences more obvious aspects of our national identity, unions may also help re-shape them.

By the early 1980s, the position of women in management, law and tertiary education was characterized by modest achievement and an increasing awareness by women of what remained to be achieved. With some 2 per cent of the women in paid work located at management level[59], there was clear ground for such concern, though it found only meagre official recognition (see for example the report of the 1982 Committee of Inquiry into Management Education).[60] In the legal profession, legal barriers against women were beginning to lift, while 'considerable inroads' had been made upon the profession's stoutest barriers, those enmeshed in attitudes, procedures and traditions.[61] In 1975, Australia's second woman Stipendiary Magistrate was sworn in,[62] and the powerful new Family Court was given a woman, Justice Elizabeth Evatt, as its Chief Judge. In 1978, Judge Robyn Layton became the first woman to be appointed to the South Australian Industrial Court[63]; by 1980, the *Australian Law Journal* called editorially for the appointment of a woman to the High Court,[64] and by 1983, Mary Gaudron was Solicitor General of New South Wales. A survey in 1982 by Jane H. Matthews, N.S.W. District Court Judge, indicated a remarkable rise in the number of women enrolling to study law at Australian universities since the 1970s. Where at Sydney University in 1970, 12 per cent of law undergraduates were women, in 1981 the figure was 39 per cent. Comparable figures at Melbourne University were 19 per cent and 39 per cent, and for 1982, 42 per cent; at the University of Western Australia, 17 and 40 per cent and 1982, 46 per cent. Figures in other institutions offering legal training were similar. Some of these women topped their classes at law studies.[65] However, in the State of Victoria there were very few women barristers until the seventies, and as late as 1980, there had never been a woman barrister elected to the Bar Council, or a woman on the State's County Court or Supreme Court benches. Women solicitors fared only a little better.[66] In 1982, Judge Matthews reported widespread complaints about male barristers from the practising women barristers she interviewed, 'the most frequent being of patronising attitudes, embodied in a failure to treat women as serious professional lawyers,'[67] while in the same year Justice Lionel Murphy of the High Court claimed there still existed 'the most glaring discrimination ... against women, all through the judiciary'.[68] Yet legal women had certainly begun to make a mark in official equal opportunity structures. For example in February 1983 Judge Jane Matthews was appointed as a temporary senior judicial member of the N.S.W. Equal Opportunity Tribunal, and solicitor Kaye Loder was also appointed.[69]

In tertiary education during the 1970s[70] the main increase in women's employment occurred at junior and non-tenured levels, though there was some progress at tenured levels. In universities women reached an all-time peak of 17.5 per cent of academic staff in 1975, but had fallen to 16.2 per cent in 1980.[71] Cuts in tertiary education funding, which hit tutorial levels hardest, provide the most likely explanation for the decline. Universities may well make their greatest contribution through an impact on the social construction of knowledge itself. This shapes at source our perception of what is real and of value. Universities make that subtle contribution above all through research, the most prestigious area of learning, and it is here that women's representation is lowest.[72] After 1977 academic women fought back and won certain ground in all areas of university life[73]; but so far their gains must be measured in terms of growing public awareness rather than job advances for women themselves.

High-tech economic tendencies forecast a likely decline in some of the ideological influence women have won to date, as it has occurred mainly in the humanities and social sciences. Now women can and should further increase their numerical presence in tertiary institutions by following the current technological infatuations of mainline men. But countervailing values and systems of knowledge must also continue to be developed with matching passion. Without rejecting or embracing in totality the hegemonic knowledge of technological corporatism, women have an important part to play in generating a democratic and humanist critique of it.

In the church, feminists might well have arrived earlier than elsewhere in Australia, Christian feminism* first appearing here in 1968 with the establishment of a group called Christian Women Concerned. Its members professed commitments of 'various kinds' to churches such as the Anglican, Catholic, Quaker, Congregational, Presbyterian and Methodist†, and along with their role as women in church and society, the group addressed issues such as peace, poverty and racism. In the seventies the World Council of Churches turned its attention to feelings of exclusion expressed by Christian women. Influenced by feminism, small but increasing numbers of Christian women expressed doubt, sometimes despair and even betrayal over what they perceived as a devalued role in their church arising from male spiritual hegemony. These Christian women took the question of language very much to heart: the most serious concerns of Christians could only be addressed in a male-oriented vocabulary. God was named in male terms. The female majority of churchgoers, Christian feminists argued, functioned mainly as arrangers of flowers, hewers of cake and drawers of raffle tickets, while men monopolized the ministry. In June 1973 the Australian Council of Churches (N.S.W.) set up a Commission on the Status of Women under the presidency of Ms Marie Tulip.[74] Later in the 1970s the World Council of Churches (W.C.C.) followed up an earlier 'Consultation on Sexism' with a project entitled 'Study on the Community of Women and Men in the Church'. This was designed

---

*Special thanks to Marie Tulip, Status of Women Commission of the Australian Council of Churches, and Sabine Willis. The responsibility for interpretation is mine.

†Members of the latter three merged as the Uniting Church.

for '"women and men ... who long for a renewed and transformed community of women and men in the church and in the world"'[75] The W.C.C. invited groups of this mind around the world to explore issues such as identity, church teaching, theological education, worship and ministry, and report findings to an international 'consultation' scheduled for August 1980. Australian Christians responded promptly. In N.S.W. for example, a 'Women and Men's Group' was formed by members of Anglican, Congregationalist, Methodist, Presbyterian, Quaker and Roman Catholic congregations, and met regularly. One member of the Status of Women Commission of the Australian Council of Churches (A.C.C.) summed up the position of women in these words:

It is not an exaggeration here in Australia to speak of the church's rigidities in the area of sexism. Men hold effective power in almost every area of the church's life - administration, theological education, local churches, and also in writing theology, hymn book compilation, evangelism campaigns and so on. God is indubitably male, as are most of 'his' priests and ministers, and the dominant culture of the church is a patriarchal culture.[76]

During 1978 Australian Christian women learned of 'the transformation of the church's ministry' in New Zealand, Sweden, the United States and Canada as 'significant numbers of women became active participants'.[77] Again they responded. In April 1978 twenty 'theologically trained' women met in Adelaide, 'seeking to find forms of ministry that are valid at this time', while in July a N.S.W. group of women who described themselves as 'in some way feminist and in some way associated with the church' met 'to explore together what it is we want to affirm as women ...' Other such gatherings followed. Then in September 1978 the A.C.C.'s Status of Women Commission set up four task forces: on Sexist Language and the production of non-sexist devotional literature, on Theological Colleges, on Sexuality, and Feminist Theology. The Commission also sponsored a 'Living Female Conference' in September 1980. In September 1981 the General Synod of the Anglican Church in Australia passed a bill which, if approved by individual dioceses, would lead to the 1985 General Synod proposing enabling legislation to permit the ordination of women to the Anglican priesthood. Meantime, though feminism has caused some women to leave the church, it has prompted others to pursue the feminist strand of liberation theology within it, and others still to enter ministry.

Finally, let us draw together earlier points bearing on the women's movement and feminist theory. Exploring themes of women and identity in late twentieth century Australia, we showed that during the seventies, the gap in status between Australian women and those in comparable countries tended to close as the overall position of women here improved. Women also emerged as a sector of the new corporate élite. But they remain concentrated at its junior and middle levels, and as ideologies of egalitarianism become increasingly widespread, such concentration generates intensified gender-based rivalries. All this is of direct relevance to the women's movement and feminism. Yet just as was true for the nineteenth century, the historical significance of feminism far transcends issues of its immediate social origins.

Australian feminism today can be analyzed in terms of three main groups: radical, reform and socialist feminists.[78] It is, to begin with, unusual in the extent of its centralist orientation. Overseas feminists show more familiarity with the long-standing debate in labour, liberal and conservative circles alike, about the implications for autonomy of an escalating government presence. But with few exceptions the debate itself seems unknown to Australian feminists, so that – despite their dedication to autonomy for women – the three main feminist groups display few reservations in committing themselves to an apparently unlimited growth of government, and hence to the accelerated erosion of citizen autonomy.

By contrast with the American story, in Australia radical feminists initiated the women's movement. Most radical feminists were young, broadly middle class and educated to tertiary level. But here as elsewhere, reform feminists have shown greater staying power – indeed radical feminists sometimes become reform feminists as they grow older, though in the main they drop out of organized feminist activity. While it is influenced by radical feminist thinking, Australian reform feminism is at core a version of the mainstream American feminist ideology first articulated during the 1960s. That ideology was built around liberal bourgeois principles of formal equality and social justice developed after the late eighteenth century.

Radical feminists not only provided the women's movement with much of its initial energy, but from the start contributed most in terms of theory. As Dinnerstein puts it, the 'hate, fear, loathing, contempt, and greed that men express toward women so pervade the human atmosphere that we breathe them as casually as the city child breathes smog', and much of radical feminism's contribution can be understood as an effort to sensitize us to the 'virulently anti-female feeling [permeating] our species' life'.[79] Indeed in the climate of the 1980s, only radical feminists have the courage to articulate steadily this perception (we may instance the continuing work of Adrienne Rich in America). But radical feminism deserves even more attention for its stance on gender role, for it argues that gender role is the earliest and hence prototypical form of all social domination. Some link this thesis with child development. For example, radical feminists sympathetic to psychoanalysis note that gender role acquires initial meaning for the child at about sixteen months, and in all forms of male-dominated society, they propose that female babies unconsciously experience gender in terms of social inferiority. If true, this means that an awareness of domination and subordination, thus of power in prototypical form, is acquired along with a sense of gender itself. Hence gender brings us directly and very early to the heart of issues concerning power and hierarchy, of which class, for example, is one specific form.[80] Thus from the start radical feminism generated awareness of the critical social meanings of gender, with steady ripple effects throughout feminism as a whole. Many of the most practical reform feminists, and some of the less rigidly anti-psychoanalytical socialist feminists have assimilated this core radical insight in one way or another, and it has to some extent begun to enter our social awareness.

Yet even when articulated in its most sophisticated forms, radical feminism carried from the start the seeds of the dead end in which it now finds itself. For it is built upon an implicit vision of woman as Noble Victim (or to paraphrase Juliet Mitchell, woman as pure but purely put-upon). Certainly the Noble Victim has blemishes. But they are not really hers: for they are caused by male oppression – a thought process which conceals a form of a condescension toward women and inverted aggrandisement of men worthy of the finest male chauvinist. The Noble Victim is an updated elaboration of the nineteenth century definition of woman which so marginalized her: it makes her both more than human (by placing her on the pedestal of ennobled victimhood) and less than human. For because men have caused even her blemishes, without them she would be near-enough to perfect, and because perfect, less than human. Many radical feminists seem set to share an historical fate common to many movements, set to join the ranks of society's True Believer sects. But in the meantime radical feminism has made a signal contribution to women. First it catalysed the women's movement, and then played a critical role in generating the theoretical critique of male domination which a new feminism has begun to evolve.

For its part, reform feminism adopts a vocabulary about the universal rights and needs of all women. Such universalism is standard for the great social movements of modern history, from protestantism in the sixteenth, the Enlightenment in the eighteenth, to liberalism and Marxism in the nineteenth centuries. But to date those who have reaped most benefit from reform feminism are relatively few. A significant minority of women – the most articulate, activist, and/or initially the most privileged – have gained modest footholds in the junior or middle echelons of a new corporate élite, in its bureaucratic, managerial and political apparatuses or in its promotional arm, the mass media. Aspiring or successful new female élites have commanded special attention in this chapter, as in joining their male counterparts they play an increasingly central part in the corporate system. Though the historical significance of the women's movement far transcends the concerns of aspiring and new élite women, they are nevertheless its backbone, and critical to its solidity and continuing impact. Just as the nineteenth century women's movement achieved its main social outreach through a critical minority, so too does its late twentieth century analogue. And like that of their nineteenth century counterparts in the first-wave women's movement, the function of new élite women, as we have seen, is complex and ambiguous. As many of the most talented reform feminists graduate into areas of government bureaucracy, they become an essential part of a corporate system which promotes what it requires: a passive citizenry. By contrast the ideals of feminism seek to develop greater autonomy and initiative among women. Thus the irony for the new femocrats bites deep. In the bureaucracy they do a great deal of immediate good for women. But the medium-to long-term result of their actions is not what they wanted (as is the case for most historical actors). That result has been to extend the swollen network of control which diminishes autonomy and deepens passivity among women and among men, promoting further acquiescence in an over-administered citizenry. Such passivity and diminished autonomy sabotage possibilities for real social change at their very root. Thus, genuinely seeking fuller autonomy for all women, reform feminists have certainly expanded their own. But in doing so they have also enhanced the stability and salience of the corporate presence in the Australian community. In this special sense, reform feminists therefore diminish the possibilities for autonomy of most women as of most citizens.

And there are further contradictions for the new femocrats. On the one hand new élite women consolidate the power of the corporate élite by adding women to it: the addition stabilizes the élite by siphoning off the serious internal stress that would arise from sisters, daughters and wives of the new élite being too completely excluded. On the other hand, new élite women who throw in their lot with the women's movement begin to undermine the corporate system by helping to catalyze an explicit questioning of gender role. This is an historic achievement. The institutional fabric of male-dominated society can and has repeatedly accommodated shifts in modes of domination, pre-class and class alike. But it cannot survive a fundamental change in gender role. Thus any assessment of the role of reform feminism must be couched in terms of the wayward irresolution and ambiguity which characterizes real historical achievement.

For the women's movement as a whole a good deal has altered since the mid-1970s. Despite a certain increase in media chic and political salience accompanying the 1983 Labor victory, the movement has suffered significant loss of morale, high cadre wastage and burnout. Among many activists, an earlier questing spark about long-term goals flickered low, at times smothered under the work burdens which accompanied institutional success. The movement has also suffered from real and anticipated job scarcity among the aspiring women who fuelled it so powerfully. In terms of feminist theory, the main responsibility for holding the line, as of developing feminism in response to critical new social challenge, must increasingly fall upon intellectual and academic feminists. The latter have to contend with disciplinary training which can promote a taupe-coloured attitude towards, and a fashionable miniaturization of, many of the mind's most serious concerns: by contrast the tasks of feminism demand perspectives as broad as they are bold. Paradoxically, morale and cohesiveness have declined at the very time that shallow, popularized and distorted versions of feminism are gaining an unparalleled acceptance, including a distinct if limited media exposure. One reason for loss of morale and cadres can be understood in terms of the astonishingly stubborn way gender role tugs us toward heterosexual bonding and family. If they wish to respond to this, feminists will need to stop ascribing it entirely to secondary socialization, for it goes far deeper. But to follow those American feminists who venture further into the psyche would involve a challenge to the iron hold behaviourist sociology and psychology has over Australian feminism. The women's movement also suffers from an ideological staleness. This partly reflects a sense of marginality as movement thinking here finds itself overtaken by shattering world events now obtruding into the everyday sensibility of Australians: ecothreat, signs of global economic crisis and social disintegration, together with warfare on an unparalleled scale. But the ideological staleness is exacerbated by the disappearance of many earlier feminists, who are unable to tell newcomers that they are rediscovering the wheel. Among the former are casualties of burnout produced by internecine warfare, unrealistic over-extension and overwork and/or of growing a little older.

An equally powerful but subliminal reason for the movement's present impasse lies in the sources of that female bonding so crucial to its effectiveness. Under male domination, effective female bonding is always under threat from the ambivalence inherent in the very early mother–daughter relation, an ambivalence sensitively explored by Dinnerstein and Flax.[81] And in Australia, the women's movement also suffers from a culturally determined weakness in female bonding which is the direct legacy of our brief history. Failing to adequately confront the comparatively lower status bequeathed by the past, Australian women tend instead to vent hostility to and resentment about that status on each other. Valuing each other less as a result, women then have a curtailed ability to bond. (Fanon has demonstrated the psychic mechanisms at work here for all subordinate groups.) The capacity for bonding that American women display arises in large part from the experiences of urban middle-class women in the nineteenth century. In Australia, the colonial middle-class was weaker and hence could not contribute in a similar way to the overall standing of women. Further, we had a uniquely strong input from two profoundly disadvantaged groups: pre-working-class (or casual poor) urban English women, and women from the poorest areas of rural Ireland. Female, like male, bonding tendencies are almost universal, so of course these women bonded. But their capacity for strong bonding was inevitably undercut by their historical experience. A legacy from that history operates today with anachronistic vigor and unnecessarily weakens female bonding when it is vitally needed. Women might help abolish it by dragging it into the light of day and forcing rational discourse. They would do this only in order to shrug it off: to deny its very existence as a form of 'knocking' is to slight the urgency of women's need for a stronger female bonding.

Reform feminism continues to make gains among women, especially among highly articulate and visible women in aspiring or junior ranks of the new corporate élite. And increasingly simplified versions of radical feminism operate a kind of conveyor-belt processing of young women. It rapidly draws them in only to eject them, often burned-out for all political endeavour after an astonishingly short time.* Ideologies generally become shallower as they win wider acceptance, and wider acceptance is potentially part of the way forward for feminism. But the question is whether core aspects of its major forms are leading feminism to a dead end. I argue they are, and that despite the apparent popularity of feminism at the moment, current thinking in the women's movement tends to be locked into

---

*For feminism as presently formulated, economic futures will ultimately determine whether its minimum programme on equal rights can progress far beyond the current minority. If Australians do become the poor whites of Asia, new élite women might retain their gains, and the current level of feminist media and public rhetoric might even continue. But the majority of women will make little further headway unless Australia's economic decline is reversed.

1970s forms of feminism.

Though economic downturn in the 1970s played a part, once élite footholds were won in the corporate system, the women's movement was bound to lose a lot of its impetus. Most feminists, reform, radical and centralist-socialist alike, tend to adhere to initial positions laid down in the early seventies. (In remaining locked into initial stances, feminists simply re-enact the history of most great social movements.) Hence the main thrust of feminism continues to focus on issues of formal equality and immediate social reform, issues it tends to divorce from broader social contexts or future perspectives. Thus, whatever its conscious wishes, feminism at present tends to collude in marginalizing itself and the women's movement as external forces diminish the moral power of earlier feminist aims and passionately compel our immediate attention. Those forces include looming social disintegration, accelerated shrinkage of citizen autonomy, ecothreat and an obliterative weaponry that threatens to convert the globe into one vast armed camp.

But a new feminism attuned to such frontier concerns can turn back the thrust to marginalize the cause of women. New feminism can claim the high ground for women by enriching earlier feminist insights so as to bring gender role to bear in a causal way on the central dilemmas of our time.[82] It will locate serious discourse on women within a critique of the gender grid basic to all forms of male-dominated societies, whether patriarchal or, as in the west, post-patriarchal. Modern technology now imparts qualities of deadliness to all such structures. But in the west at least – which may to some extent continue to operate as global pattern-setter – those structures are more than ripe for renewal (the very existence of feminism is a sign of such ripeness). New feminism rejects any implicit vision of Woman-as-Noble-Victim. In response to challenges which pose the alternative of real social change or disaster, it goes far beyond programmes of formal equality. In demanding that central participant-status in humanity which patriarchal ideology has always denied her, the new feminist begins by insisting that she, quite as much as man, is a central if largely unconscious actor in an ancient script – which sustains even while maiming our species – and now acts to critically retard its fuller growth – patriarchal gender role. Since she perceives its costs to her as more crippling than man does to him (he is largely blinded by the apparently superior status it awards him), she will have to take the lead in rewriting that script.

Notes

1. I am attempting here to apply to women's history an approach based on Jane Flax's writing. See 'The Conflict between Nurturance and Autonomy in Mother – Daughter Relationships and within Feminism', *Feminist Studies* 4, 2, 1978, pp. 171-89; 'Mother – Daughter Relationships: Psychodynamics, Politics and Philosophy', in Hester Eisenstein and Alice Jardine (eds), *The Future of Difference,* Barnard College Women's Centre, G. K. Hall, Boston, Massachusetts, 1980, pp. 20–40.

2. Domestic feminism focussed mainly on public remedies for issues related to women's domestic status: drink, prostitution, venereal disease, child custody, married women's property rights; and the vote – seen by such feminists largely as a means of promoting these causes.

   I owe the term 'domestic feminism' and the idea of nineteenth century women's increase in domestic status and power to Daniel Scott Smith ('Family Limitation, Sexual Control and Domestic Feminism in Victorian America', *Feminist Studies,* vol. 1, no. 3/4, Winter – Spring 1973, pp.40–57). In defining the demand for autonomy as the essence of feminism, Smith followed Aileen Kraditor (*Up From the Pedestal,* Quadrangle Books, Chicago, 1965, p. 5), and focussed upon women's control over fertility as central to autonomy. The idea of domestic feminism was explored further in 1973 by Kathryn Kish Sklar (*Catharine Beechers: A Study in American Domesticity,* Yale University Press, New Haven, Connecticut, 1973) and then Nancy F. Cott (*The Bonds of Womanhood: "Woman's Sphere" in New England, 1780–1835,* Yale University Press, New Haven, Connecticut, 1977). Yet egalitarian ideologies might have been the ultimate source of woman's changing familial status, as it was closely related to one such ideology, that of companionate marriage. For a much-needed exploration of the latter's role in nineteenth century Australia, see Patricia Grimshaw, 'Women and the Family in Australian History – A Reply to *The Real Matilda',* *Historical Studies Australia and New Zealand,* vol. 18, no. 72, 1979, pp. 412-21.

3. Jean Bethke Elshtain, *Public Man, Private Woman,* Martin Robertson, Oxford and Princeton University Press, N. J., 1981, p. 270; A. F. Davies, *Skills, Outlooks and Passions: A Psychoanalytic Contribution to the Study of Politics,* Cambridge University Press, Cambridge, Melbourne, 1980, p. 377.

4. See Jessica Benjamin, 'Authority and the Family Revisited: or, A World without

Fathers?' *New German Critique,* vol. 13, 1978, pp. 35-57; Max Horkheimer, 'Authority and the Family, in *Critical Theory,* transl. J. Cummings, N.Y., 1972 (1936); Herbert Marcuse, *One Dimensional Man. The Ideology of Industrial Society.* Sphere Books Ltd., 1968 (1964); Alexander Mitscherlich, *Society without the Father: A Contribution to Social Psychology,* Schocken Books, N.Y., 1970 (1963). In *Haven in a Heartless World: The Family Besieged* (Basic Books, N.Y. 1977), Christopher Lasch owes a heavy conceptual debt to the last three writers.

5.   Margaret Power, 'Women and Economic Crises: the Great Depression and the Present Crisis', in Elizabeth Windschuttle (ed.), *Women, Class and History: Feminist Perspectives on Australia 1788-1978,* Fontana Collins, 1980, p. 503.

6.   Bettina Cass and Heather Radi, 'Family, Fertility and the Labour Market', in Norma Grieve and Patricia Grimshaw (eds.), *Australian Women: Feminist Perspectives,* Oxford University Press, Melbourne, 1981, p. 197, 199.

7.   Mary Owen, 'Women's Employment: Past and Future', Third Women and Labour Conference 1982, *Papers* vol. 1, p. 120.

8.   Australian National Opinion Poll, commissioned by the *National Times,* 3-8 October 1977.

9.   Industries Assistance Commission, *Structural Change in Australia,* A.G.P.S., Canberra, 1977, p. 86.

10.   The census of 1976 revealed that about one-quarter of the women in Australia's paid workforce were born overseas (Australian Bureau of Statistics, *Census 30th June 1976,* Table 62, 'Occupation by birthplace, employed population, females').

11.   Mary Gaudron and Michael Bosworth, 'Equal Pay?', in Judy MacKinolty and Heather Radi (eds.), *In Pursuit of Justice: Australian Women and the Law 1788-1979,* Hale and Iremonger, Sydney, 1979, p. 169. This quotation applies to 1978, but the situation was not significantly different by the early 1980s.

12.   Linda Rubinstein, 'Women, Work and Technological Change', in E. Windshuttle (ed.), *op. cit.,* pp. 514-30; Sandra Prerost, 'Technological Change and Women's Employment in Australia', in Margaret Bevege, Margaret James and Carmel Shute (eds.), *Worth Her Salt: Women at Work in Australia,* Hale and Iremonger, Sydney, 1982, pp. 142-4.

13.   Committee of Inquiry into Technological Change in Australia, (Chairman: R. H. Myer), *Technological Change in Australia,* A.G.P.S., Canberra, 1980, vol. 1, p. 103.

14.   Women's Bureau, Department of Employment and Industrial Relations, *Women and Work Newsletter,* vol. 4, no. 4, December 1982.

15.   Australian Labor Party (N.S.W. Branch), *The Radical,* February 1983, p. 9.

16.   Kathleen Edwards, *Fragments of the Future: Final Report of the Women's Welfare Issues Consultative Committee,* Department of Social Security, Canberra, 1982, p. 3.

17.   National Women's Advisory Council, *Annual Report 1981–2*, A.G.P.S., Canberra, 1982, p. 3.

18.   M. Power, *op. cit.,* p. 504.

19.   Women's Bureau, Department of Employment and Youth Affairs, *The Role of Women in the Economy* (Position Paper presented to the O.E.C.D. High Level Conference on the Employment of Women, 1980), A.G.P.S., Canberra, 1981, pp. 13–14.

20.   M. Power, *op. cit.,* p. 50.

21.   National Women's Advisory Council, *Migrant Women Speak,* A.G.P.S., Canberra, 1979, p. 6.

22.   Women's Bureau, Department of Employment and Youth Affairs, *The Role of Women in the Economy,* p. 15.

23.   *Ibid.,* p. 12.

24.   *Sydney Morning Herald,* 6 April 1983.

25.   Women's Bureau, Department of Employment and Youth Affairs, *The Role of Women in the Economy,* p. 13.

26.   Dorothy Dinnerstein, *The Mermaid and the Minotaur: Sexual Arrangements and Human Malaise,* Harper and Row, N.Y., 1976; Nancy Chodorow, *The Reproduction of Mothering: Psychoanalysis and the Sociology of Gender,* University of California Press, Berkeley, California, 1978.

I follow Dorothy Dinnerstein in locating the deepest and most stubborn (because unconscious) roots of patriarchy in its gender role, and the key to that role in a universal cultural – not biological – custom: female near-monopoly of very early child-rearing. With such a monopoly as its core, and definitive, characteristic, patriarchy is trans-historical. (The particular historical form of family bearing this characteristic varies widely across different periods and social formations.) Other writers who (for various reasons) see patriarchy as cross-cultural and trans-historical include Juliet Mitchell and Sherry Ortner. See Juliet Mitchell, *Psychoanalysis and Feminism,* Allen Lane, London, 1974, and Sherry Ortner, 'Is Female to Male as Nature is to Culture?', in M. Rosaldo and L. Lamphere (eds.), *Woman, Culture and Society,* Stanford University Press, Stanford, California, 1974; and Sherry B. Ortner and Harriet Whitehead, 'Introduction: Accounting for Sexual Meanings', in Sherry B. Ortner and Harriet Whitehead (eds.), *Sexual Meanings: The Cultural Construction of Gender and Sexuality,* Cambridge University Press, Cambridge, 1981, pp. 1–27.

27.   Australian Labor Party, 'National Committee of Inquiry Recommendations', *The Radical,* vol. 10, no. 2, May 1979.

28.   N.S.W. Labor Women's Conference, Sydney, 28 May 1983. Opening by Senator Susan Ryan, Minister for Education and Youth Affairs, and Minister Assisting the Prime Minister on the Status of Women.

29.   *National Times*, 27 February to 5 March 1983. But compare that to the *Age*, 3 October 1980.

30.   *Sydney Morning Herald*, 19 February; *Australian*, 19 February 1983. See the Women's Electoral Lobby Letter to Members, Sydney, 21 February 1983, for the text of a telegram sent to the main party leaders on behalf of W.E.L., Australian Federation of Business and Professional Women, Australian Women's Education Coalition (N.S.W.); National Association for Community Based Child Care; Children's Services Action; Feminist Legal Action Group (N.S.W.); Women and Development Network of Australia, and other groups.

31.   *Australian*, 16 February 1983.

32.   *The Radical*, February 1983, p. 9.

33.   Liberal Party of Australia (Federal Secretariat), Press Release, File 472/75, 3 December 1975.

34.   Liberal Party of Australia, *Federal Platform*, 1982, p. 15, 38.

35.   For the similarity between W.E.L. and the Liberal Party over certain core women's issues (shared often with the Labor Party), see 'Lobbying – Women's Electoral Lobby – the last ten years and the future', Paper presented at the National Conference of the Women's Electoral Lobby, October 1982.

36.   Earlier professionalization and expansion of welfare (perhaps the most striking example of early domestic feminist politics) was associated with the considerable power of women in the Liberal Party. See Cynthia Turner, 'Welfare and Women: Changing Conceptions of Welfare and Women's Identity in Australia', in N. Grieve and P. Grimshaw (eds.), *op. cit.*, pp. 168–77.

37.   *Age*, 10 March 1983.

38.   Liberal Party of Australia (Federal Secretariat) Current Political Notes: 'Women in Politics', September 1981.

39.   R. A. Craig, *Women and the Rural Class Structure*, Roseworthy Agricultural College, Roseworthy, South Australia, 1979.

40.   National Party of Australia, *Platform*, A.C.T., n.d. (1981?); National Country Party (N.S.W.), *State Platform*, Sydney, 1981.

41.   *Australian Women's Weekly*, 7 July 1976.

42.   A. Bunning, 'Living within Economic Constraints', *The Country Woman in Australia Looks Ahead*, National Conference, La Trobe University, 16–19 August 1979; A. Bunning and M. Gibbs, 'Women on Family Farms in Australia: the Underestimated Workforce', *Rural Marketing and Policy*, 10, 4, 1980.

43.   National Committee on Discrimination in Employment and Occupation, *First Annual Report: Towards Equal Opportunity in Employment*, A.G.P.S., Canberra, 1974, p. 31.

44.   Chris Ronalds, 'To Right a Few Wrongs: Legislation against Sex Discrimination', in Judy MacKinolty and Heather Radi (eds.), *op. cit.*, p. 192. In 1976, South Australia and New South Wales passed anti-discrimination laws, and Victoria followed suit in 1978. Reform feminists in the Women's Electoral Lobby played an important part in each state.

45.   Office of the Status of Women, 'A Guide to the United Nations Convention on the Elimination of All Forms of Discrimination against Women', June 1983. Members of the N.S.W. Women's Liberal Network supported Senator Ryan. However for opposition to the Sex Discrimination Bill from sections of the Liberal Party, the National Party, from the Council for Free Australia and from Women Who Want to be Women, see *Sydney Morning Herald,* 15, 17, 20, 22 September 1983.

46.   Statement – 'Australian Senate', 14 July 1983.

47.   Minister for Education, News Release, 10 August 1983.

48.   For an analysis of the privileged situation of labour in the national identity, see Miriam Dixson, *Greater than Lenin? Lang and Labor 1916–1932,* Melbourne Politics Monograph, Melbourne, 1976, ch. 8 and *passim.*

49.   Kate White, 'An Assessment of Women and Unions in Australia', *Papers* (Third Women and Labour Conference) vol. I, 1982, pp. 161.

50.   Zelda d'Aprano, *Zelda: The Becoming of a Woman,* Widescope International, Melbourne, 1978, *passim.*

51.   Anna Pha, 'Women in Trade Unions: A Literature Survey', *Papers* (Third Women and Labour Conference) vol. I, 1982, p. 179.

52.   Mary Owen and Sylvie Shaw, *Working Women: Discussion Papers from the Working Women's Centre, Melbourne,* Sisters Publishing Ltd, Carlton, Vic., 1979. The Working Women's Centre addressed a wide range of working women's problems: discrimination in pay, superannuation, promotion, training and retraining, and child-care. It operated through a multi-lingual newspaper, leaflets, submissions to committees of enquiry and government departments, and its data generated interest here and in educational, health and welfare institutions. Because the Centre adopted the feminist view that sex-role conditioning forms the basis of discrimination, it also worked with teachers and vocational guidance officers interested in non-sexist approaches.

53.   Kay Hargreaves, *Women at Work,* Penguin, Ringwood, Vic., 1982, pp. 305–19.

54.   Consider some of the implications of this incident, for example: a builders' labourer was reported as saying, upon seeing a woman driving a hoist on a building site: '"… it makes me feel so inadequate, it makes me feel as if my job is not what I think it is – sheilas can do what I'm doing!"' (cited in Meredith Burgmann, 'Revolution and Machismo: Women in the New South Wales Builders Labourers' Federation, 1961–75', in E. Windschuttle (ed.), *op. cit.,* p 456).

55.   Heather O'Connor, 'V.T.U. Elimination of Sexism Committee: A Study of Women and Politics', *Papers* (Third Women and Labour Conference) vol. I, 1982 pp. 149-60.

56.   Some teachers actively promote 'counter-sexism' among girls and young women. See *Women at Work Kit,* produced jointly by the Technical Teachers' Association, the Victorian Secondary Teachers' Association and the Victorian Teachers' Union Sexism in Education Project and the Working Women's Centre, Melbourne, 1979.

57.   *Sydney Morning Herald,* 18 June 1981; National Women's Advisory Council, *Annual Report, 1981-2,* A.G.P.S., Canberra, 1982, p. 97; *Sydney Morning Herald,* 15 September 1983.

58.   Community Research Action Centre, *Women and Unions,* Monash University Union, Melbourne 1981; Anna Pha, *op. cit.,* pp. 176-9; Kate White, *op. cit.,* pp. 164-65.

59.   *Australian,* 8 March 1978; see too *National Times,* 13-18 March 1978.

60.   Committee of Inquiry into Management Education (Chairman: J. T. Ralph), *Report,* A.G.P.S., Canberra, 1982, pp. 91-3.

61.   Daphne Kok, Joan O'Brien, Ruth Teale, 'In the Office and at the Bar. Women in the Legal Profession', in Judy MacKinolty and Heather Radi (eds.), *op. cit.,* pp. 181-8.

62.   *Sydney Morning Herald,* 29 August 1975.

63.   *Australian,* 10 March 1978.

64.   *Age,* 22 October 1980.

65.   *The Australian Law Journal,* vol. 56, no. 12, 1982.

66.   *Age,* 22 October 1980.

67.   *The Australian Law Journal, loc. cit.*

68.   *Sydney Morning Herald,* 11 September 1982.

69.   *ADB-INK,* Newsletter of the N.S.W. Anti-Discrimination Board, no. 13, February 1983.

70.   For a general discussion of gender role socialisation and higher education in Australia, see Shirley N. Sampson, 'Socialisation into Sex Roles', F. J. Hunt (ed.), *Socialisation in Australia,* Australia International Press and Publications Pty Ltd, Melbourne, 1978, pp. 270-6.

71.   Jennifer M. Jones and Josie Castle, 'Women in Australian Universities 1945-80', *Vestes,* vol. 27, no. 2, 1983, p. 19. For a general analysis of women's position in the academic professions, see Bettina Cass, 'Woman's Place or Domestic Contradictions?' in Bettina Cass, Madge Dawson, Diane Temple, Sue Wills, Anne Winkler (eds.), *Why So Few? Women Academics in Australian Universities,* Sydney University Press, 1983, p. 122.

72.   Jill Blewett, 'Women: The Perpetual Tutor', in *From the Gilded Cage,* Women's Electoral Lobby, 1974, pp. 27-9; Federation of Australian University Staff Associations, *Report of the Committee on the Status of Women,* November 1977; Jennifer M. Jones and Frances H. Lovejoy, 'Discrimination against Women Academics in Australian Universities', *Signs,* vol. 5, no. 3, 1980, pp. 518-26.

73.   For example, in 1977 the Federation of Australian University Staff Associations issued the report of an inquiry it commissioned into the overall status of academic women. At Sydney University, women set up the Association of Women Employees in the University of Sydney, and in 1981, a report relating to women's academic status was adopted by the University Senate (*National Times,* 14-20 June 1981). For Macquarie University, see Sabine Willis, 'Affirmative Action at Macquarie University', University and Academic Staff Association of N.S.W., *UASA News,* November 1982; for the University of New England, see *Vestes,* organ of the Federation of Australian University Staff Associations, November 1982; for Melbourne University, see the Victorian Equal Opportunity Board and the Commissioner for Equal Opportunity, *Equal Opportunity Forum,* no. 12, March 1983, Government Printer, Melbourne, p. 7. See too Bettina Cass, Madge Dawson, *et al., op. cit.* At the same time, the Chair of the Victorian Ministerial Equal Opportunity Advisory Committee, Dr Shirley Sampson, claimed that in late 1982, fewer women held top level positions in Victorian primary and secondary education than in 1977 *(Equal Opportunity Forum,* no. 12, March 1983, pp. 11-13).

74.   See Sabine Willis (ed.), *Enquiry into the Status of Women in the Church,* Commission on the Status of Women, Australian Council of Churches, N.S.W., Sydney, 1974; Commission on the Status of Women, *Liberation Theology and Feminism,* Australian Council of Churches, N.S.W., Sydney, 1975.

75.   'Magdalene: A Christian Newsletter for Women', March 1979.

76.   Marie Tulip. 'Women and the Kingdom', in 'Community of Men and Women in the Church: A Report from an Australian Group', Australian Council of Churches, Sydney, N.S.W., April 1980, p. 8. Written as a background document for the World Council of Churches Conference 'Your Kingdom Come' in Melbourne, May 1980. First published in *The International Review of Mission,* vol. LXXX, no. 274, April 1980. See too Marie Tulip, *Women in a Man's Church: Changes in the Status of Women in the Uniting Church in Australia 1977-1983,* Commission on the Status of Women, Australian Council of Churches, N.S.W., Sydney, 1983.

77.   'Magdalene', October 1978.

78.   See Miriam Dixson, 'Women', in A. F. Davies, S. Encel, and M. J. Berry (eds.), *Australian Society: A Sociological Introduction,* Longman Cheshire, Melbourne, 1977, pp. 118-25; Marian Simms, 'Conservative Feminism in Australia: A Case Study of Feminist Ideology'. *Women's Studies International Quarterly,* vol. 2, no. 3, 1979, pp.

305–318, and 'The Australian Feminist Experience', in N. Grieve and P. Grimshaw (eds.), *op. cit.*, pp. 227–39.

79. Dorothy Dinnerstein, *op. cit.*, pp. 88–9.

80. For the girl baby's simultaneous learning of gender role and social inferiority, see Jane Flax, 'The Conflict between Nurturance and Autonomy in Mother – Daughter Relationships and within Feminism', p. 173; and for a general argument about domination-subordination, power and the early mother-child relation, see Dorothy Dinnerstein, *op. cit., passim.*

81. Jane Flax analyses key aspects of this ambivalence through exploring the concepts of 'nurturance' and 'autonomy' within and between women. Dinnerstein proposes that the most significant implications of such ambivalance may be best understood as part of human predicament itself.

82. This is done in Dorothy Dinnerstein's work *The Mermaid and the Minotaur.* I am greatly in debt to this book, a work transcending that of de Beauvoir, Norman O. Brown and Freud in its project of linking male and female gender role to the human predicament. For the best Australian attempt to state and appraise Dinnerstein's thesis, see Norma Grieve and Michael Perdices, 'Patriarchy: a refuge from maternal power? Dinnerstein's answer to Freud', in N. Grieve and P. Grimshaw (eds.), *op. cit.*, pp. 25–38.

Chapter 8

Eager Ghosts

'The past is our mortal mother, no dead thing. Our future constantly reflects her to the soul . . . We are pushed to [our fortune] by the hundreds of days we have buried, eager ghosts. And if you have not the habit of taking counsel with them, you are but an instrument in their hands.'

(GEORGE MEREDITH, *Harry Richmond*, XXXII)

The central theme of this book, first published in 1976, was that Australian history had left its mark on our sexual relations in ways that needed understanding because they needed changing. (Saying, I think now, too little about the ways that did not need changing because they were 'good enough'.[1]) To this day I do not know whether the book really captured or conveyed my sense of what was different and lacking in our sexual ambience. But after trying to suggest what it was, I looked to the past for a lead on how, with gentle hands, we might go about effective change. From the start, the purpose of *The Real Matilda* was to explore 'misogynous influences arising from Australia's history so as to shrug off the faster those . . . we feel impoverish us as we live out our present.' (p. 13). Again, this assumes there will be a lot we do not want to shrug off because we don't feel it impoverishes us. Having brought into being a culture which a critical and comparative analysis must rank with the world's most benign and fortunate, much of our basic cultural script (this includes gender) needs to be left alone to continue its 'holding'[2] work as best it can in the face of an increasingly fragmented planet. The process of changing our gender relations was imagined by analogy with the psychoanalytic model: through insight which owed everything to the climate of respect and trust in which it was won, we would venture warily, slowly, upon modest alteration of the old – but only if and because we'd first fashioned something that might work better. (Since 1976, Lacan's academic chic and Habermas's respect for the psychoanalytic encounter as model for ideal human intercourse have made the general idea of psychoanalysis more relevant to Australians.)

To attempt change realistically is to understand what needs changing, and that begins with realistic naming. Australian gender patterns could never have been cast in the classic modern middle-class pattern, even if only because of a massive, partly pre-modern 'formative' input into our overall identity from the Irish. 'Irish residual clan-collectivism in Australia' this book related to 'a persisting clan structure . . . associated with a pre-modern "collect-ivism" ' (p. 156). (Writers such as Robert Hughes and Patrick O'Farrell have since taken up the theme of Irish 'residual clan-collectivism'.[3]) What could have sat more awkwardly with the individualism of the English, the world's premier modernizers, unless – and this is a fateful rather than merely awkward lack of fit – we count the communalism of the Aborigines, among the world's premier collectivists? While Australian gender patterns certainly must be theorized in terms of the western bourgeois model, if to the pre-modernism of the Irish we add the equally formative cultural input of convict 'nomad tribalism',[4] we cannot adopt that uniquely individualist model neat, so to speak: a certain modification is needed.

We might say that what applies to other aspects of national identity goes for gender too: our glosses on the western model were and remain in many ways beneficial. For example with 'a unique national identity which rejects bombast, flim-flam, and pretentious-ness',[5] we are more egalitarian than the English and even the Americans. Our gender patterns might well always have been less paternalistic (which is not necessarily to say more comfortable), if only because from the start the father's role lacked the great patriarchal buttresses of an aristocratic, church and military establishment. And thus the father's role was sharply contested by the sons. All true. However at this point we are not talking good or bad, richer or poorer, but different. In two main ways, *The Real Matilda* tried to pin down our differences from the western gender model. First, Australian women had a less assured sense of confidence, a relative lack most immediately manifest in the public arena and only visible in comparative perspective. Historian Patricia Grimshaw challenged this, proposing among other things, that any female public diffidence was the correlate of a high domestic profile.[6] There is a good deal in her criticism. Yet the famous mateship ambience linked with single brotherhood, so very powerful in our formative experience, seems to have found its way into the domestic arena, and into marriage itself, not just into marriage among the 'lower orders'. As we will see shortly, from convict times, irresistible if far from unchallenged, mateship seems to have moved up the social hierarchy.

Just the same, since 1976 the book's theme about a lesser female confidence, especially in relation to the public sphere, has lost something, in certain ways much, of its force. Women's own struggles figure as a central but by no means the sole explanation for this. In addition, men's role as fathers and workers has been signally weakened, and as a result women appear to have gained, certainly to have become more culturally salient. As with their earlier versions in the previous chapter, explanation here for these changes must in large part be directed to the economy.[7] In a very short time, we have lived through an historically unprecedented transformation of work, with dramatic consequences for manufacturing, farming and small business. Service industries, in which women are strongly represented, have grown considerably. Expanded too is the presence and weight in the community of government and hence of bureaucracy. New class women (Barbara Ehrenreich's 'professional middle class'[8]), the prime bearers of feminism, have found significantly increased employment opportunities on all such counts – though the historical meaning of feminism, as the last chapter emphasized, ranges far beyond questions of class origins. For one thing, feminist 'initiation of public discourse on the ... "basic gender script" characteristic of ... male-dominated societies ... has to be rated an achievement without historical parallel.'[9] We also saw in the last chapter that women of the new class are now much more publicly visible and confident in media, politics, the professions and, to a lesser extent, management. In this the women's movement is a significant cause.

This brings us to the other main way in which *The Real Matilda* proposed that our sexual relations appear different in comparative perspective. It might best be summed up in terms of a relative lack of comfortableness and fellowship, perhaps thus even of affection, between the sexes. Of Irish marriage, V.S. Pritchett, we recall, once wrote:

It is often said that the sexes do not like each other and fear sexual life . . . One has the impression of Irish love being militant flirtation, a meeting of enemies who unite for a moment and then return chastely to their own separate ways of living . . .[10]

Because historically the Irish transferred great slabs of their soul to Australia, there is a certain 'ethnopoetic' justification – a rightness both ethnic and poetic – in imagining Australian gender as a much-modified version of Pritchett's 'Irish love'. But pushed very far, the comparison would seriously mislead: for one thing, the English, at top and bottom rungs of the status hierarchy, played no minor role. Though in this we would see convictism as analytically distinct from ethnicity, it implicated both the English and Irish, while for their part, élite Australians registered the effect of the English élite's narrowing reaction against a sunnier eighteenth-century sexuality. And we may suspect other intangibles to do with the extreme difficulty – its causes psychic as much as material – in which all relationships, from the primary level upwards, took shape in harsh early days hostile to coherent community.

Former Wimbledon champion Arthur Ashe testified that when he lived in Australia during the 1960s, 'women seemed to be mainly second-class citizens who existed to serve men sexually and in any other way that men wished.'[11] Much, very much has changed. But the sense of a relative lack of fellowship between the sexes continues to find expression, though it is rarely direct and varies greatly. In 1982, himself clearly dissenting, novelist Thomas Keneally said: 'We pride ourselves on being the greatest oppressors of women in the world.'[12] In understanding this, we must first assume a degree of jokiness (though Freud insists jokes let us express truths otherwise forbidden). And in strictly status and material terms, the proposition no longer holds as clearly – material gaps between classes may well have outrun gender gaps within them. How then should we best read Keneally here? If he's getting at anything at all, it is at something of great importance. Because women mother, even Australians who think infancy and childhood have very little to do with adulthood might well feel that if remotely true, Keneally's point says a lot about

Australian men as well as women. And indeed something about our sexual ambience continues to jar, to evoke disquiet in a range of ways. In 1988, after more than a decade in Australia, American scholar Kay Schaffer found that 'representation of women in culture . . . is particularly negative . . . marked by inferiority in culturally specific ways which are quite different from, say, notions of the feminine in the cultural discourses on American national identity, or those of Canada, or New Zealand'.[13] In 1993 Andre Thornelowe, a young English computer systems analyst living here, put things more bluntly: 'This is the worst country for sexism that I have lived in. It's worse than in Egypt. I don't think Australian men respect women much.'[14] But the feeling much more often surfaces as an obscure sense of malaise. '[A]n unconscious but unavoidable sense of incompletion': this was the phrase used in 1991 by George Watt, Dean of John XXIII College at the Australian National University, and it goes some way towards catching that feeling in its most general manifestation.[15]

In some cases it is associated with an underdeveloped link with convictism. Reviewing *The Fatal Shore*, Robert Hughes' study of Australian convicts, historian Lloyd Robson wrote: 'I think Hughes overlooks the great fact of transportation. This was the extraordinary disproportion of adult males and females transported. If there is or was a social effect on colonial society that is where it is.'[16] We cannot know whether Robson thought the social effect of transportation cut out with federation, but Robert Hughes does not. He writes: 'it may also be that Australian sexism receives some of its force from the brutal legacy of carceral life.' Asked what changes he would make in a second edition of *The Fatal Shore*, Hughes included an 'offhand sexism' among possible long-term effect of transportation:

I think I pulled my punches too much. I think I was too cautious. Now I would be much more speculative about the effects of transportation . . . the offhand sexism in Australia, for example. And I think there is some part of mateship which can be traced to the convicts.[17]

Some knowing or unknowing comparison with the sexual ambience in other communities is implicit in this, and as an Australian, Hughes must surely have met up with himself in making it. Is there a sense of mourning, obscure malnourishment, in these expressions of unease? The gestation in feeling of such a thought would surely have involved sadness, regret – though because the unconscious deals only in extremes, profound sadness, deep regret? In 1988 Ita Buttrose was moved to anger on Australian domestic violence. Perhaps one can catch a remote buried anguish in the fierceness of her reaction, in an extravagance discouraging credibility. She was responding to a 1988 survey by the federal government's Public Policy Research Centre. Commissioned by the Office of the Status of Wo.nen, its findings took Buttrose directly back to convict sexual relations: 'Australian women have advanced nowhere. Our perceived success is made worthless by this revelation of the acceptance of violence. It must be said that in this our Bicentennial year things haven't improved much since our convict days.'[18]

If I were writing *The Real Matilda* today, in trying to come to grips with my own sense that there is a relative lack of fellowship and affection between the sexes, I'd now also take account of the relative strengths of male and female bonding. Our male bonding, mateship, though very much attenuated by the forces of post-industrialism, remains one of the strongest in the western world. To offset it, women would have needed comparably strong ties. But as a result of colonial legacies, Australian women did not experience bonding comparable to, say, that of English and American women. Women's bonding underpins women's politics, and in order to strengthen both, we need to begin by looking with sympathy, with empathy if possible, into circumstances of origin which diminished its force. Bonding, a transcultural and transhistorical constant, is an invariable fact of human society but comes in all shapes and sizes and, as Australian women, we would be less rueful about men's bonding (mateship) if we felt more richly rewarded by our own. Sturdy female bonding can enter the subjectivity of the individual woman so as to tilt in her favour that subliminal negotiation process present in the sexual relation. Comparative studies in women's history suggest female bonding elsewhere is often stronger than ours. The remarkable political clout of American women, for example, owes its start to the originary strength of women's bonding, village-based from the seventeenth century, then small town- and finally city-based. American geography was kinder by far to female bonding – through rivers which encouraged multiple town settlement and thus the ready access of women to sociability with other women; and through rainfall which encouraged family-based farming. Moreover, the central role played by religion not only helped underwrite bonding in the deepest way, but provided that unique apprenticeship in public affairs American women experienced, from the time of Anne Hutchinson, the seventeenth-century radical puritan leader,[19] to the Second Great Awakening after the 1790s. Underpinned by a fairly robust female bonding and secularized, the impetus carried American women to a world leading role in women's rights politics during the nineteenth and twentieth centuries. The Australian record in this is remarkable, with more than its share of courageous, spirited and dedicated women. But historical factors more strongly empowering women in cousin communities operated less effectively here. By comparison with that of Britain and America, overall, Australian religion was informed by distinctly less passion, and was more concerned with religious observation than with issues of salvation and the transcendental. Through no fault of our own, for bonding purposes we lacked comparably enabling historical and geographic factors. Some by contrast were on balance disabling. Convicts enter the picture again here. Women convicts played the cards history dealt as best, indeed as gallantly, as they could. But they necessarily furnished poor models of female bonding. For the structure and ethos of convictism itself, together with the negative light in which it sought to cast convict women – with, I will argue, a certain success – was hostile to robust bonding. (As to how and why convict women internalized negative hegemonic views, more later.)

Our version of male bonding, mateship, originated in colonial history among what earlier centuries were pleased to call the 'lower orders' rather than the 'middling kind' or 'the quality'. Contemporary observers still draw attention to the mateship mode in full cry among today's equivalent to the 'middling kind', the 'new class' of professionals, managers and bureaucrats. We can indeed pick up an unusual interpenetration of two broadly class-based masculine modes, with middle or new class men demonstrating patterns historically associated with, and arising from, less educated and poorer men, broadly working-class men (since the term 'lower order' belongs to earlier centuries). In Australia, the second masculine style ultimately takes us back to convicts. Scholars exploring colonial gender patterns are able to point us towards this same phenomenon of interpenetration in the late nineteenth and early twentieth centuries. Evidence for it emerges in a study of the Australian family from 1788 to the 1980s by historian Patricia Grimshaw, where she demonstrates the effects of mateship in the culture at large and thus in marriage across classes. 'A large number' of colonial men could not marry because of a shortage of women, and they therefore

formed emotional bonds with other men as a form of psychic defense against . . . loneliness. From such bonding arose a countervailing ideology to familial values which injected negative attitudes *to domestic life in general* [emphasis added] and women in particular into Australian culture.

The 'countervailing ideology' of single mateship men made itself felt in marriage as well as outside it.[20] Grimshaw thus demonstrates the interpenetration of what feminist Marilyn Lake, in an article to be seen as a 'watershed' text in national identity discourse,[21] later described as two distinct models of masculinity. In 1986 Lake construed the 1890s as marked by two 'competing ideals of masculinity', the unmarried 'Lone Hand' mateship man versus 'Domestic Man'.[22] The 'Lone Hand' stands for our broadly working-class (originally convict) 'mateship' mode of masculinity, 'Domestic Man', for our middle-class mode. Asserting the relevance of gender to the debate on national identity, Lake's picture is fruitful in its own right. Yet what the 1890s, that curious bridging decade, also reveals is a degree of interpenetration between the two models of masculinity which is possibly unparalleled in the west. On the ground, these two models actually coexisted, jostled one another, indeed flowed one into the other. The origins of this interflow, like the origins of mateship itself, take us back to convict society. They speak to the importance of the sexual ambience of that formative time for our gender patterns and the national identity itself.

First published in 1976, *The Real Matilda* has dealt with domination in a major way, bringing together concerns with national identity, class, race and gender and framing them within colonialism. Situating these within a modified version of Hartz's fragment theory, the book awarded early historical influences a disproportionate role in cultural dynamics. It thus proposed that in seeking sources of our cultural distinctiveness, we focus on an early configuration of class, race and gender within (what a comparative perspective shows to be a remarkably benign) colonialism. Domination figured importantly though not exclusively within that configuration – power, as we scarcely need Foucault to remind us, assumes enabling as well as disabling forms! From the 1970s, psychoanalysis began to change the ways social theory set about understanding ideologies centrally implicating domination, increasingly prompting social theory to look for the ways 'primary attachments, drives, fantasies, and structures of unconscious desire' help shape ideologies of domination.[23]

Offering a theory of intermeshing domination structures relevant to women and identity, in 1976 *The Real Matilda* adopted an approach which lends itself to and is deepened by a reading in terms of the 'object relations' tradition in psychoanalysis. (This includes the work of Melanie Klein and her followers.) The tradition involves the 'internalisation by the subject of mental images of the parental figures, and the foundation of . . . personality on a persisting phantasy relationship to . . . unconscious "internal objects" ' In short, it conceptualizes a mental structure which is 'an unconscious representation of the self related in phantasy to others.'[24] The book's early chapters on the free pre-working class poor, the convicts and the Irish invoked a kind of proto-object relations approach used by Frantz Fanon, a 'psychiatrist working with the Algerian Liberation Forces' (p. 162).[25] (This early theorist of colonialism has influenced thinkers from Sartre to Edward Said.[26]) Exploring more recent issues of women and identity, the second edition explicitly invoked the object relations tradition through the writings of Dorothy Dinnerstein, Nancy Chodorow and Jane Flax (pp. 229–57). We now briefly outline some key aspects of that tradition. One reason is that it enables a fruitful reworking of central concepts used to explore women's relation to intermeshing domination structures, and thereby expands the explanatory power of those concepts. Having outlined aspects of object relations' thought, we then use them to look again at earlier notions used to understand élite, Irish and convict women. A second reason for introducing object relations brings us to hotly contested ideological terrain. The recent growth of interest in psychoanalysis has come about mainly as a spin-off from post-structuralism. Key post-structuralist tenets find important legitimation in Lacan's quite particular reading of the early Freud. If we challenged post-structuralist claims – for example, that a linguistically and socially constructed being, shot through with division and contradiction, construes selfhood as consoling but fraudulent defense – we might well be referred to Lacan as their major legitimator. The object relations tradition associated with Melanie Klein, Donald Winnicott and others, based on over fifty years clinical experience, contests Lacan on the above and other basic issues. Of major relevance to our woman and identity project is the way object relations foregrounds women, so that one authority refers to the 'feminisation of psychoanalytic theory ... this tradition has accomplished.'[27] The object relations approach focuses not on Lacan's reading of early Freud texts in terms of post-structural linguistics, nor on an abstract idea of language itself, but on clinical understandings of the prelinguistic early mother–child relationship. While opening to readings of culture that are both historical and transhistorical, object relations is immediately concerned with mechanisms laid down long before language evolves, embodied in explosively creative and potent psychic scripts centring around the 'internal objects' in a little twenty-four-hour-a-day theatre of the unconscious.

Of the major forms of domination, racism and sexism share a prime emphasis on the body, their roots in our earliest unconscious structures. Michael Rustin, a social theorist aligned with socialist and Kleinian thinking, explores the early psychic mechanisms on which racism draws. Precisely because these begin to operate so early, though sexism carries vastly different meanings to racism, Rustin's views are relevant to sexism. Indeed his views recall the thesis proposed in the last chapter by that dazzling feminist theorist, Dorothy Dinnerstein, and the similarity endorses radical feminism's original sense that sexual domination is the prototype for race and class domination. (Aspects of Kleinian thinking may well bear out radical feminism in a remarkable way.) Discussing the psychic roots of racism, Rustin writes that beliefs about race, when 'suffused with intense feeling, are akin to psychotic states of mind.'[28] These states of mind, in the Kleinian view, characterize the so-called 'paranoid-schizoid position', Klein's first model of early mental functioning.[29] Here, splitting tendencies and feelings of persecution dominate the psyche. After the child reaches about three months, this first model yields centre-stage to a second which involves a greater capacity to integrate and is called the 'depressive position'. In the first or paranoid-schizoid position, the psyche, split, fragmented to a greater or lesser degree, is dominated by fears for the safety of the self, these fears being experienced as feelings of persecution. By contrast the greater integration of the self characterizing the depressive position means the self feels safer, and therefore has a somewhat greater capacity to feel concern for others (for 'the object'). The direction of concern is thus reversed. Though henceforth sidelined, the first model (the 'paranoid-schizoid position') continues to coexist with the second, so that splitting and feelings of persecution remain throughout life as 'universal, original and latent components of human mentality, never wholly banished from the self . . .'[30] They are normally operative in routine daily life, but tend to reassert themselves with special force, tend indeed to reclaim their old primacy, in times of personal or social trouble. Varying in form and intensity with historical circumstance, racism and sexism, because rooted in the paranoid-schizoid position, foreground splitting tendencies, feelings of persecution, and a curtailed ability to experience others. Thus they demote rationality, place it on hold, may threaten its purchase on mental life. In sum, the psychic mechanisms operating in the domination ideologies of racism and sexism involve splitting objects into an extreme form of the good and the bad, projecting unwanted parts of the self onto external targets, and suffusing thought processes with intense but unrecognized emotion.

Thus despite their radical difference, ideologies of sexism and racism do tap into the same unconscious mechanisms. So in seeking the Australian gloss on western sexism, as a point of departure, this book used Frantz Fanon's work on racism in the setting of colonialism. Hegemonic ideologies, with their myths and stereotypes, Fanon argues, find their way into the subjectivity of the dominated, and recent scholarship rightly argues that the psychic mechanisms he proposes lend themselves to a reading in terms of the object relations tradition.[31] Seeking the mechanisms whereby the oppressed themselves 'internalize' or absorb and adopt, at an unconscious level, aspects of the negative valuation placed upon them by the oppressor, Fanon called attention to the coiled, paradoxical routes by which the oppressed collude with even while passionately resisting the oppressor. The oppressed, he insisted, always contest the negative valuation of the oppressor, with varying degrees of energy and success according to available symbolic and moral resources. But to contest is not to banish. If we cast it in object relations terms, and be prepared for a duly modified application to colonial Australia, Fanon's thesis could read this way: the oppressed unconsciously take in, and up to a point, identify with negative evaluations (the 'internal objects' and 'part-objects' projected into them) by the oppressor. But just how might this transaction take place? The process centrally involves what Melanie Klein saw as the 'dominant mechanism'[32] of the paranoid-schizoid position, known as 'projective identification'. Juliet Mitchell describes it: 'In this the ego projects its feelings into the object which it then identifies with, becoming like the object which it has already imaginatively filled itself with.'[33]

Unwanted aspects ('bad objects') of the self may thus be handled by projecting them into others and then 'relating to them, so to speak, through hatred or fear, externally and in a relatively objectified form.'[34] And so in a domination structure, whether colonialist, racist or sexist, the oppressor dumps unwanted unconscious bits of the self into an external 'container' by projecting them into the oppressed. The oppressed will in turn unconsciously take in these expelled unwanted bits, thereby partly becoming what the oppressor claims he/she is and has forever been: dumb, sneaky, lazy, promiscuous, dirty . . . No matter how bravely he/she tries, the oppressed can never contest this with anything like complete success, in the first place because the oppressor is so powerful, controls socialization mechanisms, sets cultural agendas. Disturbingly, however, unconscious collusion adds a further reason, intransigent, doggedly and often successfully resistant to educative and political endeavour pitched at rational levels. Again we can use race as example: the further reason is that in some ways 'the black man wants to be like the white man.' (Reporting this thesis of Fanon's, a black scholar recently described him as 'very, very painful for a black person to read.')[35] Yet the cycle of projective identification continues, for the oppressor *then takes back into him/herself, reabsorbs*, aspects of the oppressed now changed for the worse precisely because the latter has internalized expelled negative objects dumped by the oppressor. Thus, through projective identification, two imaginary collectivities engage in a powerful transitive communication in which the oppressed are far from passive and by which each may be much altered. The dialectic of class domination broadly follows this model, and is equally contingent on historical context.

We've set down here a kind of worst-case scenario, with the model necessarily drawn at an abstract level. History demonstrates more benign (if always ambivalent) outcomes. To cast the process in terms of Fanon's conceptualization of racism is to focus on darkest potentials, and the culture of colonial Australia of course enabled radical development beyond these. As one of the most early and basic aspects of communication, projective identification will equally figure along more constructive axes in the benign aspects of intersubjectivity – the analyst, for example, might use the way projective identification shows up in her own feelings as best evidence of what the analysand is unconsciously experiencing. But as we see, processes of domination can also mobilize and enfold projective identification along negative axes. In such cases it operates as 'a self-reinforcing dynamic, in which the evidence of damage inflicted on projected internal objects generates still more violent persecution, which is again projected on to powerless victims.'[36]

Though an important part, domination, we know, constituted only part of everyday experience in colonial Australia. Life was varied, in some ways a feast of experience, harsh but in stark, bleak moments never without challenge, real joy, beauty. From the start, the emergent symbolic tapesty contained rich threads which registered the complexity of colonial society as a fragment of the world's vanguard modernizing nation: changing family and gender configuration, religious and ideological travail, an emerging respect for individual dignity only then starting to make its presence strongly felt. The powerfully 'rebellious' strain among the 'plebs' which E.P. Thompson highlights in traditional eighteenth-century British culture,[37] helped shape an Australian culture in other ways uniquely modern. How then should we see our early selves? Modernity, so central to our experience, itself represented and represents a development in human affairs at once flawed, massively contradic-

271

tory yet containing unparalleled potential. A development on which the jury of history is still out.

While a mechanical application will certainly mislead, it is possible to read black–white relations in colonial Australia at least partly in terms of the way projective identification operated within a dialectic of domination. And, as we will argue later, we can read convict relationships, in this case those of convict women, in terms of a modified version of it. An entire culture will certainly register the effects, sometimes powerful in impact, sometimes relatively mild, of its main domination 'couples'. The mechanisms of projective identification are at work in some form wherever there are structures of domination. So where we suspect that eager ghosts from the past still walk among us, where therefore we might want to understand what we hope to modify, it's worth trying to unravel the workings of this central psychic mechanism, so strange yet curiously familiar.

Domination was pervasive in colonial life, part of all we've come through and not entirely put behind. The foundational nature of convictism guaranteed this. A heavy state presence at once deepened and consolidated the whole experience, with the two great convict-era churches – Anglican and Roman Catholic – also playing a complex part in shaping formative scripts. The 'dialectic of domination' we have proposed, applies to major social groupings: thus, among others, to the Australian colonial élite in relation to its British counterpart, to Aborigines in relation to Europeans, to the Irish in relation to the English, to convicts in relation to administrators. And to the women within each group in relation to the men in each group.

For the Australian élite in relation to its British counterpart, a passionate desire to conform to the latter's metropolitan standards affected the whole culture through a heavy burden falling directly and in the first instance on élite women: 'colonial respectable classes' wanted 'to distance themselves in the strongest possible way from the convict "stigma" ', and so 'in most Australian colonies, the legacies of convictism converted a general Western bourgeois preoccupation with female respectability and domesticity into the extremely defensive version of ultrarespectability and ultra-domesticity.'[38]

An earlier chapter examined the way the Irish internalized hegemonic English attitudes over the centuries. Illuminating the position of other major groups, this throws poignant light on the dialectic of domination. In migrating to Australia, Irish males, 'the victims of long centuries of English colonial . . . contempt', did not 'shake off their past heritage, neither its treasures, its dreams nor its nightmares.' The English defined them as 'wretchedly unworthy beings.' But like all colonial subjects, even as the Irish 'passionately rejected[ed]' this definition, 'a deep and treacherous corner of the heart accept[ed] it', turning it 'inward in . . . self-denigration.' Thus brave, even triumphalist, nationalist ideologies contained as well as contested the colonial masters' negative definition of their victims. And the dynamic of victimhood inevitably implicated women, for while Irish males turned part of their self-denigration 'outwards on to the Anglo-Saxon Protestant master . . . part, alas, [they turned] on to Irish women. Irish women [were] thus the "victim of victims"' (pp. 155–6). Hence the Irish are shown as internalizing even while contesting, and partly displacing on to women, the dominant view of them held by the colonial English.

But before meeting the élite and before meeting the Irish, the reader was introduced to the dialectic of domination where it concerned the free women from among whom our convicts tended to come – the 'casual poor'. Because the 'attitude capitalist hegemonic strata felt towards women . . . came to be reflected, in varying ways, down the entire status ladder', a man might be expected to have wanted his 'woman to experience greater feelings of unworthiness than he did, and . . . it was an aim widely achieved among the casual poor. This process, largely unconconscious, operated . . . at all levels of the status ladder' (pp. 90, 91). Free casual poor people could and did become convicts, and the book's argument then moved to convict men and women. At the time it was first published, research had already begun to suggest that only some 25 per cent of convict women could be ' "designated prostitutes" '. This the argument accepted, along with the possibility put forward by demographer Peter McDonald in 1974 (later established as fact by historian Portia Robinson), that ' "a large proportion" ' of convict marriages ' "may have been stable unions" ' (p. 135).[39] These were of course vital matters. But if they had a decisive impact upon the overall psychic implications of domination, such implications would need to be addressed. They have not been addressed. Indeed, like feminist historiography, convict historiography tends to back away from cultural implications of the domination inherent in convictism.

Coerced migration 'played a significant role in the development of Australia right up to Federation', with several states remaining dependent on convict labour for more than a generation after transportation legally ended.[40] At a formative period in our history, domination, through convictism, laid its imprint on relationships, values, attitudes at a deep level. Therefore theorizing domination in its cultural rather than its legal, political or economic register takes us much further than the legal end of transportation. Among and far beyond the ranks of convicts, roles – whether of worker, citizen, husband, father, wife, mother – engaged with and were affected by the sense of domination inherent in the convictism. Relative to the free poor of the day, convicts were comparatively well fed, clothed and housed, and this is sometimes taken as a warrant for denying or underestimating the effect of unfreedom, or of domination, on convict selfhood. Because oppressors project negative views about the oppressed onto the oppressed, and the oppressed partly internalize them, domination, we saw, operates on and in the self significantly through stereotyping. To clear the way for examining the role of domination and negative stereotyping, let us, like some recent historians, assume for the moment that negative stereotypes were largely inaccurate. This will set us free to focus on the power, as distinct from the accuracy, of such stereotypes.

This book argued that, accurate or inaccurate, negative views about convict women possessed real power. Early chapters examined mechanisms by which the oppressed internalized negative views projected onto them by the oppressor. Singling out convict women, we recall that they 'were regarded . . . I stress the words "were regarded" . . . as . . . of trivial economic importance . . . , were defined as economically irrelevant'. In addition to this, 'the English élite thought of convict women . . . mainly as a kind of sexual servicing outcast group.' If free poor men at that time evinced strongly negative views towards their women, convict men, degraded through their lack of freedom, compounded such negativity: 'with convictism, the issue of . . . "the iron dominion exercised . . . by the masters", . . . of *dominance*, came to . . . eat more deeply into personality' than among free poor men. Seeking reasons for a lack of self-esteem, we could therefore 'simply point to manifest aspects of society's view of [convict women] and leave it at that.' Language gives us a 'hint of the fact that [convict women] were treated as outcasts of a sort' (pp. 122–4), and it's possible that the language of convict men, their own men, bit deepest into their hearts. Taken with the expressed disapproval of the élite and of respectable everyday women and men ('popular revulsion'), *irrespective of accuracy*, all this added up to negative stereotyping of extraordinary potency. Through an examination of the mechanism known as 'projective identification', the present chapter has more closely explored these culturally formative transactions between oppressor and oppressed.

Keeping in mind our analysis of the psychology of domination, we turn now to convict studies by Manning Clark, Robert Hughes and David Neal,[41] where domination receives an unusual amount of attention though women do not. In Manning Clark's history, subjectivity commands centre stage. He had a strong tendency to engage with individual characters in such a way that the social loses salience, but this is probably least in evidence for the convict era. Here the reader can almost feel domination as social presence, one hovering over the whole historical canvass. Clark linked some of our current habits of the heart with convictism, and about the Australian gloss on sexism Clark wrote: 'Others . . . have traced to the convicts . . . all the humiliations . . . to which men subject women in Australia.'[42] Robert Hughes, like Clark, is a writer in whom the painter and the poet help the historian to convey a subjectivity drawn with passions in conflict, and we can understand Hughes' work partly in terms of the project on domination associated with Marcuse and Foucault. Using Australia as case-study, *The Fatal Shore* might be construed as a similar meditation on the meaning of domination in the modern west. Concluding pages of Hughes' book raise the possibility of configurational analogies between convict and allegedly current Australian attitudes: cynicism about authority yet conformism with orthodoxy; mateship and egalitarianism. We recall too his earlier speculation that 'Australian sexism' may receive 'some of its force from the brutal psychic legacy of carceral life.' The last pages of *The Fatal Shore* dismiss such questions as 'a sterile line of enquiry', on the headcounting grounds that 'the vast majority of European

Australians' did not descend from pre-1850 stock.[43] But as we saw, a later interview suggested a different approach: 'Now I would be much more speculative about the effects of transportation . . . the offhand sexism in Australia, for example'.

In David Neal's study of law, politics and convictism, domination moves into sharp focus through an emphasis on the role of punishment. Punishment is the 'dominant', though not exclusive, characteristic of society. Legal changes, which other writers argue softened the social effect of punishment,[44] certainly lessened its arbitrary incidence. But Neal insists that 'legal protections against flogging . . . should not be overstated', as even with them, 'the rate of floggings and the number of lashes was enormous.' While flogging 'may not have been an everyday spectacle', convicts were forced to witness it, and '[p]aradoxically', the effect 'on those . . . who had not actually seen or experienced a flogging but had heard the stories, may have been heightened.' As to psychological effects, while flogging was 'brutalizing to those who underwent it', it was '[a]t the very least . . . degrading and probably much feared' by those who did not.[45] In short, an 'enormous incidence of physical coercion' and punishment 'stamped the mental world of New South Wales', 'determined much of the relevant tradition of New South Wales' and was crucial 'in shaping the tone and character' of society.[46] We might fairly conclude that an entire social climate was affected, surely with a special significance for women, their confidence, and their sense of belonging. Those who left accounts of floggings – 'people familiar with the use of corporal punishment in other contemporary contexts – left no doubt about their horror of what they saw in the colony.' Despite hyperbole, the horror punishment evoked registered feelings whose mobilization was necessary as the culture struggled to transcend its effects. This mobilization began a process of confronting radical moral and human drawbacks built into convictism which we may yet have to overcome completely.

In relation to domination and the effects of power, convict studies by Portia Robinson, Stephen Nicholas and Deborah Oxley[47] form a clear contrast to the works just mentioned. Portraying 'convict men . . . as workers and convict women as wives and mothers . . .'[48], Robinson, Nicholas and Oxley effectively divorce these roles from the context of domination. They offer a picture of personality shaped almost exclusively by material concerns, one which thereby imputes a dismaying one-dimensionality to convict subjectivity. In portraying convictism as a 'productive' and 'efficient' system, Nicholas, for example, offers us convicts as 'human capital', but loses them as human beings. The three writers portray the convict as worker, wife and mother in such a way that these roles, variously 'respectable', 'productive', 'efficient' and 'assertively' executed, are essentially sheared off from social context and the lived experience of punishment and power. An overpowering emphasis on the material glosses all roles as economic, almost as if, without intending to, historians were at once brightening and flattening the historical record so as to underpin 1980s econocrats in the drive for a productive 'enterprise culture'.

Arguing that convict women ' "laid the foundation for all that followed" ' in New South Wales,[49] Robinson gives detail on convicts as workers, wives and mothers that is as fascinating as it is valuable. From the start within the penal setting, potent forces worked towards shaping a society she seems to portray in terms of a basically standard model of the modern west. Work is inflected as entrepreneurial, family as bourgeois, woman as assertive.[50] Robinson's research rightly throws the vital forces of modernity into focus. But what remains overwhelmingly with the reader, driven home time and again, is a sense of the near-automatic power of the material to effect transformations of unquestioned psychic depth. We hear virtually nothing of the complex influences, psychic as much as physical, internal as much as external, reining in if not partly undermining courageous effort to transcend domination. For Robinson, roles, enacted in a new and materially expansive setting, function as apparently automatic solvents of earlier cultural legacies. Given the nature of that early society, stable pairing and marriage rightly receive Robinson's close attention as a major achievement, both by individual women and men and by the institutions of colonial society. Yet we receive no hint that the inner climate of marriage/pairing was as likely to reproduce as to delete prevailing gender patterns and social attitudes, and with them, negative stereotypes. To be sure, material opportunity and upward mobility modified the effects of intermeshing structures of domination on women's lives and sense of self. But we could scarcely expect them to have banished such effects. The legacies of domination are not so easily exorcized. Modernizing forces – work as entrepreneurial, family as respectably bourgeois – arguably encountered stronger opposition here than in any comparable society, and in crucial ways *the very contest involved is what makes us distinctive.* We cannot be judicious or insightful about Australia while we try to understand ourselves in terms of such a straightforward version of the bourgeois west. That contest which does much to make us distinctive, engaged us at the deepest levels, and was one in which the question of domination played an important part. To assess past achievements and current dilemmas is to confront that engagement and its consequences.

The virtual absence of this whole rich drama leaves Robinson's work, for all its absorbing detail, conceptually thin, and the reader with a sense of walking over surfaces. Finally, in *The Women of Botany Bay*, a complex oppositional literature on negative stereotyping is given a perfunctory, generally dismissive treatment. Negative stereotyping with its effects on women *and through them on the entire culture*, is very largely ignored. Those who have addressed it in their various ways are labelled rather than analysed, written off in the main as pure merinos, bigoted colonial bourgeois or their legatees today among mainstream and feminist historians.[51]

Stephen Nicholas' book, *Convict Workers. Reinterpreting Australia's past*, contains one chapter on 'Female Convicts' by Deborah Oxley. Like Robinson's, this account is at once accurate in detail and grievously reductionist in outcome, conjuring up a vision of personality without depth and beyond the workings of power. Implicitly and at times explicitly intervening in the historiography on female convict identity, Oxley reads that identity almost wholly in terms of economic role. We seem meant to accept Oxley's market interpretation of motherhood and prostitution for the convict woman, as if it accounted for her total selfhood. Thus, in urging us to see convict women as 'talented and skillful workers . . . mainly young women [with] the ability to bear children and to create and perpetuate the future labour force', Oxley offers a picture of female convict subjectivity in keeping with a book which basically portrays 'convicts as "human capital" '. Having children, becoming a mother, Oxley conflates with the marketplace and class, naming motherhood in terms of 'creat[ing] and perpetuat[ing] the future labour force'.

278

She proposes that we should understand prostitution 'as an occupation, quite receptive to reclassification as legal, and thus as evidence of a woman's working class origins.' Oxley argues that convict women were not 'professional criminals', but 'casual pilferers', not 'prostitutes', but poorly paid 'workers' who 'probably cushioned the impact of economic fluctuations by turning to prostitution.'[52] Clearly true. But the blunt reductionism of Oxley's approach diminishes our ancestors. Identity is once more brought back to economics and a view of role significantly emptied of rounded subjectivity. In relation to negative stereotyping, Oxley, like Robinson, assumes that to challenge its accuracy is to dispose of its power.

Domination acted on the subjectivity of convict women in large part through negative stereotyping. The convict studies we have just discussed basically sidestep the cultural implications of domination and negative stereotyping by conflating questions of the latter's accuracy with questions of its power. The facts about convict women are clearly more complex than these writers imply. But even if we completely adopt the 'inaccuracy' standpoint and accepted their more favourable verdict on convict women in all contested areas, this would not close the question of negative stereotyping because we would have failed to address its power. Placed so vulnerably in a system involving a generally harsh form of domination, convict women could not have failed to be deeply affected by negative stereotyping. To return to Frantz Fanon and his Algerian *colons*: Algerians contested negative views about them promulgated by French colonial rulers. But as Fanon tells us, Algerians were still profoundly affected by those views, not only in practical matters (economic, social and political) but – for Fanon, the most bitter of ironies and for us, the issue most relevant to convict women – also in terms of their own self-definition. Historians can and should revisit archives and challenge stereotypes on grounds of accuracy. But to challenge accuracy is not to challenge power. Each demands a separate kind of challenge. In this case, power needs to be addressed, as Foucault might argue, in terms of the ways stereotypes have their effects, of the mechanisms by which they set up their place in the subjectivity of the oppressed. Our earlier sketch of projective identification in the context of racial domination attempted to identify such mechanisms.

Whether convict women worked productively, enjoyed upward mobility and embraced respectability, whether they married, had children, engaged in prostitution, whether they carried out these roles assertively or otherwise, *at the same time* they were profoundly influenced by stereotypes partly constitutive of the culture. The achievements of Australian women deserve to be measured in terms of where they really began, in terms of the means by which, and the degree to which, they transcended initial difficulties, cultural quite as much material. Far more than material, we might argue. Denial of those difficulties, for a start holds us back from appreciating women's real experience and achievement. But more, it also undermines the broader project of understanding how past patterns have helped to shape the present, and thereby condition options for the future. For where some past patterns enriched, others diminished us and while denied, will no doubt continue to do so. If we want to loosen the power of clamant 'eager ghosts', the poet's verdict on them bears repeating: 'if you have not the habit of taking counsel with them, you are but an instrument in their hands.'

In these times of global uncertainty, along with basic 'holding' structures such as family and *ethnie*, the nation attracts increasing attention in Australia and throughout the west. We now therefore turn to more recent feminist interventions on national identity. Positioning women, however marginally inscribed in basic texts, as central to the reality of the nation and its core culture, in 1976 *The Real Matilda* explored the idea of formative inputs into both by different categories of women: in terms of class, élite and poor women; in terms of ethnicity, Irish women; and in a category unique among formative groups in the western context, convict women. With Kaye Schaffer's 1988 study, *Woman and the bush*, feminists explicitly re-entered Australian discourse on national identity. Schaffer indicted that discourse with marginalizing woman and portraying her more negatively than did its western counterparts. Influenced by post-structuralism and its crucial legitimator, psychoanalyst Jacques Lacan, Schaffer's analysis is often congruent with one grounded in the object relations tradition. For her, the 'construction of the bush as cruel mother, compounded by the stereotype of women as God's police, continues to affect the culture's consciousness of women.'[53] In the figure of woman as mother-aligned-with-nature, each part is etched into the unconscious as non-nurturant. We might think of Lindy Chamberlain, or A.D.Hope's woman whose breast remains 'tender but within the womb is dry.'[54]

Where Schaffer targetted constitutive cultural elements of national identity in relation to women, other feminists addressed mainstream historical discourse. In 1991 historian Gail Reekie too argued for its basic irrelevance to women. Proposing that 'the work of feminist historians shows how women have repeatedly been sacrificed to the nation', Reekie offers an overview of Australian feminist historiography. While apparently omitting convict women, according to her, it instances women as

bearers of class distinction, as wartime heroines, as workers worth two-thirds of a man's wage, as the unpaid housekeepers of the workingman's paradise and the liberal democratic society, as helpmate and slave to the pioneer settler, as the silent victims of domestic conflict, as mothers of the nation responsible for national prosperity and security, and as a metaphor for an Australian landscape that constituted the object of men's desire.[55]

In a major way women figure here as victims: 'sacrificed', 'slave', 'silent victims', 'the object of men's desire'. We know that sexual and racial relations differ in the most profound way. Yet however differently inflected in each culture, each contain victim and oppressor aspects. As we've seen in relation to racism, object relations psychoanalysis shows that while engaged in bitter contest, victim and oppressor also collude at unconscious levels. Though for racism the ratio of contest to collusion is much greater, we need to theorize sexism in a similarly doubled, ambivalent way. Reekie *demonstrates* collusion but fails to *theorize* it. Following Benedict Anderson, for her the nation is 'imagined as a fraternal community'[56] and so is rightly seen as integral to patriarchy. Earlier in the same work, Reekie suggests that women might collude with men in this patriarchal project. Thus for example, women's work in 'production, reproduction, domestic labour, social reform . . . may have been consistent with an allegiance to the fraternal community'. Elsewhere, collusion is more clearly suggested: 'Many women have undeniably been just as enthusiastic nationalists as men.' Because discourse on the nation omits or marginalizes women, Reekie suggests that one way to offset this, while making gender itself visible, is to examine 'the ways in which women have been actively involved, perhaps complicit in . . . nation-formation.'[57] What does this complicity or collusion mean? The underlying issues of agency, contest and collusion recur in later feminist engagements with the nation. In the article discussed earlier, Marilyn Lake compellingly explores a *contest* between women and men over gender in the 1890s.[58] But at the level of class, this 'watershed' text also makes it clear that women *colluded* with men around issues of 'respectability', and so helped build the more stable and controlling form of (patriarchal) capitalism we meet in the 1920s. Historically, gender collusion itself appears over so great a range of issues as to demand central and explicit focus in feminist theory.

Gail Reekie is unusual in calling explicit attention to women's collusion in patriarchal projects. But since she fails to explore the meaning of collusion, we're probably justified in thinking she does not find it especially problematic. In fact, it points to a crucial *aporia* in feminist theorizing, for psychoanalytic feminist theory makes it clear that such complicity goes much deeper than ideological manipulation by patriarchal élites. Similarly Benedict Anderson's 'imagining' of the nation as a 'community . . . [pivoted around] a deep, horizontal comradeship . . . [a] fraternity' points far beyond the conscious levels on which he and most others seem to conceptualize it,[59] or Reekie invokes that conceptualization. The last chapter examined Dorothy Dinnerstein's 1976 work, *The Mermaid and the Minotaur*. Drawing on object relations as well as classical psychoanalysis, Dinnerstein argued that the pre-oedipal child, male or female, flees from its archaic sense of maternal power to embrace the power of the father. Because he becomes 'vivid' for the child when its own mental apparatus is less primitive, the father's power appears to it as less immense, arbitrary and hence more limited and safe. Dinnerstein therefore proposed that at the unconscious level, women and men colluded in the genesis and perpetuation of patriarchal gender: in the west today, without such collusion patriarchy would be 'a pushover'. Feminist theory since Dinnerstein has usually refused to address the possibility of this kind of unconscious collusion, whether in relation to patriarchal gender itself, to the fratriarchal nation, or a host of other central issues. Collusion of this sort represents a particular kind of agency. Feminist theory is generally unwilling to examine agency in terms of the unconscious. But on the one hand, it is quick to invoke agency by way of rejecting imputations of female passivity, while on the other hand, as with Reekie, it often finds a path back to explicit or implicit versions of victimhood – and thus passivity. Listening with the third ear, many people pick up this contradiction, the fact that women collude with as well as contest men's endeavours. If we fail to incorporate it into our theorizing of patriarchy and its projects, while these days no one will say so, many feel it can't be so wrong to continue writing as if women are implicitly present in inclusive accounts. Thus failure to directly acknowledge the fact that women *both contest and collude with* patriarchy must undercut the ability to challenge women's virtual exclusion from mainstream discourse on national identity.

We turn finally to recent issues linked with women and identity in Australia. Since 1976 when this book was first published, women have chalked up palpable victories. Valuable legal initiatives inspired by feminism have encouraged formal equality. In the government sector, especially within areas such as education, health and community services, feminist influence has made itself widely felt.[60] Along with humane toleration, internationalism, anti-racism, support for mass immigration and for state intervention as something like a principle, feminism became part of a virtual symbolic badge or kit for ascendant post-1970s layers of the new class. Through this class above all, the decades since the 1970s transformed much of the vocabulary of public discourse, and feminism figured centrally in that transformation. Political scientists here as elsewhere in the west claim that politics is undergoing 'feminization', pointing to the new profile of the 'soft' or feminine issues of ecology, social welfare, child-care. Variously defined, feminism penetrated beyond the level of public discourse into issues of child-raising and gender formation.

Yet radical change was in the making, and as the 1980s came to an end, oppositional politics of all kinds had fallen on dark days. Increasingly it seemed that global corporatism faced no real rivals. Dominant economic rationalist policies minimized the possibility of major gains for women. All this found its reflection in feminism. As oppositional politics and with it, the women's movement, lost their mass base, feminism joined the move by liberal and radical intellectuals to displace lost power into cultural rhetoric. Thus much of feminist theory embraced the post-structuralist philosophy of textuality and difference, together with the politics of micro-issues. The latter had the effect of focusing feminist energy onto local, fragmented micro-power structures. Though women often consti- tute a majority, women's oppression consequently now tends to find itself situated in a list of minority concerns, and in their Foucauldian proscription of the general concept, feminist post-structuralists find it hard to contest this marginalization of women. Partly because global issues of no matter what urgency fall under post- structuralism's blackban on the large-scale, intellectual feminists now tend to show little interest in bold feminist alternatives in public policy, whether in environmental resource allocation, law and industry policy, feminist concepts of urban planning, or social welfare.

If this suggests political reasons for feminism to think again about the influence of Foucault, there are equally cogent theoretical reasons. Foucault's thought finds significant legitimation in Lacan- ian psychoanalysis. Feminist theory urgently needs to compare the tenets of Lacan, along with those of Foucault himself, with those of a tradition in psychoanalysis in general opposition to the Lacanian, that is, the object relations tradition (Klein, Winnicott, and in feminist theory, Dinnerstein, Chodorow, Flax).

In the 1980s, government strategy to address economic crisis set out to restructure the economy and build an 'enterprise culture'. We suggested earlier that for convict historiography, this found echoes in a 'productivist' tendency which diminished the complexity of convict subjectivity and failed to address the power, as distinct from the accuracy, of negative stereotyping. Government strategy had an even clearer impact on feminism. Government, business leaders and major union officials drew up an 'Accord' and established an Australian corporatism. As they accepted executive and policy- making positions in a much-expanded bureaucracy, many feminists, especially though not exclusively the liberal feminist descendants of first-wave feminism, became part of this. Given the celebrated Australian 'talent for bureaucracy',[61] such 'femocrats' soon formed a major presence within feminism. Though often highly ambivalent about Accordist political culture, femocrats commonly had to adopt market-dominated values. Has all this been of major benefit to everyday women? Feminists themselves are refreshingly honest in evincing doubt. Political theorist Anna Yeatman suggests that femocrats abetted Labor moves by which women were forced to settle for the appearance rather than the substance of equality. Labor administrations, Yeatman writes, developed 'elaborate discourses of access and equity', and these operated as 'symbolic smokescreens' to legitimize social policies signally failing to alleviate major everyday problems.[62] In like vein, former leading femocrat and feminist theorist Hester Eisenstein judged it to be 'a matter for debate as to how widespread and effective feminist campaigns have been, and how in particular the outcomes of the campaigns, in terms of legislative reform, have benefitted the women *for whose sake they were undertaken*' [my emphasis].[63] However this verdict needs important qualification. While taking into account the real, often passionate dedication of many femocrats, it is true that they have 'conspicuously improved their [own] position'. But we need to remember that as a 'small but socially significant minority crucial to feminism', one with a 'secure niche in the system', femocrats 'provide an enduring base for continuing social discourse on the meaning of gender'[64]. Such discourse is now firmly positioned in new class ranks, and through them, in society at large. An institutional base in the bureaucracy, though extraordinarily ambivalent in its consequences for feminism, remains vital to its continuing influence.

As to the broad reach of feminism, clearly a good deal has been achieved, but to what extent has fundamental symbolism changed? In her 1988 study of our basic texts, Kay Schaffer portrays the 'particularly negative' 'representation of women in culture' as an ongoing reality.[65] Consider the symbols Prime Minister Keating invoked, positioning himself as historic leader in the run-up to elections. In a 1993 Australia Day speech calling on Australians to meet the 'challenge to secure their future' in lean times, he defined the essential Australian:

Out there at Bowral in the twenties, young Donald Bradman must have imagined himself making centuries at the Sydney Cricket Ground – and somewhere else in NSW the young Bill O'Reilly probably imagined himself getting him out. I don't know whether Ben Lea ever imagined he'd play in the Vienna Philharmonic, but I suspect he did. And against all the odds, the young Lionel Rose no doubt imagined himself one day a world champion and a national hero. If they can do it, we can.[66]

Thus in 1993 the Prime Minister basically perpetuated the womanless iconography enshrined in the Convict–Jolly Swagman–Digger–Hoges symbolic cluster. The overall social climate has, if anything, become more hostile to the most basic values sustaining community itself along with women's central role in it. For example, though more women host talk shows and play the lead in sitcoms, nationally and internationally the mass culture industry's portrayal of women contains a good deal of routine trivialization and contempt/hate. Far more damaging though, is the development of a 'kill culture' here as throughout the west:

Sado-sexual violence is on the ascendancy. Its symbols, cinema, literature, music, art, style . . . from Rage to Romper Stomper, from splatterpunk to serial savagery . . . [form] the iconography of everyday life . . . Groovy, gothic, ironic, fun, fashionable, post-modern . . . [in it we glimpse] the 'imagery of today'.[67]

A near-saturation of media with physical and psychic violence – the news, ramboist films whether flagged as high art or serious social analysis – suggests that values traditionally associated with women are under relentless and escalating assault. If television and film penetration of the child's pre-oedipal psyche carries the radical implications some suggest, the results of media colonization may only be starting to come in.

Thus besides the material gains for women mentioned earlier, there have been other developments, ambiguous, ambivalent, which lie at a deeper level in western culture as a whole. Some still await decoding. The redundancy notice twentieth-century western culture served on the patriarchal father has been accompanied (I believe in part caused) by an increasingly strong maternal role in child-rearing. Women have also assumed a modest but increasing public role. Partly as a result of these changes, whole reaches of social and political life in the west show capacities for compromise, flexibility, negotiation. They demonstrate a respect for the person significantly greater than in cultures where women occupy less important roles.

In the end, though, all this might be a spin-off from the fact that in the west, fratriarchy has replaced patriarchy. In the long historical perspective, fratriarchy, the rule of the brothers, might prove to be the form of male domination adopts in the era of global monopoly capitalism. What would this mean for women?

Notes

1. 'Good enough' is borrowed from Donald Winnicott's famous phrase, 'good enough mothering'. Winnicott was a pediatrician and psychoanalyst of the 'British object-relations' school, closely linked with Melanie Klein. See D. W. Winnicott, *The Family and Individual Development*, Tavistock, London, 1964.

2. 'Holding': this is another Winnicott term. Cut from the prototype of the mother physically holding the baby and psychically holding or containing its fragmenting anxieties, in broad cultural terms the word denotes integrative, anti-splitting tendencies inherent, as reality and potential, in social relationships, structures and symbolic activity. See *Holding and Interpretation: Fragment of an Analysis*, The Hogarth Press and The Institute of Psycho-Analysis, London, 1986.

3. Robert Hughes, *The Fatal Shore. A History of the Transportation of Convicts to Australia, 1787-1868*, Collins Harvill, London, 1987, p. 593; Patrick O'Farrell, *The Irish in Australia*, New South Wales University Press, Kensington, N.S.W.: 'an Irish Catholic tribe' (p. 40); 'quasi-tribal drinking and riotous behaviour' (p. 41); 'quasi-tribal unity of the Irish proletariat' (p. 43).

4. Henry Mayhew uses the phrase 'the nomad races' of English poor (*London Labour and the London Poor*, 1861-2 edition, Frank Cass, London, 1967). See too M. B. and C. B. Schedvin, 'The Nomadic Tribes of Urban Britain: A Prelude to Botany Bay', in John Carroll (ed.), *Intruders in the Bush. The Australian Quest for Identity*, Oxford University Press, Melbourne, 1982, pp. 82-108. See too Russel Ward, *The Australian Legend*, Oxford University Press, Melbourne, 1958.

5. Peter Robinson, *Sun-Herald*, 27 Jan. 1991.

6. Patricia Grimshaw, 'Women and the Family in Australian History - a reply to *The Real Matilda*', *Historical Studies*, vol. 18, no. 72, April 1979, pp. 412-21.

7.   Michel Aglietta, *A Theory of Capitalist Regulation: The U.S. Experience,* trans. David Fernbach, New Left Books, London, 1979; Manuel Castells, *The Informational City: information, technology, economic restructuring and the urban-regional process,* Basil Blackwell, Oxford, 1989; Saskia Sassen, *The Global City: New York, London, Tokyo,* Princeton University Press, Princeton, New Jersey, 1991; Belinda Probert, 'Restructuring and Globalization: What Do They Mean?' *Arena Magazine,* April–May 1993, pp. 18–22.

8.   Barbara Ehrenreich, *Fear of Falling. The Inner Life of the Middle Class,* Harper Collins, New York, 1990.

9.   Miriam Dixson, 'Gender, Class and the Women's Movements in Australia 1890, 1980', in Norma Grieve and Ailsa Burns (eds), *Australian Women. New Feminist Perspectives,* Oxford University Press, Melbourne, 1986, pp. 14–15.

10.   V. S. Pritchett, *Dublin: A Portrait,* London, Bodley Head, 1967, pp. 90–1.

11.   'Love, sex and death' excerpts from the posthumous autobiography of Arthur Ashe, *Age* (Melbourne), 19 June 1993.

12.   Constance Casey, 'Australians Observed', *National Times,* Aug. 22–28, 1982.

13.   Kay Schaffer, *Women and the bush. Forces of desire in the Australian cultural tradition,* Cambridge University Press, Cambridge, 1988, p. 15.

14.   Sun–Herald, 20 June 1993.

15.   George Watt was reviewing Joy Hooton, *Stories of Herself When Young. Autobiographies of Childhood by Australian Women,* Oxford University Press, Melbourne, 1990 (*Australian,* 21/22 July 1990).

16.   Lloyd Robson, review of Robert Hughes, *The Fatal Shore. A History of the Transportation of Convicts to Australia, 1787-1868.* (*Times on Sunday,* 1 February 1987).

17.   Robert Hughes, interview with Lloyd Robson, *Times on Sunday,* 1 February 1987.

18.   Ita Buttrose, 'Time to stop accepting violence', *Sun–Herald,* 13 March 1988. At the time, Buttrose was editor-in-chief of the *Sun–Herald.*

19.   G. J. Barker-Benfield, 'Anne Hutchinson and the Puritan Attitude toward Women', *Feminist Studies,* vol. 1, no. 2, Fall 1972, pp. 65–96.

20.   Patricia Grimshaw, 'The Australian Family', in Ailsa Burns et al. (eds), *The Family in the Modern World. Australian Perspectives,* Allen and Unwin, Sydney, 1983, p. 36.

21.   Susan Magaray, Sue Rowley, Susan Sheridan (eds), *Debutante Nation. Feminism Contests the 1890s,* Allen and Unwin, Sydney, 1993, p. xx.

22. Marilyn Lake, 'The Politics of Respectability: Identifying the Masculinist Context', *Historical Studies*, vol. 22, no. 86, pp. 116-131. Reprinted in Susan Magaray et al. (eds), *Debutante Nation*, pp. 1-15.

23. Anthony Elliott, *Social Theory and Psychoanalysis in Transition. Self and Society from Freud to Kristeva*, Blackwell, Oxford, 1992, p. 162.

24. Michael Rustin, 'Kleinian Psychoanalysis and Cultural Theory', in Michael Rustin, *The Good Society and the Inner World. Psychoanalysis, Politics and Culture*, Verso, London, 1991, pp. 181-3.

25. In this book, see too pp. 145, 248. Fanon's works include *Black Skin, White Masks* (*Peau Noire, Masques Blancs*, 1952, transl. Charles Lam Markmann), Paladin, Hertfordshire, 1970; *The Wretched of the Earth (Les Damnés de la Terre)*, Penguin, Harmondsworth, 1967.

26. See for example Albert Memmi, *The Colonizer and the Colonized*, Beacon Press, Boston, 1967; Edward Said, *Culture and Imperialism*, Chatto and Windus, London, 1993.

27. Michael Rustin, 'Kleinian Psychoanalysis and Cultural Theory', p. 197.

28. Michael Rustin, 'Psychoanalysis, Racism and Anti-Racism', in Rustin, *The Good Society*, p. 62.

29. For this section, I'm grateful for help from Joan and Neville Symington.

30. Michael Rustin, 'Psychoanalysis, Racism and Anti-Racism', p. 62.

31. Dr Fakhry Davids, 'Frantz Fanon: the Struggle for Inner Freedom'. Paper given at Psychoanalysis and the Public Sphere, Sixth Annual Conference sponsored by Free Association Books, The Human Nature Trust and the Sociology Department, University of East London, 30-31 October 1992, Stratford, London.

32. Neville Symington, *The Analytic Experience. Lectures from the Tavistock*, Free Association Books, London, 1986, p. 266.

33. Juliet Mitchell (ed.), Introduction to *The Selected Melanie Klein*, Penguin, Harmondsworth, 1986, p. 20.

34. Michael Rustin, 'Psychoanalysis, Racism and Anti-Racism', p. 64.

35. Frantz Fanon, *Black Skin, White Masks*, p. 9; see too p. 162; Dr Fakhry Davids, 'Frantz Fanon: the Struggle for Inner Freedom'.

36. Michael Rustin, 'Psychoanalysis, Racism and Anti-Racism', p. 66.

37. E. P. Thompson, *Customs in Common*, The Merlin Press, London, 1991, p. 9.

38. Miriam Dixson, 'Gender, Class, and the Women's Movements in Australia 1890, 1980', p. 19.

39. The possibility of 'stable unions' was put forward by demographic

historian Peter F. McDonald, *Marriage in Australia*, Australian Family Formation Project, Monograph no. 2, Department of Demography, Institute of Advanced Studies, A.N.U., Canberra, 1974, p. 30; Portia Robinson, *The Hatch and Brood of Time. A study of the first generation of native-born white Australians 1788-1828*, vol. 1, Oxford University Press, Melbourne, 1985; *The Women of Botany Bay. A reinterpretation of the role of women in the origins of Australian society*, The Macquarie Library, Macquarie University, Sydney, 1988.

40. Stephen Nicholas and Peter R. Shergold, 'Transportation as Global Migration', in Stephen Nicholas (ed.), *Convict Workers. Reinterpreting Australia's past*, Cambridge University Press, Cambridge, 1988, p. 29.

41. C. M. H. Clark, 'The Origins of the Convicts Transported to Eastern Australia, 1787-1852', *Historical Studies, Australia and New Zealand*, vol. 7, 1956, pp. 121-35, 314-27; *A History of Australia*, vol. I, *From the Earliest Times to the Age of Macquarie*, Melbourne University Press, Melbourne, 1962; vol. II, *New South Wales and Van Diemen's Land 1822-1838*, Melbourne University Press, Melbourne, 1968; Robert Hughes, *The Fatal Shore*; David Neal, 'Free Society, Penal Colony, Slave Society, Prison?', *Historical Studies*, vol. 22, no. 89, October 1987, pp. 497-518; *The Rule of Law in a Penal Colony. Law and Power in Early New South Wales*, Cambridge University Press, Cambridge, 1993. For Clark's sense of the formative cultural effect of convictism, see Miriam Dixson, 'Clark and National Identity', in Carl Bridge (ed.), *Manning Clark*, Melbourne University Press, Melbourne, 1994.

42. C. M. H. Clark, *A Short History of Australia*, Mentor, the New American Library, New York, 1963, p. 118.

43. Robert Hughes, *The Fatal Shore*, p. 596.

44. See, for example, Nicholas, *Convict Workers*, p. 195.

45. David Neal, *The Rule of Law* pp. 50-52. Reviewing *The Fatal Shore*, historian Lloyd Robson wrote: 'Hughes's case in terms of brutalisation is overwhelming' (*Times on Sunday*, 1 February 1987).

46. David Neal, 'Free Society, Penal Colony', p. 508-511.

47. Portia Robinson, *The Women of Botany Bay; The Hatch and Brood of Time*; Stephen Nicholas (ed.), *Convict Workers*; Deborah Oxley, 'Female Convicts', in Stephen Nicholas (ed.), *Convict Workers*, pp. 85-97.

48. Marion Aveling, Review of Robert Hughes' *The Fatal Shore*, in *Historical Studies*, no. 90, April 1988, pp. 127-8.

49. Portia Robinson, *The Women of Botany Bay*, p. 239.

50. For Robinson's treatment of the role of material prosperity, enterprise, upward mobility, marriage and respectability, see *The Women of Botany Bay*, *passim*, and especially pp. 3-5, 37-8, 63, 99-100, 122, 214, 236, 239.

51. Robinson, *The Women of Botany Bay*, pp. 7-8; 207, 214, 236, 276, n. 17.

52. Oxley, 'Female Convicts,' pp. 86-95.

53. Kaye Schaffer, *Women and the bush*, p. 177.

54. A. D. Hope, 'Australia', *Penguin Book of Australian Verse*, Penguin, London, 1958, p. 119.

55. Gail Reekie, 'Contesting Australia', in Gillian Whitlock and David Carter (eds), *Images of Australia. An Introductory Reader in Australian Studies*, University of Queensland Press, St Lucia, 1993, p. 155.

56. Benedict Anderson, *Imagined Communities. Reflections on the Origin and Spread of Nationalism*, Verso, London, 1982.

57. Reekie, 'Contesting Australia', pp. 148-9.

58. In Susan Magaray *et al.*, (eds), *Debutante Nation*, pp. 1-15.

59. Benedict Anderson, *Imagined Communities*, p. 16.

60. Marion Sawer, *Sisters in Suits. Women and Public Policy in Australia*, Allen and Unwin, Sydney, 1990.

61. A. F. Davies, *Australian Democracy. An Introduction to the Political System*, Longman's, Green and Co., Melbourne, 1958, p. 3.

62. Anna Yeatman, *Bureaucrats, Technocrats, Femocrats. Essays on the contemporary Australian State*, Allen and Unwin, Sydney, 1990, p. 172.

63. Hester Eisenstein, *Gender Shock. Practising feminism on two continents*, Allen and Unwin, Sydney, 1991, pp. 92-3.

64. Miriam Dixson, 'Gender, Class and the Women's Movements in Australia: 1890, 1980', pp. 22-4.

65. Kay Schaffer, *Women and the bush*, pp. 15, 177, 181.

66. 'Keating appeals to national imagination', *Australian*, 26 Jan. 1993.

67. Richard Neville, former editor of Oz magazine, in *The Independent Monthly*, April 1993.

Conclusion

This book has explored historical influences shaping identity for women in Australia, and in doing so has been concerned to underline the disproportionate role of early, formative inputs. It is past-into-present and past-for-the-present history, and so many of its central concerns remain relevant to women today.

In this most spectacular of all democracies, notwithstanding the unique role of the 'lower orders' in shaping identity, the role of our élite was more important. Historically, the nineteenth century must rate as the 'century of the bourgeoisie'. Males from all layers of the nineteenth-century Australian élite tended to experience profound uncertainty about issues of authority and identity, though we have singled out the old middle class, then the cultural pattern setter for the entire west. Marxists used to claim that imperial powers systematically kept colonial élites (the 'compradore bourgeoisie') in a relatively modest material condition; set alongside comparable colonial élites, Australia's was especially thin in terms of self-confidence and material prosperity. By contrast with the United States, for example, our élite was notably lacking in both. It also failed to experience the boost to confidence that came with the clarified family, hence self, boundaries the United States achieved through the 1776 War of Independence. This functioned as a powerful ritual helping American sons to separate from a British father.

The book has proposed a range of explanations for the relative disabilities experienced by Australian colonial women, one being the disproportionate strengths of female bonding and male bonding (mateship). But it is important to re-emphasize one cause that is central: Australian women inevitably had to reflect the self-doubt of their men. This is a law of male-dominant society, even in the fratriarchal form I claim prevailed from the start in Australia, and has contributed to a characteristically uncertain, indefinite feel about national identity itself. Australian male colonists developed (sometimes overly defensive) ideologies which contested negative imperial views about them. Such ideologies helped sustain colonial self-belief (we might see ockerism as a late twentieth-century legatee). Yet Australians continued to experience massive uncertainty about authority, an issue psychoanalysis locates near the centre of selfhood. Elite Australian males were apt to fall back on an unconscious compensatory mechanism whose outcome was that men insisted that their women stand lower in the appropriate class-status niche. The result was to make women less certain of themselves, and so more constricted, indeed often in a defensively extreme way, in their own self-definition. To take an example originating among élite women: colonial women practised an ultradomestic version of the nineteenth-century western bourgeois female role. Bound into this version is the exile of central human concerns from the social gathering, together with an encompassing timidity about mind (it wasn't 'nice' to be passionately intellectual.) Who can gauge the effects these things had, even if only through their impact on the attitudes of intellectuals to middle Australia?

By the end of the nineteenth century, the Australian élite (administrators, politicians, landowning, merchant, financial, emergent industrial and professional strata) had by no means thrown off those thin and derivate qualities standard for any colonial ruling class. Intellectuals then often spurned association with the ruling class (indeed with much energy), but wherever that class was notably deficient in confidence, so were intellectuals. In Australia, the élite's deficit of confidence indirectly helped prompt some intellectuals to devalue the mind, in potential the most democratic of all human resources. Intellectuals no doubt thereby avoided some of the consequences of appearing élitist in the most egalitarian society then (and still) in existence, but the strategy nevertheless failed to bring them notable social respect or confidence. Though women novelists showed early signs of the remarkable gifts to remain their hallmark, that devaluation of mind may help explain why Australia's female intelligentsia numbered fewer who identified with the women's movement. By contrast, in countries such as England and Sweden where intellectuals were somewhat less ambivalent in identifying with élites, intellectual women played a more prominent part in that movement. In the United States, where women enjoyed a head start in access to higher education, the role of women with higher education in the women's movement was outstanding, contributing in no small way to its world pre-eminence.

This book proposed a cluster of historical factors to explain some of the traditions most relevant to women and identity. Respecting the impact of economy and class on culture, it noted the impoverishing effect on women's cultural standing of the high valuation placed from formative times on single-male staffed 'robber' and 'raping' industries (whaling, sealing, fishing, wool and mineral extraction). The book also emphasized the relatively low valuation placed on family-centred agriculture. Women are central to family, and because successful family-centred agriculture entails a certain wooing of 'mother nature', women might have achieved a higher standing had colonial agriculture flourished more widely, hence acquiring a more solid social niche. (We emphasize the word 'might' because cross-culturally this varies with other traditions relevant to women.) The book also stressed the implications for women and identity of a formative social weight exercised by early free and convict pre-working-class English women, and by tragically poor Irish peasant women. In the Australian 'fragment' (Hartz), countervailing inputs from other traditions and groups (for example, from the British craft and farming ethos, or from British élites) were, of course, much slighter than in lands of origin. (The argument was thus one about countervailing forces operating dialectically within an early overall configuration of values.)

Designed as an exploration of women's identity in the context of and constitutive of national identity, *The Real Matilda* set out to assess the role of early value patterns enshrined in institutions and habits of the heart. Its argument does not deny the existence of extremely robust forces associated with a wide range of groups and traditions. Nor does it deny that people from disadvantaged situations responded positively (indeed often in amazing and moving ways) to the opportunities offered to them in Australia. Though the insistent theme of the Loser as Hero in our classic texts may partly contradict the point, this book also assumes that early Australians generally made the best of the hand of cards history dealt them: most people did and do. But the book holds in steady focus certain 'cards' generally ignored in national identity discourse: those associated with early domination ideologies (about class, colony, race and sex), which were absorbed into originary patterns and into the person. The cards history dealt our founding generations thus included psychic patterns and cultural legacies. Such 'eager ghosts' from the past, where unwelcome, need not figure as big players in present scripts. Open to creative exorcism, they pale to the extent that honest, tolerant conversation succeeds in summoning them into the light.

The book's argument cannot legitimately be contested by cata-loguing examples of those who did well, or of those who did the best they could. Their existence is built into the very model on which *The Real Matilda* is constructed (forces balanced against counter-vailing forces), and it takes care to demonstrate their existence in our history. But as indicated, the argument assumes that attitudes and values, including those of the unconscious, were also part of the hand history dealt our founding mothers and fathers. They were an even more important part, perhaps, than the opportunity for material advancement which bulks large in recent historical discourse. Some of this, indeed, seems to form a kind of counterpoint to current official and semi-official projects of lightening up, or even 'inventing' an Australian identity.

If we now pursue our quarry (woman within national identity) into the last decades of the twentieth century, there are real signs of progress for women. There is a new awareness that reaches beyond its immediate strata of origin in the post-1970s new class, into the community at large – though to be sure, women's progress at the end of the twentieth century contains ambivalent implications, as it did at the end of the nineteenth.

The colonial women's movement was an integral part of moder-nization while up to a point, its successors today reflect the radical modernization some call post-modernism. Partly for this reason, any final judgment about either period is difficult: on the modern epoch as a whole the historical jury is still out. At the end of the twentieth century, many women have registered only modest advance. Dif-ferences in life chances between social classes continue to widen even as the gulf between men and women within classes tends to close. The main immediate beneficiaries of the second-wave women's movement tend to be found among vanguard activists from the 1970s on: initially disadvantaged but aspiring female members of the post-1970s new class which now constitutes a, if not the main, cultural pattern-setter. Therefore an important by-product of women's advancing status has been to broaden in sexual composition, and so consolidate, the position of the new class itself as part of corporatism's ruling configuration. An analogous process took place in the nineteenth century, when class was just as relevant. (Then, the ruling strata was broadly bourgeois or old middle class, its capital in property; now, the latter find themselves increasingly edged aside by new class managers, bureaucrats, professionals, media personnel, their capital in knowledge.) Finally, at the public level, women's progress in Australia may no longer trail that of women in comparable countries. But there could well remain a difference in sexual ambience to the taste of neither sex, one which we might understand in terms of a relative lack of comfortableness and fellowship, and thus even of affection.

Notwithstanding these and other ambiguities, women's progress has been real, with a strong if limited social base, and may still turn out to constitute the most serious challenge the system confronts. Like all systems of male-dominated society, corporatism is most vulnerable in relation to its gender-base, where the child's earliest, hence most powerful, cues about power are either learned or critically shaped.* (In learning her gender, the baby girl simultaneously learns her social inferiority.) Yet now, as part of a process arguably unmatched in significance for humanity's future, women have begun to question basic gender scripting, and some even to question their own unconscious collusion in transmitting and perpetuating it. If gender does significantly underpin the power dimension in all institutional structures, to challenge gender in its formative moments may be to challenge those structures at core. Such change as emerges will scarcely bring utopia, which is for some other species on some other planet. But it may bring real change,

---

* Foucault rightly insists on the near-foundational psychic role of power. However, his 'genealogical' strategy leaves women defenceless and men much empowered in the face of patriarchy's transhistorical and cross-cultural reach.[1]

and that is saying a good deal: all previous revolutions of modern history have been betrayed revolutions which, with startling speed, have ushered in new modes of domination and subordination. Changing gender roles may represent a strategy for undermining at source the *need* for domination, not for revamping the mode of domination.

Yet this brings us up hard against a dilemma. If the old is dying and the new lacks power to be born, what is to be our role? Do women settle for the fratriarchal form of male domination? Global capitalism is establishing this around the whole west while further entrenching it in Australia. Women may feel they do better as sisters under the rule of the brothers than as daughters under the rule of the father. If, however, there are altogether richer ways of arranging human relations, and current feminist theory cannot turn its gaze from the text in order to address them, we must hope other women and men can. None of us are bystanders in this astonishing drama.

Note

1.   I. D. Balbus, 'Disciplining Women. Michel Foucault and the Power of Feminist Discourse', in Selya Benhabib and Drucilla Cornell (eds), *Feminism as Critique. Essays on the Politics of Gender in Late-Capitalist Societies*, Polity Press, Cambridge, 1987, pp. 110–27.

A Kind of Glossary

In what follows I set out the meaning I attach to certain out-of-the-way words or terms used in this book. I'm not offering definitive statements, and probably most readers will have their own working definitions of the contents in any case. Over the years I recruited these terms to help explore woman and identity.

Androgyny.   The first half of this word comes from the Greek for 'man', the second for 'woman'. An androgyne can be biologically a male or a female, but has access to the full range of human qualities. These we have brutally separated by labelling some 'feminine' (inwardness, insight, compassion, nurturance, gentleness, creativity . . .) and hence second-rate; and some masculine (courage, daring, initiative, enterprise, wisdom, high and sustained capacity for intellectuality, perseverance). Because they are allegedly masculine, these are valued as first-rate.

Barbara Thiering in *Created Second?* suggests that to think androgynously in Christian terms is to think of God's creation before the Fall, which fractured an essential human unity into two impoverished polarities, 'feminine' and 'masculine'. To think of us androgynously is to agree with Betty Roszak that there is a 'human continuum'. She writes:

Human characteristics belonging to the entire species have been crystallized out of the living flow of human experience and made into either/or categories. This male habit of setting up boundary lines between imagined polarities has been the impetus for untold hatred and destruction.

Machismo (or 'macho').   This is one socially defined way of being a male. It is an exaggerated version of another socially defined way of being a male which is known as 'masculine'.

John Wayne is a kind of bridge or transitional specimen between the two ways. Originally, 'machismo' ('macho') was a Latin-American style of being male, but the term is now widely used by feminist women and men, heterosexual and homosexual, to designate 'protest' or 'Marlboro Country' masculinity. Warren Phillips in *The Liberated Man: Beyond Masculinity* describes a macho well. He is dedicated to the 'stubborn pursuit of . . . male values [which] produce impotence, clockwork executives, high-level mediocrities, self-alienation, passive marriage . . . and violence.'

In general, macho males are bad value for women. They often look promising, but don't wear well.

Misogyny.   Misogyny involves a spectrum of conscious and unconscious negative feelings about and attitudes towards women. They range from a vague uneasiness and desire not to be with them more than absolutely necessary, through dislike, to contempt, hostility and hate. Envy is generally involved.

Patriarchal Society.   Most, but not all, literate societies are patriarchal. Since a good deal of our learning comes to us through the written word, women in patriarchal society are seen and see themselves in a curious and impoverished way. In patriarchal societies the value structure (that crucial though intangible essence of all communities) and thus the institutions, are invisibly and implicitly shaped by what David Riesman calls the 'pace-setting and boundary creating men'. We noted earlier John Kenneth Galbraith's remark that 'the labor of women to facilitate consumption [is] not valued in national income or product', a fact 'of some importance for its disguise'. We can apply this to women's role in the entire patriarchal value structure, thus to our institutions and culture as a whole. It's quite crucial to the 'disguise' that the role of the pace-setting men be invisible and implicit, and there is extraordinary resistance, at conscious and unconscious levels, to making the processes explicit. Karl Marx remarked once that, as the end of the rule of a particular group approached, sections of the group itself broke away to join its opponents. An exemplary patriarch, Marx was, of course, referring to men and class struggle, but his point has a relevance he did not envisage. John Stuart Mill, a nineteenth-century feminist, 'broke away' in the cause of human liberation, and drew amazing invective. The breaking-away is gathering momentum again today. R. V. Sampson in *The Psychology of Power* and Warren Phillips in *The Liberated Man: Beyond Masculinity* are current examples. Their appearance makes the pace-setter's invisibility more difficult. For example, I had no real idea, it turns out, of how male chauvinism works, until I read Michael Korda's *Male Chauvinism: How it works*. Similarly, the proliferation of men's liberation, or men-against-sexism, or men's consciousness-raising groups is going to tear aside crucial veils and shatter the invisibility without which patriarchy, like the emperor in the fairy tale, will be seen to have no clothes on . . .

Pace-setting males are a smallish group. They tend to crowd the main decision-making and climate-moulding structures, and they con other men, and most women, into believing theirs is *the* way of being, not just a male, but a worthwhile human being. Would-be pace-setters often lead movements not currently dominant, and bring about reforms and revolutions by which they then become pace-setters. In the course of pace-setting games, males jam communities into deathly situations, and then reproach non-pace-setters, female and male alike: 'How can you prattle about your sort of issue at a time like *this*. Wait till after (the revolution, the depression, the crisis, the end of the world . . .)'. One thing the most deadly (literally *deadly*) enemies amongst pace-setter males share: rage at and contempt for non-pace-setters (men, women or children) who question, or want to change, the rules of their game.

Patricentric-Acquisitive Societies. Erich Fromm's phrase, but I understand and use it in this way: The explicit ideologies of patriarchal societies vary. However by far the most, if not all, of them award their highest accolade to the acquisition of material things, to power, competitiveness and status, defined in terms of a male-dominated value structure. (We recall Dr H. C. Coombs' description of ' "male" values . . . power, status, force and greed'.) Dr Coombs was referring to Australia, and we should note that these are predominant 'male' values only in 'patricentric-acquisitive' societies such as our own. There are other, far richer ways of being a male.

Role Model. A child takes shape (its identity evolves) partly around and through role models, good, bad or indifferent. The child is most likely to use those available in the family. These may be directly and physically available, or, as in the case of my grandmother, partly through 'traces' transmitted through a parent. However, visible, socially valued and relevant models in the wider society are also crucial to the process of identity formation. While the most sensitive phases of that process occur early in life, the work of identity formation, as Erikson shows, spans the whole life cycle. Hence role models, good, bad and indifferent are, and presumably always have been, of critical importance for the entire community.

Substitute Gratification. The connotation most relevant for our purposes concerns man-woman relations and sexuality. Applied to these in mass consumer patriarchal society, 'substitute gratification' often involves a deep unconscious conviction that the only way men can relate sexually to women is by superiority and, commonly, phantasies associated with domination. This way shades over into various degrees of psychic sadism. As the wise Satchmo said, it takes two to tango, and this particular form of substitute gratification fails where women refuse to accept a complementary substitute for authentic sexual pleasure. That complementary form involves women believing, on unconscious if not conscious levels, that women can relate sexually to men only by *being* dominated. Phantasies associated with this spill over into varieties of psychic masochism. (A complication: both domination and subordination, and sadism and masochism, are dialectically opposed twins which always go together, carrying roughly the same emotional energy charge in the make-up of a specific individual. The individual who prefers to own up to a given degree of psychic sadism will always carry an unavowed and proportional degree of masochism. That individual may be a man or woman.)

But since it does take two to tango, either man or woman can refuse substitutes and hold out for the real thing (which can take time and courage, but the pay-off is worth it). If one partner refuses to play, the whole game has to be called off. A woman, for example, might refuse to be a dolly-bird, refuse to enact deference rituals, self-put-downs, etc., in a relationship with a man. They then either begin a new scenario together, or each move on in search of other partners.

Index

Aboriginal women, 74, 197–9, 228, 234, 260
  influence on attitude towards all Australian women, 197–9
Aborigines, 179–80, 198, 260
  and frontier 'imprinting' experience, 17
  and national guilt, 74
  white women's violence towards them, 198
Ackermann, Jessie, 212
Adams, Francis, 117
Addams, Jane, 139
Administrative and Clerical Officers' Association, 238
Agriculture
  family-based in colonial N. America, 22
Akademiskt Bildade Kvinnors Förening (Swedish University Women), 206
A Lady's Visit to the Gold Diggings of Australia in 1852–1853, 99
Allport, Gordon, 126
Alternative Trade Union Women's Conference, 237
American women, 22, 37–8, 76, 134, 184–5, 194–6, 222, 243, 262–3
  and historiography, 76, 179
  de Tocqueville on, 196
  in the early labour movement, 37–8
  in the 1970s, 243
  nineteenth century women's movement, 262–3
  on the colonial frontier, 134, 194–6
  on the nineteenth century frontier, 134, 184–5, 194–6

Anderson, Benedict, 281
Anglican Church, 242
D'Aprano, Zelda, 237
Australian Clerical Officers' Association, 237
Australian Council of Churches (N.S.W.)
  Commission on the Status of Women, 241
Australian Council of Salaried and Professional Officers' Associations, 237, 239
Australian Council of Trade Unions, 237–9
Australian Federation of Business and Professional Women, 253
Australian Labor Party, 47, 229, 230
  and feminism, 229 ff.
  National Committee of Inquiry, 1979, 230
Australian Women's Education Coalition (N.S.W.), 253
Autonomy
  and women, 221, 269–70

Blackhouse, James, 98, 131–2, 142
Banner, Lois, 139
Barrett, Kate Waller, 136
Barrow, Sir John, 193
Barrow women, 92
Bartley, N., 190
Bathurst, Earl Henry, 135
Bayly, Nicholas, 135
Baynton, Barbara, 77, 185–6, 191
Bear-Crawford, Annette, 211
Beaumont, Lady, 203

Bennet, Hon. H. Grey, 134–5, 193
Bernard, Jessie, 40
Bigge, J. T., 125, 128–9, 130, 140,
    160, 193
Blackstone, Alice, 140
'Black velvet', 14, 197
Blainey, Geoffrey, 58, 106, 191
Bligh, Governor William, 122
Bolton, Geoffrey, 57
Bolton, Margaret, 96
    see also the *Carthaginian*
Bonding
    see female bonding, mateship
Bonwick, James, 193
Bourgeoisie
    a colonial bourgeoisie, 34, 59,
        179, 199–200, 229, 248, 261
    and domestic feminism, 223, 263
    and intellectuals, 262
    cultural weight in Australia, 34
    in Sweden, 82
    materially and culturally in
        Australia, 59, 179, 199–200,
        229, 248, 261–2
    see also pattern-setting strata
Bourke, Governor Richard, 107, 131,
    208
Bowes, Surgeon, 124
Braim, T. H., 136
Brazil
    as a Hartzian 'fragment', 70
Brooks, Ivy, 210
Brooks, Rev. S. W., 105
Brown, Norman O., 65, 197
Browning, Elizabeth Barrett, 68, 204
Brunskill, Sarah, 182–3
Bulletin, 77
Bunbury, Sir H. E., 135
Bush women, 198
Bussell, Charlotte, 180
Butler, Samuel, 68
Buttrose, Ita, 264

Calhoun, A. W., 194
Cambridge, Ada, 205
Capitalism
    and democracy and women, 73
    and attitudes towards women, 90
    enlarges 'relational distance'
        between the sexes, 69
    industrial capitalism and cruelty,
        64–5
Carthaginian, 96
    see also Margaret Bolton
Cass, Bettina, 39
Caste, 131–3
'Casual poor', 78, 80
    English mental-universe
        reproduced in Australia, 99
    males' contempt for 'their'
        women, 89
    women in England and
        Australia, 93–4
    women's self-concept, 94
Catholic Press, 169
'Character-armour' of English élite,
    160
Childbirth, 97
Childhood
    of a nation, 61
Children
    among the casual poor, 103–5
    'latchkey', 48
    used by women as compensatory
        mechanism, 67
Chisholm, Caroline, 96, 139, 209
Church of England, Sydney Diocese
    submission to Royal Commission
        on Human Rights, 1975, 49
Clacy, Mrs Charles, 108
Clan-collectivism and Irish, 156
Clark, C. M. H. (Manning), 74, 89,
    115, 116, 118, 119, 120, 145, 194
    199, 275
Class
    domestic power of women varies
        with, 221

structure in colonies, 34
see also bourgeoisie, new class,
  pre-working-class, working
  class
Clayton, J. R., 104–5
Cobb, Joan, 194, 203, 208, 209, 212
Collectivism, 63
  among Irish, 156
  industrial proletariat, 156
Colonial
  élite males, 73
  élite strata, 74
Colonial Times, 141
Colony
  see colonial élite males
Committee of Inquiry into Manage-
  ment Education, 239
Committee of Inquiry into Techno-
  logical Change in Australia, 227,
  251
Commodity-fetishism, 63
  see also Marx, Karl
Commonwealth Conciliation and
  Arbitration Commission, 36
Commonwealth Department of
  Labour, 35
Commonwealth Department of
  Labour, Women's Bureau, 36
Connell, R., 121
Consensual union
  see 'pairing'
Consumerism, 13
Contraception, 63
Convictism, 115 ff.
  and children, 143–4
  and family, 144–5
  and standing of women, 89
  as a form of slavery, 73
Convicts, 263–6, 273–6
  as sources of female identity,
    121–45
  as sources of male identity, 24
  statistics on, 119 ff.
Convict women, 115 ff., 276–80

as outcast group, 145
as role-models, 115
punishment of, 140–3
Conway, Jill K., 65–6
Conway, Ronald, 12, 24, 31, 67
Cook, Professor Alice, 35
Coombs, Dr H. C., 24, 39
Cooper, Mrs Maria, 165
Cooper, The Very Reverend W. M.,
  Dean of Sydney, 105
Core culture, xii, 280
Corporate élite, 223, 243, 245, 248,
  266
Coster women, 92, 93
Council for Free Australia, 254
Council of Australian Government
  Employees Organisations
  (C.A.G.E.O.), 237
Country Women's Association, 234
Crawford, Virginia, 206
Cult of 'true womanhood', 204
Cunningham, Peter, 94, 125

Darling, Governor Ralph, 160
Darling, Lady Eliza, 207
Darwin, Charles, 125, 143
Democracy
  and differences, 70
  and misogyny, 82
  and racism, 70
  and sex, 70–71
  shaping of value-structure, 80
  unique qualities of Australian
    democracy, 80–81
Department of Labour Women's
  Bureau, 36
Déraismes, Maria, 206
De Tocqueville, Alexis Clérel, 57,
  63, 65, 118, 140, 157
  and American women, 196
Dickens, Charles, 93
Dinnerstein, Dorothy, 221, 244, 270,
  266–8, 282, 284

Domestic feminism, 223, 233, 250, 263
Domination-subordination and sexuality, 18, 23
Douglas, Mary, 131–2
Drinking
    and casual poor women, 101
    and Irish, 170
    and mateship, 169
    heavy drinking in Australia, 71
    sublimatory, 28
Drinking habits, 47
    of Australian men, 28, 29, 30, 31
    of Australian women, 33
    of Irish, 170
Drysdale, Ann, 122

Eade, Susan Margaret, 212
Earl Grey, 107, 165
Economy, 121–2, 224–9, 263
Eden, Charles H., 72
Edgar, Don, 39
Education
    and women, 39, 40, 239–41, 256
Ehrenreich, Barbara, 261
Eisenstein, Hester, 285
Eldershaw, P. R., 115
Eliot, George, 204
Elite strata, 293–4
    and the military, 200
    early Australian, 74
    in colonies, 73, 261–2
    uncertainty of identity, 72
    see also pattern-setting strata
Elite women, 202 ff., 222, 229, 245–6, 266
    and Aboriginal women, 198
    and convict women, 198
    as role-models, 198
Encel, S., 22, 26, 33, 34, 38–9, 80, 81
Endleman, Robert, 78
Engels, Frederick, 78–9

Equality
    and women, 232, 235–7
Equal pay, 36, 232, 237
Equal Remuneration Convention, 35
    see also International Labour Organization
Erikson, Erik, H., 14, 80, 91, 183, 188, 197
    table of human virtues, 69
'Erotic' sex
    versus 'pornographic' sex, 109
Evans, Estyn, 164
Evatt, Elizabeth, 239
Evening Observer (Brisbane), 77
Everton, Mrs E. M., 186
Ey, Anna, 183

Fairlie, 107
Family
    contradictions within, 267–8
    higher status in colonial America, 49
    late beginnings in eastern Australia, 196
    male parental commitment in Australia, 49
    under stress in late twentieth century, 224
Fanon, Frantz, 145, 162, 248, 267–71, 279, 289 n. 25
Farmers
    and Australian national identity, 76, 263
Federated Clerk's Union, 238
Female
    bonding weak in Australia, 247–8, 260, 264–5
    identity formation in Australia, 81
Female (Convict) Factory
    Hobart, 68, 127–8, 132–3, 144
    Parramatta, 125, 127, 129, 131 207, 209
Feminine conservatism, 16

Femininity
  nineteenth-century, 69
Feminism, 223, 243 ff.
  Christian, 241–3
  domestic, 223, 263
  new, 245, 249–50
  nineteenth century, 33, 205–7,
    210–13
  1970s forms marginalize women,
    223
  1970s forms dominated by
    behaviourist sociology and
      psychology, 247
  radical, 223, 243–5, 248
  reform, 223, 243, 245–6, 248
  socialist, 223, 243
Feminist Legal Action Group
  (N.S.W.), 253
Feminists
  anti-feminist critique, 268–9
  see also feminism
Femocrats, 246, 284–5
Fenian Sisterhood, 168
Ferguson, Rosina, 183
Fiedler, Leslie, 188–9, 198
Finland, 23, 47, 48, 80, 156
Finnish National Council of
  Women, 211
Finnish women, 106, 230
  and politics, 44–5, 211
Fitzpatrick, Kathleen, 131
Flax, Jane, 250, 267
Flynn, Elizabeth Gurley, 38
Forbes, Lady, 201, 209
Formative
  experiences, 28, 61, 62, 64, 72, 73,
    247, 259–60
  Aborigines and the Australian
    formative experience, 74
  times, 12, 21, 42, 49, 80, 143
  see also 'imprinting' experiences
Forward, Ann, 238
Foucault, Michel, 267, 275, 279,
  284, 297, 298

Fowler, Frank, 104, 137
Franklin, Lady Jane, 141
Franklin, Miles, 77
Fraser, Malcolm, 231–2
Fratriarchy, 260, 282, 286, 293, 298
Freeman's Journal, 169
Freud, Sigmund, 23, 61, 187
Friendship, 136
Fromm, Erich, 15, 21, 65, 70
Frontier, 134
  and Aboriginal women, 179
  and women, 179, 184–5
  and women as 'monsters of virtue'
    or gentling heroines, 198
  see also American women
Froude, J. A., 204
Fry, Elizabeth, 68, 209
Furphy, Joseph, 32

Galbraith, John Kenneth, 13, 34
Galvin, Paddy, 160
Gardiner, John, 182
Gardiner, Mary, 182
Gaudron, Mary, 239
Gender role, 246–7, 249–50, 265, 268
  as form of social domination, 244,
    267
  core aspects learned unconsciously,
    259–60
  female inferiority and early gender
    socialization, 257
  gender, power, class and status,
    244, 246, 259
  male in post-industrial society, 254
  socialization, 255
Gender script, 223, 266–8
Gilbert, Mrs John, 186
Gilmore, Mary, 205
Gipps, Governor George, 96, 200, 208
Giroud, Françoise, 48
Goddard, Rosemary, 194
Golding: Annie, Belle, Kate, 211
Goldman, Emma, 38

Gold rushes, 71
  and children, 105
  and women, 104-5, 108
  historians' neglect of impact on
    women and children, 105
Goldstein, Vida, 206, 210
Gorer, Geoffrey, 35, 195
Gorman, J. V., 161
Grimshaw, Patricia, 260-1, 266
Guardian, 109
Guilfoyle, Dame Margaret, 227

Habermas, Jurgen, 259
Hale, Amy, 180
Hargreaves, Kaye, 238
Hargreaves, Mary, 181
Harris, Alexander, 98, 123, 164
Harris, Max, 32, 121
Harrison, Inspector C. E., 104
Hart, Lucy, 183
Hartz, Louis, 28, 59, 60, 62, 70, 266,
  295
  Hartz thesis and status of women
    in Australia, 67
Hawke Labor Administration, 235
Hawke, R. J., 36, 232
Hayter, Kezia Elizabeth, 68
Hegemonic values
  bourgeois hegemonic values, 90
Hell's Angels, 91, 109
  and 'negative identities', 79
Henry, Alice, 38
Henry, Reverend William, 135
Henty, Jane, 180
Herbert, Xavier, 29, 118
Hernton, Calvin, 70
Hill, J. W., 138
Hill, Rosamond and Florence, 101,
  105, 123, 209
Hirst, Mrs Alexander, 210
Historians
  and women, 76, 188-91, 198
  attitudes of, 17

on national identity and women,
    58-9
Hobsbawn, E. J., 157-8
Hodge, Mrs Baldwin, 186
Holden, Frances Gillan, 210
Homosexuality
  and mateship, 81
  in patriarchal society, 25
  latent, 24
Hood, John, 199
Hope, A. D., 280
Houseman, Laurence, 97, 100, 109
Hughes, Robert, 260, 263, 275
Human Rights Commission, 236
Hunter, Governor John, 124, 128,
  131, 201
Hutchinson, Mary, 133, 208, 209
Hutchinson, R. C., 125, 208
Ibsen, Henrik, 23, 134
Identity, 14
  class, ethnic, national, 23
  'negative identity', 79
  male identity in industrial and
    post-industrial society, 230
Ideology, 91, 259
  and personality structure, 221
  and status, 259
  and individual 'internalizing'
    hierarchical values in childhood,
    60, 79
Illegitmacy
  among casual poor, 100
Immigrants ships, 95
  Immigration Committee Inquiry,
    1842, 96
Imperialism
  and Ireland, 157 ff.
  Swedish, 156
Imperial Review, 90, 171
'Imprinting' experiences, 61
  see also formative experiences
Industrial revolution, 59, 65, 70
  and Australia, 66-7
  and women, 37

Industries
  'robber' (sealing, fishing, wool, mining), 22
Inglis, K. S., 58, 158
Intellectuals, 293–4
  women, 204
International Labour Organization, 35, 46, 235
  see also Equal Remuneration Convention
Ireland, David, 102
Irish, 21, 30, 61, 73, 272–3, 287 n. 3
  and Governors Darling, Hunter, King, Macquarie, 160–1
  as a main source of Australian identity, 24
  as 'victims', 155–6, 160, 162–3
  children and sex-roles, 172
  clan-collectivism and women, 157
  clannishness in Australia, 164–5, 250
  clan structure, 163–4
  contribution to Australian value-structure, 80
  convicts, 120
  drinking patterns, 170
  male dominance causes high female mortality, 173
  male identity, 59
  orphan girls, 67, 107
  sex roles, 155
  sexuality, 170–1
  women, 89, 248, 260–1
  women's use of compensatory mechanisms in family, 261
  women and politics, 167–9
  women as drudges, 161
Irving, Baiba, 40, 42
Irving, T. H., 121

John Bull and Co., 210
Johnson, Ester, 122
Jones, 'Mother', 36
Jung, Carl, 45

Kelly, Ned, 12
Keneally, Thomas, 262
Key, Ellen, 207
Keynes, John Maynard, 27
Kiddle, Margaret, 96
Kimbal, Solon T., 172
King, Governor Philip Gidley, 124, 128, 133
Kingston, Beverley, 103
Klein, Melanie, 267–8, 270

Lacan, Jaques, 259, 267–8, 280
Lacour, Léopold, 206
Lady Penrhyn, 120, 124
Lake, Marilyn, 266, 282
Lang is Greater than Lenin, 75
Lang, John Dunmore, 208
Langenhand, Emma, 107
Lansbury, Coral, 37
Lasswell, H. D., 45
Lawrence, Hannah, 107
Lawson, Henry, 12, 77, 185
Lawson, Louisa, 211
Layton, Robyn, 239
Lee, June, 191–2
Leijon, Anna Greta, 47
Lenin, V. I., 89, 116
Lerner, Gerda, 194
'Les Origines du Féminisme Contemporaine', 206
Lewis, George Cornewall, 164
Liberal-National Coalition, 231
Liberal Party, 230–3
  Victorian Liberal Feminist Network, 233
  Federal Women's Committee, 233
Life Against Death, 197
Loder, Kay, 240
London Missionary Society, 135
Lovejoy, Frances, 40
Loveless, George, 141
Lowenthal, Leo, 64
'Lower orders', 60, 99

and marriage, 90
and national pride, 59
Lumpenproletariat, 78
Luxemburg, Rosa, 34, 74
Lying-in, 101
and Sydney Benevolent Asylum, 99
Lyons, Dame Enid, 233

Macarthur, Elizabeth, 122
Macarthur, James, 119, 193, 202
McCarthy, M. J. F., 170, 172
MacDonagh, Oliver, 61, 158
MacDonald, Louisa, 23
McDonald, Peter, 121, 146 n. 30, 273
McEnroe, The Venerable,
   Archdeacon of Sydney, 161–2
McGirr, J. J., G., 102
McKenzie, Charlotte May, 180
MacKenzie, Jeanne, 32
MacKenzie, Norman, 21, 25, 26,
   196, 212
McLerie, Inspector, J. M., 104, 137
Maconochie, Alexander, 116
Macquarie, Elizabeth, 207
Macquarie, Governor Lachlan, 129,
   130, 131, 135–6
Macqueen, Thomas, 125
Machismo, 13, 15, 16, 50
Madgwick, R. B., 193
Magee, Martha, 95
Maley, Mrs J. S., 181
Marcus, Steven, 64
Marcuse, Herbert, 14, 15, 23, 65–6,
   91, 109, 275
Marjoribanks, Alexander, 127
Markievicz, Constance de, 169
Marriage
   English upper class, 67–9
   in early N.S.W., 135
   nineteenth century form, 90
Marsden, Samuel, 128, 129, 130, 135
   and Irish, 159–60
Martin, Jean, 35

Marx, Karl, 63, 157
Masculinity
   nineteenth century form, 69
Massachusetts, 134
Mateship, 12, 27, 81, 101, 229–30,
   264, 266, 293
   and heavy drinking, 169
   and Irish, 157
   Barbara Baynton on, 77
   barrier to women in A.L.P., 229–30
   celebrated by Australian writers, 77
   cultural universe of, 185
   Judith Wright on, 77
   see also Ockerism
Matilda, 11
'Matriduxy', 48
Matthews, Jane H., 239–40
Mattson, Lisa, 42
Maxwell, Constantia, 161
Mayhew, Henry, 89, 90, 92, 161–2
Mead, Margaret, 170
Melanesian men's houses and the
   military, 200
   see also women and the military
Men Against Sexism, 211
   see also mens' consciousness-raising
      groups
Men's consciousness-raising groups,
   211
Meredith, Mrs Charles, 144, 169–70
Meudall, G., 138
Migrant women, 226, 228
Military
   as 'imprinting' élite influence, 200
Mill, J. S., 49–50, 60, 68, 211
Milett, Kate, 200
Misogyny, 12, 13, 23
   and democracy, 82
Mitchell, Juliet, 244, 270
Moberg, Wilhelm, 161
Models
   see role models
Molesworth, Sir William, 116
Montefiore, Dora, 212

Moran, Cardinal Patrick Francis, 168
Moran, Herbert M., 155, 171
Morgan, Molly, 121
Morrison, Arthur, 93, 108
Mother – daughter relationship
 ambivalence in, 247, 257
 Dinnerstein and Flax on, 247
Mothering
 and self-concept of women, 100
 and casual poor women, 103
Motherly love
 a modern invention, 100
 and contraception, 100
Mumford, Lewis, 23
Munday, G. C., 127
Murphy, Lionel, 240
Murray, Terence, 158
Myrdal, Gunnar, 71
My Secret Life, 90

National Council of Women, 203,
 204, 210, 226
National Health and Medical
 Research Council, 1971, 169
National identity
 Australian historians on, 13, 57,
  75, 263
 characteristics of, 21–51, 260–6
 'core culture', xii, 280
 feminist interventions in
  historiography of, 280–3
 mateship and, 260–1, 265–6
 theory of, xii, 57–83, 271–3, 293–6
 variations on western bourgeois
  model, 260–1, 272, 277–8
 Women, ignored in analyses of,
  76
National Party, 234, 254
National pride
 and the 'lower orders', 59
National Society for Prevention of
 Cruelty to Children, 1881, 103
National Women's Advisory

Council, 227
'Naughty'
 term for sexual intercourse, 27
Neal, David, 275, 276
Ned Kelly syndrome, 79
'Negative identity', 92
New Class, 261, 283, 296–7
Newcomb, Caroline, 122
Newman, Dorcas, 95
Nicholas, Stephen, 276
Nightingale, Florence, 34
Nineteenth century historians'
 treatment and women's
 experience, 73
Norton, Caroline, 69, 203
N.S.W. Corps, 201
N.S.W. Labor Council, 238
N.S.W. Women's Liberal Network,
 254
Nurturance, 221, 269–70
 defined as uniquely female, 66

O'Brien, Eris, 166
Ocker, 30
 place of women in Ocker culture,
  11
 nineteenth-century Ockers, 12
Ockerism, 27, 30, 224, 262
 see also mateship
Organization for Economic
 Co-operation and Development,
  36, 228
O'Farrell, Patrick, 118, 260, 287 n. 3
O'Neill, William L., 61, 190, 194
O'Rell, Max, 210
Orphan Immigration Committee,
 107, 165
Osborne, Alick, 125
Outcast, 124, 128, 222
 casual poor women, 95, 101
 convict women, 143, 260
Oxley, Deborah, 276, 278–9

'Pairing'
in early Australia, 196
Palmer, J. H., 104
Palmer, Vance, 75, 77
Parkes, Clarinda, 98
Parkes, Henry, 98, 116
Parkin, Frank, 91
Parramatta Female Convict Factory
see Female Factory
Pattern-setting strata, 222-3, 229,
235, 245-6, 266
see also bourgeoisie
Payne, H. S., 127
'Performance principle', 23, 91
Perth Gazette, 187
Phar Lap, 12
Phillip, Governor Arthur, 128
Phillips, A. A., 77, 200
Phillips, Marion, 129
Phillips, Sophia, 138
Pike, Douglas, 75, 118
Politics
relevance to women, 42
see also women
'Pornographic' sex, 109
Positive discrimination, 231
Post-structuralism, 267-8, 283
Potter, David, 184
Power, Margaret, 36
Praed, Mrs Campbell, 185, 188, 192
Pre-working-class, 229, 248, 259
see also 'casual poor'
Prichard, Katharine Susannah, 186
'Principle of stratified diffusion', 63
see also De Tocqueville
Pritchett, V. S., 170, 262
Professions
and women, 38, 39, 239-41
Prostitutes, 99, 102
'get' innocent men, 102
Prostitution, 71, 89, 101, 104, 133-40,
193, 195
among children, 1859, 104
and humiliation, 102

Protestantism
in Australia and women, 179
Psychoanalysis, 259
and social theory, xii, 267
and feminism, 244
'Feminisation of', 268
Lacan, Jacques, 267-8, 280
'object-relations' tradition, 267,
284: Chodorow, Nancy 284;
Klein, Melanie, 267-8, 270,
284, 287 n. 1; Rustin, Michael,
268; Winnicott, D. W., 268,
284, 287 n. 1, 2. As
oppositional to Lacan, 284
'Projective' identification', 270-2

Race, 70
see also sex
Racism
and Australian sexism, 197,
268-70
and guilt, 197
as component of national identity,
74
and psychoanalysis, 268-71
Rainwater, Lee, 71, 102
Rape, 108
Raphael, Alderman, J. G., 100
Räsänen, Leila, 48
Rawson, Lady, 204
Reekie, Gail, 281-2
Reiby, Mary, 121
Reich, Wilhelm, 90
Reid, Elizabeth, 46-7
Rich, Adrienne, 244
Rickard, John, 265
Riddell, Elizabeth, 29
Riegel, Robert E., 139
Riesman, David, 15
Riksdag (Sweden)
and women parliamentarians, 42
Roberts, Sarah, 181
Roberts, Stephen, 190

Robinson, Portia, 273, 276–8
Robson, L. L., 89, 119, 120
Roe, Jill, 32
Roe, Michael, 75, 200, 201–2, 203
Role models, 40
    and upper social strata in Australia,
        179
    for women in Australia, 81, 199
    for women on Australian frontier,
        179
    range constricted by colonial class
        structure, 179 ff.
Roman Emperor, 67, 161
Roper, Edna, 44
Roszak, Theodore, 15, 65–6, 75, 134
Royal Commission on Human
    Relationships, 49
Royal Society for Prevention of
    Cruelty to Animals, 1824, 103
Rumsby, Anne, 129
Rural women, 226, 263
    feminist insensitivity towards, 234
Rustin, Michael, 268, 288 n. 24, 289
    n. 27, 28, 30, 34
Ryan, Susan, 231, 235–6
Rye, Maria S., 181

Said, Edward, 267, 289 n. 26
Sampson, R. V., 17–18, 23, 49
Sanger, Dr William, 139
Scandinavia, 17
Schaffer, Kay, 263, 280, 285
Scott, Rose, 211
Select Committee
    on the Condition of the Working
        Classes of the Metropolis
        (N.S.W.), 1859–60, 103–4, 137
    on Emigration from the United
        Kingdom, 1826, 163
    on the Employment of Children,
        (N.S.W.), 1875–6, 205
    on Irish Female Immigration,
        (N.S.W.), 1858, 161
    on Prevalence of Venereal
        Diseases (N.S.W.), 1915, 101
    on the State of Ireland, 1831, 163
    on Transportation, 1812, 119
    on Transportation, 1837, and
        1837–8, 116, 125, 131, 135, 136,
        144, 193, 208
Serle, Geoffrey, 71, 204
Sex
    and race, 70
    artificial sexual polarization of
        human qualities, 66
    Australian attitudes towards, 28,
        29, 31
    'erotic' sex versus 'pornographic'
        sex, 109
    women as objects of sexual use, 49
Sex Discrimination Bill 1983, 235
Sex ratio, 134
    among convicts, 120–1
    and low standing of women in
        Australia, 193–6
Sex role, 12, 15, 39, 45, 49
    see also gender role
Sexism
    and Australian racism, 197
Sexual
    relevance/irrelevance of females, 92
    power relationship, 17
Sexual relations
    in Australia, 17
Sexuality, 18, 23, 27, 62, 101
    and adolescents, 108
    'de-eroticized', 109
    mateship and sublimated
        homosexuality, 81
    of Australian women, men's
        attitudes to, 31
    repressive de-sublimation of, 109
    working class, 102
Shaftesbury, Lord, 103
Shann, Margaret Bertha, 187
Shaw, A. G. L., 115, 143, 145
Sillanpää, Miina, 44

Simmel, George, 82
Slater, Phillip, 16, 22, 72, 105, 145
Slavery
  and sexuality, 143
Smallholders
  see farmers
Social Democratic Women
  International Conference, 1972, 44
Soldiers' Women, 29
Sombart, Werner, 65
Sorell, Lieutenant Governor
  William, 130
South Australian Destitute Asylym,
  101
Spence, Catherine Helen, 206
Status
  of women, 66, 89
  of women and trade unions, 35, 37,
    38
  of women in democracies, 81
  of women in early N.S.W., 79
  of women in Australian workforce,
    35
  of women in working classes, 90,
    92
  of Australian women (international
    comparison), 26
  changing status of women, 38
  debasement of status of women,
    109
  lower in Australia, 73
  United Nations Commission on
    Status of Women, 46
Status hierarchy, 60, 91
Stedman Jones, Gareth, 78
Stephen, A. G., 77. 205
Stowe, Harriet Beecher, 143
The Subjection of Women, 211
Subraon, 95
'Substitute gratifications', 16, 17, 18,
  101
Suicide rate, 33
Sullerot, Evelyne, 38, 41, 45, 63, 100
Sweden, 47, 80

as imperialist power, 156
civic standing of women compared
  to Australia, 82
Swedish University Women
  see Akademiskt Bildade Kvinnors
    Förening, 206
Sydney Benevolent Asylum, 99, 100
Sydney Gazette, 122
Sydney Women Graduates'
  Association, 212
Symons, J. C., 97

Taft, Ronald, 33
Taine, Hippolyte, 104
Teachers' Unions
  and sexism, 238, 255
Tebbutt, Margaret, 21, 26
Tennyson, Lord Alfred, 13–14
Terry, Rosetta, 121
Therry, J. J., 158, 166
Therry, Roger, 127, 158
Thompson, Emma Lucille Frances,
  180
Thompson, E. P., 271
Thompson, Roger, 94, 134, 194–5
The Timber Getters, 186
The Times, 29
Tone, Wolf, 166
Torsh, Dany, 39
Trade unions, 21, 81, 230, 236
  and status of women, 35, 37, 38
  attributes to women, 103
  bureaucracy and women workers,
    238
Trench, W. Steuart, 164
Trotsky, Leon, 34, 74
True Colonist, 133
Tulip, Marie, 241
Tuominen, Eeva-Eliza, 48
Turner, Frederick Jackson, 62
Turner, Ian, 58
Twopeny, R. E. N., 138

Ullathorne, W. B., 116, 125, 158
Unemployment
    and women, 227–8
Union of Australian Women, 226
Unions
    see trade unions
United Australia Party, 233
United Nations, 33, 235–6
    Commission on the Status of
        Women, 46
    Convention on the Political Rights
        of Women, 42
    Declaration on the Elimination of
        Discrimination against Women,
        46
Upward social mobility, 98, 260
    effects on basic folkways and
        values, 78
Value structure, 61
    and women's self-attitudes, 94
    in democracies, 80
    in male-dominated societies, 106
    of casual poor, 79
    relation to status, 91
    see also hegemonic values
Veblen, Thorstein
    and women as badges of
        'conspicuous consumption', 63
Venereal diseases, 101, 102
'Victim'
    Allport's definition, 123
Victims
    Irish as, 162–3
    psychodynamic mechanisms used
        by, 126, 162–3
    see also Fanon, Frantz
Violence, 50, 71, 95, 97
    towards children, 79
    towards coster women, 93
    towards women, 12, 48, 60, 79
Virginia, 134

Waelder, Robert, 61

Waldersee, James, 158, 165, 166
Walker, Mrs Eliza, 99
Walker, Robin, 105
Waltzing Matilda, 11
Ward Russel, 24, 58, 59, 62, 75, 80,
    89, 120, 155, 183, 196
Ware, Helen, 27
Waterson, Duncan, 187
Weber, Max, 65
Welter, Barbara, 194
White with Wire Wheels, 29
White, Patrick, 32
Whitlam Administration, 230, 235
Whitlam, E. G., 36
Wilberforce, William, 160
Wilkinson, F., 107
Williamson, David, 29
Willis, Dr Charles, N.S.W.
    Department of Public Instruction,
        101
Willis, Sabine, 241
Windeyer, Lady, 138, 211
Woman
    as Noble Victim, 244, 249, 268
Womanhood
    see cult of 'true womanhood'
Womanhood Suffrage League of
    N.S.W.
    Rules of, 14–15
Women
    and compensatory mechanisms in
        family, 48
    and the military, 200–1
    and the moral economy, 94
    and paid work, 34, 39, 46, 48, 99,
        225–9
    as Noble Victim, 244, 249, 268
    as transmittors of male value
        systems, 18
    concept of in national identity, 57
    differential situation in Australia,
        33–4
    discrimination in Australia
        education, 39, 239–41

professions, 33, 239–41
Public Service, 33
universities, 240–1
immigrants, 96, 226, 228
in agriculture, 22, 234–5
in America, 22, 37–8, 76, 134,
184–5, 194–6, 222, 243, 262–3,
271
in the church, 241–3
in the economy, 22, 121–2, 224–9
in education, 39, 239–41, 271
in the legal profession, 239–41
in management, 239–41
in parliament, 42–4, 233, 235
in politics, 40, 41, 43, 45, 229–35
in the professions, 33, 239–41
in the Public Service, 33, 227
in universities, 240–1, 256
intellectual women, 206, 262, 271
'internalize' required male
definitions, 106–7
male influence on their
self-concept, 59
novelists, 262
on the frontier, 198
see also bush women
outside power structures, 49–50, 67
profile in Australia contradicts
reputation as leading democracy,
82
psychodynamics of self-concept
formation, 106–7, 257, 259–60
treatment by historians in
discourse on national identity,
75 ff., 264–6
trivialized by historians, 76
Women Who Want to be Women, 254
Women's Action Committee
(Melbourne), 237
Women's Christian Temperance
Union, 211, 271
Women's Club, 203
Women's Electoral League,
Queensland, 41

Women's Electoral Lobby, 226, 230,
232, 254
Women's Liberal League, N.S.W., 41
Women's Movement
Nineteenth century
general, 209, 211, 212, 213, 218
and historians, 58
in international perspective,
203–4, 206–7, 210–13
role of intellectual women in,
206–7
1970s
general, 221, 247–50
main divisions, 221, 243–50
reasons for downturn, 247–50
1990s, 283–5
Women's status
lag in Australia, 17, 33
see also status of women
Women's suffrage, 42
South Australia, 228
Woods, G. D., 108
Woolf, Virginia, 76
Workforce
women in, 225–9
Working Bullocks, 186
Working class
as input into Australian male
gender script, 24
as contribution to Australian
hegemonic values, 71, 82
gender role, 238, 254
influence on national identity, 82
male view of women, 103
males imitate bourgeois males, 63
Working Women's Centre, 237, 254
Working Women's Charter, 237
World Council of Churches, 241
Wright, Judith, 77, 180, 185
on mateship, 77

Yeatman, Anna, 285
Young Liberal Movement, 234